Economics Entrepreneurship and Taxation

Economics Entrepreneurship and Taxation

Dr. Ashok Purohit

RANDOM

RANDOM PUBLICATIONS

NEW DELHI (INDIA)

Economics Entrepreneurship and Taxation

ISBN 978-93-5111-810-7

Published in 2016 in India by
RANDOM PUBLICATIONS
4376-A/4B, Gali Murari Lal, Ansari Road
New Delhi-110 002
Phone : +9111-43580356, 011-23289044, 011-43142548
e-mail: sales@randompublications.com,
info@randompublications.com, randomexports@gmail.com

Reprinted 2026

Type Setting by : Friends Media, Delhi-110089

Preface

Entrepreneurial economics is the study of the entrepreneur and entrepreneurship within the economy. The accumulation of factors of production per se does not explain economic development. They are necessary inputs in production, but they are not sufficient for economic growth. Human creativity and productive entrepreneurship are needed to combine these inputs in profitable ways, and hence an institutional environment that encourages free entrepreneurship becomes the ultimate determinant of economic growth. Thus, the entrepreneur and entrepreneurship should take center stage in any effort to explain long-term economic development. Early economic theory, however did not lay proper attention to the entrepreneur.

A tax is a financial charge or other levy imposed upon a taxpayer by a state or the functional equivalent of a state to fund various public expenditures. A failure to pay, or evasion of or resistance to taxation, is usually punishable by law. Taxes are also imposed by many administrative divisions. Taxes consist of direct or indirect taxes and may be paid in money or as its labour equivalent. Few countries impose no taxation at all, such as the United Arab Emirates and the kingdom of Saudi Arabia.

Entrepreneurship plays a pivotal role in sustained U.S. economic growth and improved standards of living through lower prices, higher wages, and advances in healthcare. There are many factors involved in bringing an idea to the market, but we know surprisingly little about the role of government, and taxation specifically, in attracting foreign entrepreneurs and spurring.

The book will be useful both as a text book for the students of the agroforestry as well as a compendium of the foresters and scientists. The prose is quite simple and readable without any ambiguity in meaning.

– Author

Contents

1

Principles of Entrepreneurship

The workshop participants were introduced to various aspects of entrepreneurship, namely the importance of getting ideas for an enterprise, how to get ideas, identifying the appropriate trade, factors to consider in selecting a business, factors to consider in deciding to initiate an enterprise, and the functions of an enterprise.

The topics discussed during the session are as follows:

- *Importance of Getting Ideas for an Enterprise*:
  - Basic ideas are required in all cases to perform any work successfully
  - One should acquire the basic concepts of entrepreneurship before getting involved in running an enterprise
  - This knowledge helps an entrepreneur to run the enterprise smoothly and also to explore the possibility of taking new initiatives
  - It also helps in correct decision making
- *How to Get Ideas*:
  - Consult with those who are currently in the business
  - Observe other enterprises to identify problems and think about possible solutions
  - Discuss with friends and neighbours
  - Get ideas from the existing available merchandise in the market
- *Identifying the Appropriate Trade*:
  - Be selective in identifying one's trade.
  - Select just as to the ability and interest of the entrepreneur.
  - Decide only after getting enough relevant information about a particular trade or business. It will help to:

a. Run the business smoothly

b. Avoid loss from major mistakes

- Factors to Consider in Selecting a Business
  - Possibilities of success
  - What risks are involved
  - Profitability
  - Attractiveness
- Factors to Consider when Deciding about Initiating an Enterprise
  - Availability of experienced and knowledgeable persons to consult with
  - Mobilization of sufficient capital
  - Adequate demand for the products/goods in the market
  - Facility for marketing
  - Facility for storage of goods
  - Availability of raw materials
  - Ability to get support from Government
- Functions of an Enterprise
  - Preparing business plan
  - Surveying the market
  - Mobilizing capital
  - Analysing costs
  - Pricing goods
  - Marketing products
  - Keeping accounts
  - Identifying risk factors
  - Looking for ways to become self-reliant

MEANING

Entrepreneurship is the act of being an entrepreneur, which can be defined as "one who undertakes innovations, finance and business acumen in an effort to transform innovations into economic goods". This may result in new organizations or may be part of revitalizing mature organizations in response to a perceived opportunity. The most obvious form of entrepreneurship is that of starting new businesses; however, in recent years, the term has been extended to include social and political forms of entrepreneurial activity.

When entrepreneurship is describing activities within a firm or large organization it is referred to as intra-preneurship and may include corporate venturing, when large entities spin-off organizations. Paul Reynolds, entrepreneurship scholar and creator of the Global Entrepreneurship Monitor, "by the time they reach their retirement years, half of all working men in the United States probably have a period of self-employment of one or more years; one in four may have engaged in self-employment for six or more years. Participating in a new business creation is a common activity among U.S. workers over the course of their careers." And in recent years has been documented by scholars such as David Audretsch to be a major driver of economic growth in both the United States and Western Europe. Entrepreneurial activities are substantially different depending on the type of organization that is being started.

Entrepreneurship ranges in scale from solo projects to major undertakings creating many job opportunities. Many "high value" entrepreneurial ventures seek venture capital or angel funding in order to raise capital to build the business.

Angel investors generally seek annualized returns of 20-30% and more, as well as extensive involvement in the business. Many kinds of organizations now exist to support would-be entrepreneurs, including specialized government agencies, business incubators, science parks, and some NGOs. In more recent times, the term entrepreneurship has been extended to include elements not related necessarily to business formation activity such as conceptualizations of entrepreneurship as a specific mindset resulting in entrepreneurial initiatives *e.g.* in the form of social entrepreneurship, political entrepreneurship, or knowledge entrepreneurship have emerged.

DEFINITION OF ENTREPRENEURSHIP

Entrepreneurship is more than simply "starting a business." The definition of entrepreneurship is a process through which individuals identify opportunities, allocate resources, and create value. This creation of value is often through the identification of unmet needs or through the identification of opportunities for change. Entrepreneurs see "problems" as "opportunities," then take action to identify the solutions to those problems and the customers who will pay to have those problems solved. Entrepreneurial success is simply a function of the ability of an entrepreneur to see these opportunities in the marketplace, initiate change and create value through solutions.

CHARACTERISTICS OF ENTREPRENEUR

The Department of Labour predicts that the #1 employer in 2010 will be"self." An Internet poll of 25-44 year olds revealed that 90% of them hoped to own their own businesses. A survey conducted by Ernst and Young found that 75% of influential Americans believe that entrepreneurship will be the defining trend of the 21st century. Some of the factors that have attributed to the rise of the modern day entrepreneurial spirit are access to technology, a global economy and corporate stagnation. Many workers have experienced feelings of discontent - likely due to the upsizing, downsizing, and right-sizing of corporations.

But whatever the reason, modern workers want to have more control over the work they do. And they want work that is meaningful and important to them. Now is a great time to become your own boss. In fact, the number of Americans who are running their own businesses will continue to grow as we move further into the millennium.. As workers' values are changing and people want more time to do the things they love with those they love, having employment that allows for a greater balance in their lives is critical to today's worker. In fact, it is downright un-American not to believe in the principles of entrepreneurship.

We started out working on the family farm or in the family-owned grocery store but as our country became more industrialized, families were pulled apart. We had to go where the work was. We left our homes and hometowns and ventured into the big cities. Big companies, industries and corporations popped up all over the country, and we became reliant on them to take care of us. Today, with the advent of the computer, we don't even have to leave home to conduct business.

It frees us up to concentrate on the"business of life" again. The new world of work encourages the entrepreneurial mindset, in that we need to learn to use our imagination to dream up new ideas, challenge assumptions and belief systems to find a better way, and break through worn-out thinking to create new and innovative products and services.

This way of thinking is helpful whether you are working for yourself or someone else. The characteristics of entrepreneur can be defined as'anyone who undertakes a commercial risk for profit and/or tackles new challenges'. They are the change agents of society because they see a problem and want to find a way to solve it. They believe in being self-reliant and taking action to better their communities. Robert Schwartz's definition:"An entrepreneur is essentially a visualizer and actualizer. He can visualize something and when he visualizes it, he sees exactly how to make it happen." Successful entrepreneurs realise that if it is to become a reality, they are the ones to make it happen.

An entrepreneur is someone who is able to continually reinvent himself, and to rethink an entire project if he finds that something is not right. Thus, someone who has vision, flexibility, and a risk-taking nature fares very well in self-employment ventures. Of course, like anything else, there are pros and cons to becoming an entrepreneur. One pro is that you are the boss. The con is that you still have other co-workers, customers, and vendors to rely on to get the job done. People who are self-employed often only have illusions of control.

For instance, you may think you have everything under control and then something happens that puts everything out of your control.

The difference is that being the boss means that it all comes down to you. You are fully responsible for your success. For many people this level of personal responsibility is part of the challenge and enjoyment. The truth is that any successful entrepreneur rolls with the punches and moves with the winds of change. Take this test to find out if you have what it takes to be an entrepreneur.

Characteristics of Entrepreneur:

- *Check if these entrepreneurs characteristics are applicable to you*:
  - Responsible
  - Hard Worker
  - Risk Taker
  - Creative
  - Flexible
  - Follows through with ideas
  - Personable
  - Optimistic
  - Perceptive
  - Self-confident
  - Determined
  - High degree of energy
  - Innovative
  - Independent
  - Ability to anticipate needs
  - Effective communicator
  - Responsive to criticism
  - Able to take the lead
  - Learn from mistakes
  - Self-directed
- *Would you say that you are always, sometimes, or never like these statements*:
  - I am goal and action-oriented.
  - I am a self-starter.
  - I am self-confident.

- I am a persistent person.
- I like taking risks.
- I am flexible and adaptable when necessary.
- I am a problem-solver.
- I am an innovative thinker.
- I can sell myself and/or my product to others.
- I accept responsibility for my actions.
- I enjoy networking.
- I can function in an environment of uncertainty.
- I like being in charge.
- I am willing to devote whatever time and energy it takes to be successful.
- I am able to see what needs to be done and then do it

THE GROWTH OF ENTREPRENEURSHIP IN INDIA

Through unrecognized by policy statements, entrepreneurial initiative was breaking new grounds in the small industry scene over the past four decades banking mainly upon the ingenuity and determination of individuals. The late sixties and early seventies also witnessed a few sporadic attempts to create entrepreneurs from non traditional communities with a view to breaking the monopoly of the dominant groups and diversifying the entrepreneurial base in the country.

The state of Gujarat was the forefront of this movement. By the late sixties it became quite evident that two resources are the most critical for development of entrepreneurship, finance and managerial capabilities. The industrial policy exercises were woefully oblivion of these two basic factors though there were incentives and special institutions. When industrial development picked up in the sixties the bankers limited credit mainly to established industrialists and merchants for existing projects with assured success and sufficient collaterals. A study of 53 projects financed by banks and the Gujarat State Financial Corporation during the period 1965-68 revealed many interesting things. More than two thirds of institutionals loans were for diversifications and expansion of existing enterprises. Of the new new loans, 30% were given to merchants and traders with adequate financial resources and hence the required collateral.

The entrepreneur's financial stake stood very high in the transactions tat a debt equity ratio 1:1. Such policies evidently were holistic to an aspiring and an otherwise competent young entrepreneurs but without enough financial resources and tangible assets. As an innovative alternative to the conventional banking system an Industrial Investment Corporation was set up as a State company in Gujarat in 1968 with attractive and unconventional credit schemes. The task next was to identify and groom potential new entrepreneurs from a variety of socioeconomic backgrounds. The entrepreneurship development programme with well ell designed inputs for motivating, informing and skilling entrepreneurial individuals was pioneered in 1970. Something started as an experiment soon spread to other parts of the country and became a deeply entrenched strategy for new enterprise creation over the years. Difficult models and methodologies have been evolved and tasted by different organizations.

Several modifications have been carried out to suit the profile and needs of various groups of trainees. For example, potential micro enterprises in the rural sectors by the poor, whose ventures have only limited investment and low levels of technology must be addressed differently from those of enterprising women whose talents and creativity have been suppressed by age-old socio-cultural norms and practices. Both need appropriate approaches so that they become capable of manifesting their entrepreneurial competence. Despite efforts made made by a host of institutions, only less than 20% of the new entrepreneurs have access to training every year. This means that a large mass of potential entrepreneurs are still outside the reach of training interventions.

2

Entreprenurship and Market Dynamics

UNDERSTANDING THE MARKET

A market is any one of a variety of systems, institutions, procedures, social relations and infrastructures whereby businesses sell their goods, services and labour to people in exchange for money. Goods and services are sold using a legal tender such as fiat money. This activity forms part of the economy. It is an arrangement that allows buyers and sellers to exchange goods. Competition is essential in markets, and separates market from trade.

Two people may trade, but it takes at least three persons to have a market, so that there is competition on at least one of its two sides. Markets vary in size, range, geographic scale, location, types and variety of human communities, as well as the types of goods and services traded.

Some examples include local farmers' markets held in town squares or parking lots, shopping centres and shopping malls, international currency and commodity markets, legally created markets such as for pollution permits, and illegal markets such as the market for illicit drugs. In mainstream economics, the concept of a market is any structure that allows buyers and sellers to exchange any type of goods, services and information.

The exchange of goods or services for money is a transaction. Market participants consist of all the buyers and sellers of a good who influence its price. This influence is a major study of economics and has given rise to several theories and models concerning the basic market forces of supply and demand. There are two roles in markets, buyers and sellers.

The market facilitates trade and enables the distribution and allocation of resources in a society. Markets allow any tradable item to be evaluated and priced. A market emerges more or less spontaneously or is constructed deliberately by human interaction in order to enable the exchange of rights of services and goods. Historically, markets originated in physical marketplaces which would often develop into — or from — small communities, towns and cities.

TYPES OF MARKETS

Although many markets exist in the traditional sense — such as a marketplace — there are various other types of markets and various organizational structures to assist their functions. The nature of business transactions could define markets.

Financial markets

Financial markets facilitate the exchange of liquid assets. Most investors prefer investing in two markets, the stock markets and the bond markets. NYSE, AMEX, and the NASDAQ are the most common stock markets in the US. Futures markets, where contracts are exchanged regarding the future delivery of goods are often an outgrowth of general commodity markets. Currency markets are used to trade one currency for another, and are often used for speculation on currency exchange rates. The money market is the name for the global market for lending and borrowing.

Prediction Markets

Prediction markets are a type of speculative market in which the goods exchanged are futures on the occurrence of certain events. They apply the market dynamics to facilitate information aggregation.

ORGANIZATION OF MARKETS

A market can be organized as an auction, as a private electronic market, as a commodity wholesale market, as a shopping centre, as a complex institution such as a stock market, and as an informal discussion between two individuals. Markets of varying types can spontaneously arise whenever a party has interest in a good or service that some other party can provide.

Hence there can be a market for cigarettes in correctional facilities, another for chewing gum in a playground, and yet another for contracts for the future delivery of a commodity. There can be black markets, where a good is exchanged illegally and virtual markets, such as eBay, in which buyers and sellers do not physically interact during negotiation. There can also be markets for goods under a command economy despite pressure to repress them.

MECHANISMS OF MARKETS

In economics, a market that runs under laissez-faire policies is a free market. It is "free" in the sense that the government makes no attempt to intervene through taxes, subsidies, minimum wages, price ceilings, etc. Market prices may be distorted by a seller or sellers with monopoly power, or a buyer with monopsony power. Such price distortions can have an adverse effect on market participant's welfare and reduce the efficiency of market outcomes. Also, the relative level of organization and negotiating power of buyers and sellers markedly affects the functioning of the market. Markets where price negotiations meet equilibrium though still do not arrive at desired outcomes for both sides are said to experience market failure.

STUDY OF MARKETS

The study of actual existing markets made up of persons interacting in space and place in diverse ways is widely seen as an antidote to abstract and all-encompassing concepts of"the market" and has historical precedent in the works of Fernand Braudel and Karl Polanyi. The latter term is now generally used in two ways.

First, to denote the abstract mechanisms whereby supply and demand confront each other and deals are made. In its place, reference to markets reflects ordinary experience and the places, processes and institutions in which exchanges occurs.

Second, the market is often used to signify an integrated, all-encompassing and cohesive capitalist world economy. A widespread trend in economic history and sociology is skeptical of the idea that it is possible to develop a theory to capture an essence or unifying thread to markets. For economic geographers, reference to regional, local, or commodity specific markets can serve to undermine assumptions of global integration, and highlight geographic variations in the structures, institutions, histories, path dependencies, forms of interaction and modes of self-understanding of agents in different spheres of market exchange.

Reference to actual markets can show capitalism not as a totalizing force or completely encompassing mode of economic activity, but rather as"a set of economic practices scattered over a landscape, rather than a systemic concentration of power". C. B. Macpherson identifies an underlying model of the market underlying Anglo-American liberal-democratic political economy and philosophy in the seventeenth and eighteenth centuries: Persons are cast as self-interested individuals, who enter into contractual relations with other such individuals, concerning the exchange of goods or personal capacities cast as commodities, with the motive of maximizing pecuniary interest.

The state and its governance systems are cast as outside of this framework. This model came to dominant economic thinking in the later nineteenth century, as economists such as Ricardo, Mill, Jevons, Walras and later neo-classical economics shifted from reference to geographically located marketplaces to an abstract"market". This tradition is continued in contemporary neoliberalism, where the market is held up as optimal for wealth creation and human freedom, and the states' role imagined as minimal, reduced to that of upholding and keeping stable property rights, contract, and money supply. This allowed for boilerplate economic and institutional restructuring under structural adjustment and post-Communist reconstruction.

Similar formalism occurs in a wide variety of social democratic and Marxist discourses that situate political action as antagonistic to the market. In particular, commodification theorists such as Georg Lukács insist that market relations necessarily lead to undue exploitation of labour and so need to be opposed in toto. Pierre Bourdieu has suggested the market model is becoming self-realising, in virtue of its wide acceptance in national and international institutions through the 1990s. The formalist conception faces a number of insuperable difficulties, concerning the putatively global scope of the market to cover the entire Earth, in terms of penetration of particular economies, and in terms of whether particular claims about the subjects (individuals with pecuniary interest), objects, and modes of exchange apply to any actually existing markets. A central theme of empirical analyses is the variation and proliferation of types of markets since the rise of capitalism and global scale economies.

The Regulation School stresses the ways in which developed capitalist countries have implemented varying degrees and types of environmental, economic, and social regulation, taxation and public spending, fiscal policy and government provisioning of goods, all of which have transformed markets in uneven and geographical varied ways and created a variety of mixed economies. Drawing on concepts of institutional variance and path dependency, varieties of capitalism theorists (such as Hall and Soskice) identify two dominant modes of economic ordering in the developed capitalist countries,"coordinated market economies" such as Germany and Japan, and an Anglo-American"liberal market economies".

However, such approaches imply that the Anglo-American liberal market economies in fact operate in a matter close to the abstract notion of"the market". While Anglo-American countries have seen increasing introduction of neo-liberal forms of economic ordering, this has not lead to simple convergence, but rather a variety of hybrid institutional orderings. Rather, a variety of new markets have emerged, such as for carbon trading or rights to pollute. In some cases, such as emerging markets for water, different forms of privatization of different aspects of previously state run infrastructure have created hybrid private-public formations and graded degrees of commodification, commercialization and privatization.

Problematic for market formalism is the relationship between formal capitalist economic processes and a variety of alternative forms, ranging from semi-feudal and peasant economies widely operative in many developing economies, to informal markets, barter systems, worker cooperatives, or illegal trades that occur in most developed countries. Practices of incorporation of non-Western peoples into global markets in the nineteenth and twentieth century did not merely result in the quashing of former social economic institutions.

Rather, various modes of articulation arose between transformed and hybridized local traditions and social practices and the emergence world economy. So called capitalist markets in fact include and depend on a wide range of geographically situated economic practices that do not follow the market model. Economies are thus hybrids of market and non-market elements. Helpful here is J. K. Gibson-Graham's complex topology of the diversity of contemporary market economies describing different types of transactions, labour, and economic agents.

Transactions can occur in underground markets or be artificially protected. They can cover the sale of public goods under privatization schemes to co-operative exchanges and occur under varying degrees of monopoly power and state regulation. Likewise, there are a wide variety of economic agents, which engage in different types of transactions on different terms: One cannot assume the practices of a religious kindergarten, multinational corporation, state enterprise, or community-based cooperative can be subsumed under the same logic of calculability.

This emphasis on proliferation can also be contrasted with continuing scholarly attempts to show underlying cohesive and structural similarities to different markets. A prominent entry point for challenging the market model's applicability concerns exchange transactions and the homo economicus assumption of self-interest maximization.

There are now a number of streams of economic sociological analysis of markets focusing on the role of the social in transactions, and the ways transactions involve social networks and relations of trust, cooperation and other bonds. Economic geographers in turn draw attention to the ways in exchange transactions occur against the backdrop of institutional, social and geographic processes, including class relations, uneven development, and historically contingent path dependencies. A useful schema is provided by Michel Callon's concept of framing: Each economic act or transaction occurs against, incorporates and also re-performs a geographically and cultural specific complex of social histories, institutional arrangements, rules and connections.

These network relations are simultaneously bracketed, so that persons and transactions may be disentangled from thick social bonds. The character of calculability is imposed upon agents as they come to work in markets and are"formatted" as calculative agencies. Market exchanges contain a history of struggle and contestation that produced actors predisposed to exchange under c An emerging theme worthy of further study is the interrelationship, interpenetrability and variations of concepts of persons, commodities, and modes of exchange under particular market formations.

This is most pronounced in recent movement towards post-structuralist theorizing that draws on Foucault and Actor Network Theory and stress relational aspects of personhood, and dependence and integration into networks and practical systems. Commodity network approaches further both deconstruct and show alternatives to the market models concept of commodities.

Here, both researchers and market actors are understood as reframing commodities in terms of processes and social and ecological relationships. Rather than a mere objectification of things traded, the complex network relationships of exchange in different markets calls on agents to alternatively deconstruct or"get with" the fetish of commodities. Gibson-Graham thus read a variety of alternative markets, for fair trade and organic foods, or those using Local Exchange Trading Systems as not only contributing to proliferation, but also forging new modes of ethical exchange and economic subjectivities. Most markets are regulated by state wide laws and regulations. While barter markets exist, most markets use currency or some other form of money.Any investments made in markets should be carefully analysed and read through before investing if the market crashes value of stock may go down leading to heavy losses

SIZE PARAMETERS

Market size can be given in terms of the number of buyers and sellers in a particular market or in terms of the total exchange of money in the market, generally annually. When given in terms of money, market size is often termed market value, but in a distinguished sense than the market value of individual products. For one and the same goods, there may be different (and generally increasing) market values at the production level, the wholesale level and the retail level.

For example, the value of the global illicit drug market for the year 2003 was estimated by the United Nations to be US$13 billion at the production level, $94 billion at the wholesale level (taking seizures into account), and US$322 billion at the retail level (based on retail prices and taking seizures and other losses into account).

COMPETITIVE ANALYSIS OF MARKET

In formulating business strategy, managers must consider the strategies of the firm's competitors. While in highly fragmented commodity industries the moves of any single competitor may be less important, in concentrated industries competitor analysis becomes a vital part of strategic planning.

Competitor analysis has two primary activities:

1. Obtaining information about important competitors,
2. Using that information to predict competitor behaviour.

The goal of competitor analysis is to understand:

- With which competitors to compete,
- Competitors' strategies and planned actions,

- How competitors might react to a firm's actions,
- How to influence competitor behaviour to the firm's own advantage.

Casual knowledge about competitors usually is insufficient in competitor analysis. Rather, competitors should be analysed systematically; using organized competitor intelligence-gathering to compile a wide array of information so that well informed strategy decisions can be made.

COMPETITOR ANALYSIS FRAMEWORK

Michael Porter presented a framework for analysing competitors.

This framework is based on the following four key aspects of a competitor:

1. Competitor's objectives
2. Competitor's assumptions
3. Competitor's strategy
4. Competitor's capabilities

Objectives and assumptions are what drive the competitor, and strategy and capabilities are what the competitor is doing or is capable of doing. These components can be depicted as shown in the following diagram.

A competitor analysis should include the more important existing competitors as well as potential competitors such as those firms that might enter the industry, for example, by extending their present strategy or by vertically integrating.

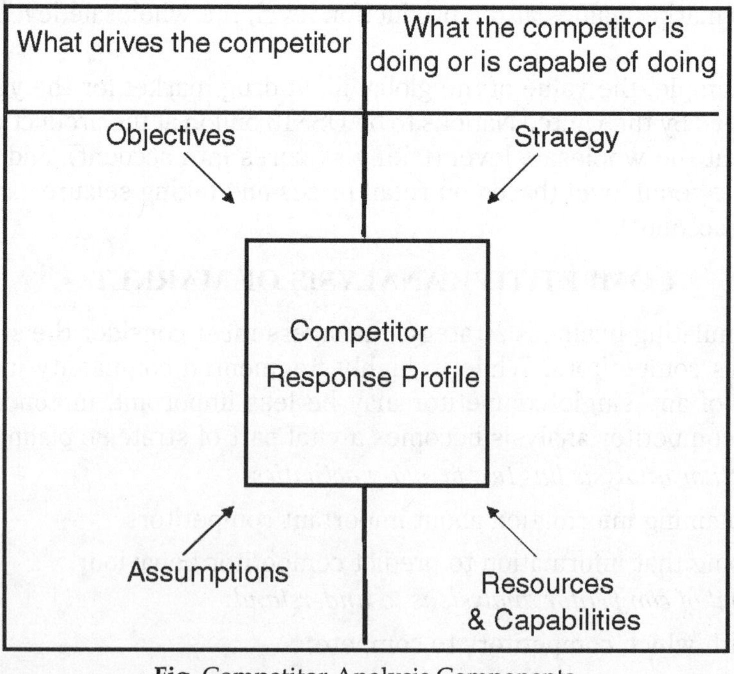

Fig. Competitor Analysis Components

COMPETITOR'S CURRENT STRATEGY

The two main sources of information about a competitor's strategy is what the competitor says and what it does.

What a competitor is saying about its strategy is revealed in:

- Annual shareholder reports
- 10K reports
- Interviews with analysts
- Statements by managers
- Press releases

However, this stated strategy often differs from what the competitor actually is doing. What the competitor is doing is evident in where its cash flow is directed, such as in the following tangible actions:

- Hiring activity
- R & D projects
- Capital investments
- Promotional campaigns
- Strategic partnerships
- Mergers and acquisitions

COMPETITOR'S OBJECTIVES

Knowledge of a competitor's objectives facilitates a better prediction of the competitor's reaction to different competitive moves. For example, a competitor that is focused on reaching short-term financial goals might not be willing to spend much money responding to a competitive attack. Rather, such a competitor might favour focusing on the products that hold positions that better can be defended.

On the other hand, a company that has no short term profitability objectives might be willing to participate in destructive price competition in which neither firm earns a profit. Competitor objectives may be financial or other types. Some examples include growth rate, market share, and technology leadership. Goals may be associated with each hierarchical level of strategy - corporate, business unit, and functional level. The competitor's organizational structure provides clues as to which functions of the company are deemed to be the more important.

For example, those functions that report directly to the chief executive officer are likely to be given priority over those that report to a senior vice president. Other aspects of the competitor that serve as indicators of its objectives include risk tolerance, management incentives, backgrounds of the executives, composition of the board of directors, legal or contractual restrictions, and any additional corporate-level goals that may influence the competing business unit. Whether the competitor is meeting its objectives provides an indication of how likely it is to change its strategy.

COMPETITOR'S ASSUMPTIONS

The assumptions that a competitor's managers hold about their firm and their industry help to define the moves that they will consider. For example, if in the past the industry introduced a new type of product that failed, the industry executives may assume that there is no market for the product.

Such assumptions are not always accurate and if incorrect may present opportunities. For example, new entrants may have the opportunity to introduce a product similar to a previously unsuccessful one without retaliation because incumbant firms may not take their threat seriously. Honda was able to enter the U.S. motorcycle market with a small motorbike because U.S. manufacturers had assumed that there was no market for small bikes based on their past experience.

A competitor's assumptions may be based on a number of factors, including any of the following:

- Beliefs about its competitive position
- Past experience with a product
- Regional factors
- Industry trends
- Rules of thumb

A thorough competitor analysis also would include assumptions that a competitor makes about its own competitors, and whether that assessment is accurate.

COMPETITOR'S RESOURCES AND CAPABILITIES

Knowledge of the competitor's assumptions, objectives, and current strategy is useful in understanding how the competitor might want to respond to a competitive attack. However, its resources and capabilities determine its ability to respond effectively. A competitor's capabilities can be analysed just as to its strengths and weaknesses in various functional areas, as is done in a SWOT analysis. The competitor's strengths define its capabilities. The analysis can be taken further to evaluate the competitor's ability to increase its capabilities in certain areas. A financial analysis can be performed to reveal its sustainable growth rate.

Finally, since the competitive environment is dynamic, the competitor's ability to react swiftly to change should be evaluated. Some firms have heavy momentum and may continue for many years in the same direction before adapting. Others are able to mobilize and adapt very quickly. Factors that slow a company down include low cash reserves, large investments in fixed assets, and an organizational structure that hinders quick action.

COMPETITOR RESPONSE PROFILE

Information from an analysis of the competitor's objectives, assumptions, strategy, and capabilities can be compiled into a response profile of possible moves that might be made by the competitor. This profile includes both potential offensive and defensive moves.

The specific moves and their expected strength can be estimated using information gleaned from the analysis. The result of the competitor analysis should be an improved ability to predict the competitor's behaviour and even to influence that behaviour to the firm's advantage.

PATENTS, TRADEMARK AND COPYRIGHT

PATENT

A patent is a set of exclusive rights granted by a state to an inventor or their assignee for a limited period of time in exchange for a public disclosure of an invention. The procedure for granting patents, the requirements placed on the patentee, and the extent of the exclusive rights vary widely between countries just as to national laws and international agreements.

Typically, however, a patent application must include one or more claims defining the invention which must be new, non-obvious, and useful or industrially applicable. In many countries, certain subject areas are excluded from patents, such as business methods and mental acts. The exclusive right granted to a patentee in most countries is the right to prevent others from making, using, selling, or distributing the patented invention without permission. It is just a right to prevent others' use. A patent does not give the proprietor of the patent the right to use the patented invention, should it fall within the scope of an earlier patent.

Under the World Trade Organization's (WTO) Agreement on Trade-Related Aspects of Intellectual Property Rights, patents should be available in WTO member states for any inventions, in all fields of technology, and the term of protection available should be the minimum twenty years. Different types of patents may have varying patent terms.

Definition

The term patent usually refers to a right granted to anyone who invents or discovers any new and useful process, machine, article of manufacture, or composition of matter, or any new and useful improvement thereof. The additional qualification utility patent is used in the United States to distinguish it from other types of patents but should not be confused with utility models granted by other countries. Examples of particular species of patents for inventions include biological patents, business method patents, chemical patents and software patents.

Some other types of intellectual property rights are referred to as patents in some jurisdictions: industrial design rights are called design patents in some jurisdictions (they protect the visual design of objects that are not purely utilitarian), plant breeders' rights are sometimes called plant patents, and utility models or Gebrauchsmuster are sometimes called petty patents or innovation patents. This object relates primarily to the patent for an invention, although so-called petty patents and utility models may also be granted for inventions.

Certain grants made by the monarch in pursuance of the royal prerogative were sometimes called letters patent, which was a government notice to the public of a grant of an exclusive right to ownership and possession. These were often grants of a patent-like monopoly and predate the modern origins of the patent system. For other uses of the term patent see notably land patents, which were land grants by early state governments in the USA, and printing patent, a precursor of modern copyright. These meanings reflect the original meaning of letters patent that had a broader scope than current usage.

History

In 500 BC, in the Greek city of Sybaris (located in what is now southern Italy),"encouragement was held out to all who should discover any new refinement in luxury, the profits arising from which were secured to the inventor by patent for the space of a year."

The Florentine architect Filippo Brunelleschi received a three-year patent for a barge with hoisting gear, that carried marble along the Arno River in 1421. In 1449, King Henry VI granted the first patent with a license of 20 years to John of Utynam for introducing the making of coloured glass to England. Patents in the modern sense originated in 1474, when the Republic of Venice enacted a decree that new and inventive devices, once put into practice, had to be communicated to the Republic to obtain the right to prevent others from using them.

England followed with the Statute of Monopolies in 1623 under King James I, which declared that patents could only be granted for"projects of new invention." During the reign of Queen Anne, the lawyers of the English Court developed the requirement that a written description of the invention must be submitted. The patent system in many other countries, including Australia, is based on British law and can be traced back to the Statute of Monopolies.

In France, patents were granted by the monarchy and by other institutions like the"Maison du Roi". The Academy examined novelty. Examinations were generally done in secret with no requirement to publish a description of the invention. Actual use of the invention was deemed adequate disclosure to the public. The modern French patent system was created during the Revolution in 1791. Patents were granted without examination since inventor's right was considered as a natural one. In the United States, during the so-called colonial period and Articles of Confederation years, several states adopted patent systems of their own. The first Congress adopted a Patent Act, in 1790, and the first patent was issued under this Act on July 31, 1790.

Law

Effects

A patent is not a right to practice or use the invention. Rather, a patent provides the right to exclude others from making, using, selling, offering for sale, or importing the patented invention for the term of the patent, which is usually 20 years from the filing date subject to the payment of maintenance fees. A patent is, in effect, a limited property right that the government offers to inventors in exchange for their agreement to share the details of their inventions with the public. Like any other property right, it may be sold, licensed, mortgaged, assigned or transferred, given away, or simply abandoned.

The rights conveyed by a patent vary country-by-country. For example, in the United States, a patent covers research, except"purely philosophical" inquiry. A U.S. patent is infringed by any"making" of the invention, even a making that goes towards development of a new invention-which may itself become subject of a patent. A patent being an exclusionary right does not, however, necessarily give the owner of the patent the right to exploit the patent.

For example, many inventions are improvements of prior inventions that may still be covered by someone else's patent. If an inventor takes an existing, patented mouse trap design, adds a new feature to make an improved mouse trap, and obtains a patent on the improvement, he or she can only legally build his or her improved mouse trap with permission from the patent holder of the original mouse trap, assuming the original patent is still in force. On the other hand, the owner of the improved mouse trap can exclude the original patent owner from using the improvement.

Some countries have"working provisions" that require the invention be exploited in the jurisdiction it covers. Consequences of not working an invention vary from one country to another, ranging from revocation of the patent rights to the awarding of a compulsory license awarded by the courts to a party wishing to exploit a patented invention. The patentee has the opportunity to challenge the revocation or license, but is usually required to provide evidence that the reasonable requirements of the public have been met by the working of invention.

Enforcement

Patents can generally only be enforced through civil lawsuits (for example, for a U.S. patent, by an action for patent infringement in a United States federal court), although some countries (such as France and Austria) have criminal penalties for wanton infringement. Typically, the patent owner will seek monetary compensation for past infringement, and will seek an injunction prohibiting the defendant from engaging in future acts of infringement. To prove infringement, the patent owner must establish that the accused infringer practices all the requirements of at least one of the claims of the patent. (In many jurisdictions the scope of the patent may not be limited to what is literally stated in the claims, for example due to the"doctrine of equivalents"). An important limitation on the ability of a patent owner to successfully assert the patent in civil litigation is the accused infringer's right to challenge the validity of that patent. Civil courts hearing patent cases can and often do declare patents not valid.

A patent can be found invalid on grounds that are set out in the relevant patent legislation that vary between countries. Often, the grounds are a subset of requirements for patentability in the relevant country. Although an infringer is generally free to rely on any available ground of invalidity (such as a prior publication, for example), some countries have sanctions to prevent the same validity questions being relitigated. An example is the UK Certificate of contested validity.

The vast majority of patent rights, however, are not determined through litigation, but are resolved privately through patent licensing. Patent licensing agreements are effectively contracts in which the patent owner agrees to forgo their right to sue the licensee for infringement of the licensor's patent rights, usually in return for a royalty or other compensation. It is common for companies engaged in complex technical fields to enter into dozens of license agreements associated with the production of a single product. Moreover, it is equally common for competitors in such fields to license patents to each other under cross-licensing agreements in order to share the benefits of using each other's patented inventions.

Ownership

In most countries, both natural persons and corporate entities may apply for a patent. In the United States, however, only the inventor(s) may apply for a patent although it may be assigned to a corporate entity subsequently and inventors may be required to assign inventions to their employers under a contract of employment. In most European countries, ownership of an invention may pass from the inventor to their employer by rule of law if the invention was made in the course of the inventor's normal or specifically assigned employment duties, where an invention might reasonably be expected to result from carrying out those duties, or if the inventor had a special obligation to further the interests of the employer's company. The inventors, their successors or their assignees become the proprietors of the patent when and if it is granted. If a patent is granted to more than one proprietor, the laws of the country in question and any agreement between the proprietors may affect the extent to which each proprietor can exploit the patent. For example, in some countries, each proprietor may freely license or assign their rights in the patent to another person while the law in other countries prohibits such actions without the permission of the other proprietor(s).

The ability to assign ownership rights increases the liquidity of a patent as property. Inventors can obtain patents and then sell them to third parties. The third parties then own the patents and have the same rights to prevent others from exploiting the claimed inventions, as if they had originally made the inventions themselves.

Governing Laws

The grant and enforcement of patents are governed by national laws, and also by international treaties, where those treaties have been given effect in national laws. Patents are, therefore, territorial in nature. Commonly, a nation forms a patent office with responsibility for operating that nation's patent system, within the relevant patent laws. The patent office generally has responsibility for the grant of patents, with infringement being the remit of national courts.

There is a trend towards global harmonization of patent laws, with the World Trade Organization (WTO) being particularly active in this area. The TRIPs Agreement has been largely successful in providing a forum for nations to agree on an aligned set of patent laws. Conformity with the TRIPs agreement is a requirement of admission to the WTO and so compliance is seen by many nations as important. This has also led to many developing nations, which may historically have developed different laws to aid their development, enforcing patents laws in line with global practice. A key international convention relating to patents is the Paris Convention for the Protection of Industrial Property, initially signed in 1883.

The Paris Convention sets out a range of basic rules relating to patents, and although the convention does not have direct legal effect in all national jurisdictions, the principles of the convention are incorporated into all notable current patent systems. The most significant aspect of the convention is the provision of the right to claim priority: filing an application in any one member state of the Paris Convention preserves the right for one year to file in any other member state, and receive the benefit of the original filing date.

Because the right to a patent is intensely date-driven, this right is fundamental to modern patent usage. The authority for patent statutes in different countries varies. In the UK, substantive patent law is contained in the Patents Act 1977 as amended. In the United States, the Constitution empowers Congress to make laws to"promote the Progress of Science and useful Arts..." The laws Congress passed are codified in Title 35 of the United States Code and created the United States Patent and Trademark Office. In addition, there are international treaty procedures, such as the procedures under the European Patent Convention (EPC), and the Patent Cooperation Treaty (PCT) (administered by WIPO and covering more than 140 countries), that centralize some portion of the filing and examination procedure. Similar arrangements exist among the member states of ARIPO and OAPI, the analogous treaties among African countries, and the nine CIS member states that have formed the Eurasian Patent Organization.

Application and Prosecution

A patent is requested by filing a written application at the relevant patent office. The person or company filing the application is referred to as"the applicant". The applicant may be the inventor or its assignee. The application contains a description of how to make and use the invention that must provide sufficient detail for a person skilled in the art (*i.e.*, the relevant area of technology) to make and use the invention. In some countries there are requirements for providing specific information such as the usefulness of the invention, the best mode of performing the invention known to the inventor, or the technical problem or problems solved by the invention. Drawings illustrating the invention may also be provided.

The application also includes one or more claims, although it is not always a requirement to submit these when first filing the application. The claims set out what the applicant is seeking to protect in that they define what the patent owner has a right to exclude others from making, using, or selling, as the case may be. In other words, the claims define what a patent covers or the"scope of protection". After filing, an application is often referred to as"patent pending". While this term does not confer legal protection, and a patent cannot be enforced until granted, it serves to provide warning to potential infringers that if the patent is issued, they may be liable for damages.

For a patent to be granted, that is to take legal effect in a particular country, the patent application must meet the patentability requirements of that country. Most patent offices examine the application for compliance with these requirements. If the application does not comply, objections are communicated to the applicant or their patent agent or attorney and one or more opportunities to respond to the objections to bring the application into compliance are usually provided.

Once granted the patent is subject in most countries to renewal fees to keep the patent in force. These fees are generally payable on a yearly basis, although the US is a notable exception. Some countries or regional patent offices (*e.g.* the European Patent Office) also require annual renewal fees to be paid for a patent application before it is granted.

Economics

Rationale

There are four primary incentives embodied in the patent system: to invent in the first place; to disclose the invention once made; to invest the sums necessary to experiment, produce and market the invention; and to design around and improve upon earlier patents.

- Patents provide incentives for economically efficient research and development (R&D). A study conducted annually by the IPTS shows that the 2,000 largest global companies invested more than 430 billion euros in 2008 in their R&D departments. If the investments can be considered as inputs of R&D, patents are the outputs. Based on these groups, a project named Corporate Invention Board, had measured and analysed the patent portfolios to produce an original picture of their technological profiles. Without patents, R&D spending would be significantly less or eliminated altogether, limiting the possibility of technological advances or breakthroughs.Corporations would be much more conservative about the R&D investments they made, as third parties would be free to exploit any developments. This second justification is closely related to the basic ideas underlying traditional property rights.
- In accordance with the original definition of the term"patent," patents facilitate and encourage disclosure of innovations into the public domain for the common good. If inventors did not have the legal protection of patents, in many cases, they would prefer or tend to keep their inventions secret. Awarding patents generally makes the details of new technology publicly available, for exploitation by anyone after the patent expires, or for further improvement by other inventors. Furthermore, when a patent's term has expired, the public record ensures that the patentee's idea is not lost to humanity.
- In many industries (especially those with high fixed costs and either low marginal costs or low reverse engineering costs - computer processors, software, and pharmaceuticals for example), once an invention exists, the cost of commercialization (testing, tooling up a factory, developing a market, etc.) is far more than the initial conception cost. (For example, the internal"rule of thumb" at several computer companies in the 1980s was that post-R&D costs were 7-

to-1). Unless there is some way to prevent copies from competing at the marginal cost of production, companies will not make that productization investment.

One effect of modern patent usage is that a small-time inventor can use the exclusive right status to become a licensor. This allows the inventor to accumulate capital from licensing the invention and may allow innovation to occur because he or she may choose to not manage a manufacturing buildup for the invention. Thus the inventor's time and energy can be spent on pure innovation, allowing others to concentrate on manufacturability. Another effect of modern patent usage is to cause competitors to design around each other's patents. This promotes healthy competition among manufacturers, resulting in gradual improvements of the technology base. This may help augment national economies and confer better living standards to the citizens.

Costs

Some of the costs to society associated with the granting of a patent are: the immediate costs associated with preparing the patent; patent office work; legal costs associated with prosecuting alleged infringements; business costs associated with those legal actions; increasing the cost of determining whether a method is covered by an existing patent, and reduced certainty in the result; restrictions on the use of the patented method (particularly in cases where the method is redeveloped independently).

The costs of preparing and filing a patent application, prosecuting it until grant and maintaining the patent vary from one jurisdiction to another, and may also be dependent upon the type and complexity of the invention, and on the type of patent.

The European Patent Office estimated in 2005 that the average cost of obtaining a European patent (via a Euro-direct application, *i.e.* not based on a PCT application) and maintaining the patent for a 10 year term was around 32 000 Euro. Since the London Agreement entered into force on May 1, 2008, this estimation is however no longer up-to-date, since fewer translations are required.

In the United States, direct legal costs of patent litigation are on average in the order of a million dollars per case, not including associated business costs, based on an American Intellectual Property Law Association survey of patent lawyers, and court documents for a sample of 89 court cases where one side was ordered to pay the other side's legal fees.

Criticism

Patents have been criticized both in principle and in implementation. In principle, patents have been criticized as a restraint of trade, for conferring a negative right upon a patent owner, permitting them to exclude competitors from using or exploiting the invention, even if the competitor subsequently develops the same invention independently.

This may be subsequent to the date of invention, or to the priority date, depending upon the relevant patent law. As state-granted monopolies, patents have been criticized as inconsistent with free trade. On that basis, in 1869 the Netherlands abolished patents, and did not reintroduce them until 1912. In implementation, patents have been criticized for being granted on already-known inventions. In 1938, R. Buckminster Fuller wrote of the patent application process in the United States:

- At present, the files, are so extraordinarily complex and the items so multitudinous that a veritable army of governmental servants is required to attend them and sort them into some order of distinguishable categories to which reference may be made when corresponding with patent applicants for the purposes of examiner citation of"prior art" disclosure. This complexity makes it inevitable that the human-equation involved in government servants relative to carelessness or mechanical limitations should occasion the granting of multitudes of"probably" invalid patent claims.

Patents may hinder innovation as well in the case of"troll" entities. A holding company, pejoratively known as a"patent troll", owns a portfolio of patents, and sues others for infringement of these patents while doing little to develop the technology itself. Other commentators suggest that patent trolls are not bad for the patent system at all but instead realign market participant incentives, make patents more liquid, and clear the patent market.

Another theoretical problem with patent rights was proposed by law professors Michael Heller and Rebecca Sue Eisenberg. Based on Heller's theory of the tragedy of the anticommons, the authors argued that intellectual property rights may become so fragmented that, effectively, no one can take advantage of them as to do so would require an agreement between the owners of all of the fragments.

Pharmaceutical patents prevent generic alternatives to enter the market until the patents expire, and thus maintains high prices for medication. This can have significant effects in the developing world, as those who are most in need of basic essential medicines are unable to afford such high priced pharmaceuticals. Critics also question the rationale that exclusive patent rights and the resulting high prices are required for pharmaceutical companies to recoup the large investments needed for research and development. One study concluded that marketing expenditures for new drugs often doubled the amount that was allocated for research and development. Other objects shed light on the problems of today's medical research. It sets wrong priorities in research and pricing, and pushes the state-run healthcare systems even of rich nations to their limits. In one response to these criticisms, one review concluded that less than 5 per cent of medicines on the World Health Organization's list of essential drugs are under patent.

Also, the pharmaceutical industry has contributed US$2 billion for healthcare in developing countries, providing HIV/AIDS drugs at lower cost or even free of charge in certain countries, and has used differential pricing and parallel imports to provide medication to the poor. Other groups are investigating how social inclusion and equitable distribution of research and development findings can be obtained within the existing intellectual property framework, although these efforts have received less exposure.

Brazil filed a proposal in 2010 with the WIPO Standing Committee on the Law of Patents about the imbalance of rights between IP title holders and the society as a whole with emphasis on the imbalance of benefits from strong IP rights between the few developed countries and the majority of member states. Such imbalance is also recognized between freedom rights and exclusion rights by the computing profession.

Concerns of a similar order have also been documented elsewhere, showing that public campaigns have had a concern for"preventing the over-reach" of IP protection including patent protection, and"to retain a public balance in property rights" of this kind. The same source also noted the shift that had taken place away from the historical classification of such rights as"grants of privilege", towards referring to them in terms of property and rights; a change that encouraged a change of view of the relation of sovereign governments towards them, away from something that the government"may grant" towards a"duty to uphold them".

TRADEMARK

A trademark or trade mark or trade-mark is a distinctive sign or indicator used by an individual, business organization, or other legal entity to identify that the products or services to consumers with which the trademark appears originate from a unique source, and to distinguish its products or services from those of other entities.

A trademark is designated by the following symbols:

- ™ (for an unregistered trade mark, that is, a mark used to promote or brand goods)
- ℠ (for an unregistered service mark, that is, a mark used to promote or brand services)
- ® (for a registered trademark)

A trademark is typically a name, word, phrase, logo, symbol, design, image, or a combination of these elements. There is also a range of non-conventional trademarks comprising marks which do not fall into these standard categories, such as those based on colour, smell, or sound.

The owner of a registered trademark may commence legal proceedings for trademark infringement to prevent unauthorized use of that trademark. However, registration is not required. The owner of a common law trademark may also file suit, but an unregistered mark may be protectable only within the geographical area within which it has been used or in geographical areas into which it may be reasonably expected to expand.

The term trademark is also used informally to refer to any distinguishing attribute by which an individual is readily identified, such as the well known characteristics of celebrities. When a trademark is used in relation to services rather than products, it may sometimes be called a service mark, particularly in the United States.

Fundamental Concepts

The essential function of a trademark is to exclusively identify the commercial source or origin of products or services, such that a trademark, properly called, indicates source or serves as a badge of origin. In other words, trademarks serve to identify a particular business as the source of goods or services.

The use of a trademark in this way is known as trademark use. Certain exclusive rights attach to a registered mark, which can be enforced by way of an action for trademark infringement, while unregistered trademark rights may be enforced pursuant to the common law tort of passing off.

It should be noted that trademark rights generally arise out of the use or to maintain exclusive rights over that sign in relation to certain products or services, assuming there are no other trademark objections. Different goods and services have been classified by the International (Nice) Classification of Goods and Services into 45 Trademark Classes (1 to 34 cover goods, and 35 to 45 services). The idea of this system is to specify and limit the extension of the intellectual property right by determining which goods or services are covered by the mark, and to unify classification systems around the world.

History

In trademark treatises it is usually reported that blacksmiths who made swords in the Roman Empire are thought of as being the first users of trademarks. Other notable trademarks that have been used for a long time include Löwenbräu, which claims use since 1383, and Stella Artois, which claims use since 1366.

Registered trademarks involve registering the trademark with the government.

The oldest registered trademarks in various countries include:

- *United Kingdom*: 1876 - The Bass Red Triangle was the first trademark to be registered under the Trade Mark Registration Act 1875.
- *United States*: Picture of Samson wrestling a lion, to Samson Rope in 1884.

Symbols

The two symbols associated with U.S. trademarks ™ and ® (the registered trademark symbol) represent the status of a mark and accordingly its level of protection. While ™ can be used with any common law usage of a mark, ® may only be used by the owner of a mark following registration with the relevant national authority, such as the U.S. Patent and Trademark Office. The proper manner to display either symbol is immediately following the mark in superscript style.

Terminology

Terms such as"mark","brand" and"logo" are sometimes used interchangeably with"trademark"."Trademark", however, also includes any device, brand, label, name, signature, word, letter, numerical, shape of goods, packaging, colour or combination of colours, smell, sound, movement or any combination thereof which is capable of distinguishing goods and services of one business from those of others. It must be capable of graphical representation and must be applied to goods or services for which it is registered.

Specialized types of trademark include certification marks, collective trademarks and defensive trademarks. A trademark which is popularly used to describe a product or service (rather than to distinguish the product or services from those of third parties) is sometimes known as a genericized trademark. If such a mark becomes synonymous with that product or service to the extent that the trademark owner can no longer enforce its proprietary rights, the mark becomes generic.

Registration

The law considers a trademark to be a form of property. Proprietary rights in relation to a trademark may be established through actual use in the marketplace, or through registration of the mark with the trademarks office (or"trademarks registry") of a particular jurisdiction. In some jurisdictions, trademark rights can be established through either or both means. Certain jurisdictions generally do not recognize trademarks rights arising through use.

If trademark owners do not hold registrations for their marks in such jurisdictions, the extent to which they will be able to enforce their rights through trademark infringement proceedings will therefore be limited. In cases of dispute, this disparity of rights is often referred to as"first to file" as opposed to"first to use." Other countries such as Germany offer a limited amount of common law rights for unregistered marks where to gain protection, the goods or services must occupy a highly significant position in the marketplace - where this could be 40% or more market share for sales in the particular class of goods or services.

In the United States the registration process entails several steps prior to a trademark receiving its Certificate of Registration. First, an Applicant, the individual or entity applying for the registration, files an application to register the respective trademark. The application is then placed in line in the order it was received to be examined by an examining attorney for the U.S. Patent and Trademark Office.

Second, following a period of anywhere from three to six months the application is reviewed by an examining attorney to make sure that it complies with all requirements in order to be entitled to registration. This review includes procedural matters such as making sure the applicant's goods or services are identified properly. It also includes more substantive matters such as making sure the applicant's mark is not merely descriptive or likely to cause confusion with a pre-existing applied-for or registered mark. If the application runs afoul of any requirement, the examining attorney will issue an office action requiring the applicant to address certain issues or refusals prior to registration of the mark.

Third, and after the examination of the mark has concluded with no issues to be addressed or an applicant has responded adequately to an examining attorney's concerns, the application will be published for opposition. During this 30-day period third-parties who may be affected by the registration of the trademark may step forward to file an Opposition Proceeding to stop the registration of the mark. If an Opposition proceeding is filed it institutes a case before the Trademark Trial and Appeal Board to determine both the validity of the grounds for the opposition as well as the ability of the applicant to register the mark at issue.

Fourth, provided that no third-party opposes the registration of the mark during the opposition period or the opposition is ultimately decided in the applicant's favour the mark will be registered in due course. Outside of the United States the registration process is substantially similar to that found in the U.S. save for one notable exception in many countries: registration occurs prior to the opposition proceeding. In short, once an application is reviewed by an examiner and found to be entitled to registration a registration certificate is issued subject to the mark being open to opposition for a period of typically 6 months from the date of registration. A registered trademark confers a bundle of exclusive rights upon the registered owner, including the right to exclusive use of the mark in relation to the products or services for which it is registered. The law in most jurisdictions also allows the owner of a registered trademark to prevent unauthorized use of the mark in relation to products or services which are identical or"colourfully" similar to the"registered" products or services, and in certain cases, prevent use in relation to entirely dissimilar products or services. The test is always whether a consumer of the goods or services will be confused as to the identity of the source or origin. An example may be a very large multinational brand such as"Sony" where a non-electronic product such as a pair of sunglasses might be assumed to have come from Sony Corporation of Japan despite not being a class of goods that Sony has rights in.

Once trademark rights are established in a particular jurisdiction, these rights are generally only enforceable in that jurisdiction, a quality which is sometimes known as territoriality. However, there is a range of international trademark laws and systems which facilitate the protection of trademarks in more than one jurisdiction.

Search

The USPTO maintains a database of registered trademarks. The database is open to the public; however a licensed attorney may be required to interpret the search results. Furthermore as trademarks are governed by federal law, state law, and common law, a thorough search as to the availability of a mark is very important. In the United States, obtaining a trademark search and relying upon the results of an opinion issued by an attorney may insulate a trademark user from being required to pay treble damages and attorney's fees in a trademark infringement case as it demonstrates that the trademark user performed due diligence and was using the mark in good faith.

Trademarks may also be searched on third-party databases, such as LexisNexis, Dialog and Compu-Mark. In Europe and if a community trademark has to be filed, searches have to be conducted with the OHIM (Community Trademark Office) and with the various national offices. An alternative solution is to conduct a trademark search within private databases.

Ability to Register

In most systems, a trademark can be registered if it is able to distinguish the goods or services of a party, will not confuse consumers about the relationship between one party and another, and will not otherwise deceive consumers with respect to the qualities of the product.

Maintaining Rights

Trademarks rights must be maintained through actual lawful use of the trademark. These rights will cease if a mark is not actively used for a period of time, normally 5 years in most jurisdictions. In the case of a trademark registration, failure to actively use the mark in the lawful course of trade, or to enforce the registration in the event of infringement, may also expose the registration itself to become liable for an application for the removal from the register after a certain period of time on the grounds of"non-use". It is not necessary for a trademark owner to take enforcement action against all infringement if it can be shown that the owner perceived the infringement to be minor and inconsequential.

This is designed to prevent owners from continually being tied up in litigation for fear of cancellation. An owner can at any time commence action for infringement against a third party as long as it had not previously notified the third party of its discontent following third party use and then failed to take action within a reasonable period of time.

The owner can always reserve the right to take legal action until a court decides that the third party had gained notoriety which the owner'must' have been aware of. It will be for the third party to prove their use of the mark is substantial as it is the onus of a company using a mark to check they are not infringing previously registered rights. In the US, owing to the overwhelming number of unregistered rights, trademark applicants are advised to perform searches not just of the trademark register but of local business directories and relevant trade press. Specialized search companies perform such tasks prior to application.

All jurisdictions with a mature trademark registration system provide a mechanism for removal in the event of such non use, which is usually a period of either three or five years. The intention to use a trademark can be proven by a wide range of acts as shown in the"Wooly Bull" and"Ashton v Harlee" cases. In the U.S., failure to use a trademark for this period of time, aside from the corresponding impact on product quality, will result in abandonment of the mark, whereby any party may use the mark. An abandoned mark is not irrevocably in the public domain, but may instead be re-registered by any party which has re-established exclusive and active use, and must be associated or linked with the original mark owner.

If a court rules that a trademark has become"generic" through common use (such that the mark no longer performs the essential trademark function and the average consumer no longer considers that exclusive rights attach to it), the corresponding registration may also be ruled invalid.

Unlike other forms of intellectual property (*e.g.*, patents and copyrights) a registered trademark can, theoretically, last forever. So long as a trademark's use is continuous a trademark holder may keep the mark registered with the U.S. Patent and Trademark Office by filing Section 8 Affidavit(s) of Continuous Use as well as Section 9 Applications for renewal, as required. Specifically, once registered with the U.S. Patent and Trademark Office the owner of a trademark is required to file a Section 8 Affidavit of Continuous Use to maintain the registration between the 5th and 6th year anniversaries of the registration of the mark or during the 6-month grace period following the 6th-year anniversary of the registration. Note, if the Section 8 Affidavit is filed during the 6-month grace period additional fees to file the Affidavit with the U.S. Patent and Trademark Office will apply. In U.S. trademark registrations are also required to be renewed on or about every 10-year anniversary of the registration of the trademark. The procedure for 10-year renewals is somewhat different from that for the 5th-6th year renewal. In brief, registrants are required to file both a Section 8 Affidavit of Continuous Use as well as a Section 9 Application for Renewal every ten years to maintain their registration.

Enforcing Rights

The extent to which a trademark owner may prevent unauthorized use of trademarks which are the same as or similar to its trademark depends on various factors such as whether its trademark is registered, the similarity of the trademarks involved, the similarity of the products or services involved, and whether the owner's trademark is well known or, under U.S. law relating to trademark dilution, famous.

If a trademark has not been registered, some jurisdictions (especially Common Law countries) offer protection for the business reputation or goodwill which attaches to unregistered trademarks through the tort of passing off. Passing off may provide a remedy in a scenario where a business has been trading under an unregistered trademark for many years, and a rival business starts using the same or a similar mark.

If a trademark has been registered, then it is much easier for the trademark owner to demonstrate its trademark rights and to enforce these rights through an infringement action. Unauthorized use of a registered trademark need not be intentional in order for infringement to occur, although damages in an infringement lawsuit will generally be greater if there was an intention to deceive.

For trademarks which are considered to be well known, infringing use may occur where the use occurs in relation to products or services which are not the same as or similar to the products or services in relation to which the owner's mark is registered. A growing area of law relating to the enforcement of trademark rights is secondary liability, which allows for the imputation of liability to one who has not acted directly to infringe a trademark but whose legal responsibility may arise under the doctrines of either contributory or vicarious liability.

Limits and Defences to Claims of Infringement

Trademark is subject to various defences, such as abandonment, limitations on geographic scope, and fair use. In the United States, the fair use defence protects many of the interests in free expression related to those protected by the First Amendment. Fair use may be asserted on two grounds, either that the alleged infringer is using the mark to describe accurately an aspect of its products, or that the alleged infringer is using the mark to identify the mark owner.

One of the most visible proofs that trademarks provide a limited right in the U.S. comes from the comparative advertising that is seen throughout U.S. media. An example of the first type is that although Maytag owns the trademark"Whisper Quiet", makers of other products may describe their goods as being"whisper quiet" so long as these competitors are not using the phrase as a trademark. An example of the second type is that Audi can run advertisements saying that a trade publication has rated an Audi model higher than a BMW model, since they are only using"BMW" to identify the competitor. In a related sense, an auto mechanic can truthfully advertise that he services Cadillacs, and a former Playboy Playmate of the Year can identify herself.

Wrongful or Groundless Threats of Infringement

Various jurisdictions have laws which are designed to prevent trademark owners from making wrongful threats of trademark infringement action against other parties. These laws are intended to prevent large or powerful companies from intimidating or harassing smaller companies.

Where one party makes a threat to sue another for trademark infringement, but does not have a genuine basis or intention to carry out that threat, or does not carry out the threat at all within a certain period, the threat may itself become a basis for legal action. In this situation, the party receiving such a threat may seek from the Court a declaratory judgment; also known as a declaratory ruling.

Other Aspects

Public Policy

Trademark law is designed to fulfill the public policy objective of consumer protection, by preventing the public from being misled as to the origin or quality of a product or service. By identifying the commercial source of products and services, trademarks facilitate identification of products and services which meet the expectations of consumers as to quality and other characteristics.

Trademarks may also serve as an incentive for manufacturers, providers or suppliers to consistently provide quality products or services to maintain their business reputation. Furthermore, if a trademark owner does not maintain quality control and adequate supervision in relation to the manufacture and provision of products or services supplied by a licensee, such"naked licensing" will eventually adversely affect the owner's rights in the trademark. This proposition has, however, been watered down by the judgment of the House of Lords in the case of Scandecor Development AB v. Scandecor Marketing AB *et al*. UKHL 21; wherein it has been held that the mere fact that a bare license (equivalent of the United States concept of a naked license) has been granted did not automatically mean that a trademark was liable to mislead.

By the same token, trademark holders must be cautious in the sale of their mark for similar reasons as apply to licensing. When assigning an interest in a trademark, if the associated product or service is not transferred with it, then this may be an"assignment-in-gross" and could lead to a loss of rights in the trademark. It is still possible to make significant changes to the underlying goods or services during a sale without jeopardizing the trademark, but companies will often contract with the sellers to help transition the mark and goods or services to the new owners to ensure continuity of the trademark.

Comparison with Patents, Designs and Copyright

While trademark law seeks to protect indications of the commercial source of products or services, patent law generally seeks to protect new and useful inventions, and registered designs law generally seeks to protect the look or appearance of a manufactured object. Trademarks, patents and designs collectively form a subset of intellectual property known as industrial property because they are often created and used in an industrial or commercial context.

By comparison, copyright law generally seeks to protect original literary, artistic and other creative works. Continued active use and re-registration can make a trademark perpetual, whereas copyright usually lasts for the duration of the author's lifespan plus 70 years for works by individuals, and some limited time after creation for works by bodies corporate. This can lead to confusion in cases where a work passes into the public domain but the character in question remains a registered trademark.

Although intellectual property laws such as these are theoretically distinct. For example, the particular design of a bottle may qualify for copyright protection as a non-utilitarian, or for trademark protection based on its shape, or the'trade dress' appearance of the bottle as a whole may be protectable. Titles and character names from books or movies may also be protectable as trademarks while the works from which they are drawn may qualify for copyright protection as a whole.

Drawing these distinctions is necessary, but often challenging for the courts and lawyers, especially in jurisdictions where patents and copyrights pass into the public domain, depending on the jurisdiction. Unlike patents and copyrights, which in theory, are granted for one-off fixed terms, trademarks remain valid as long as the owner actively uses and defends them and maintains their registrations with the competent authorities. This often involves payment of a periodic renewal fee.

As a trademark must be used to maintain rights in relation to that mark, a trademark can be'abandoned' or its registration can be cancelled or revoked if the mark is not continuously used. By comparison, patents and copyrights cannot be'abandoned' and a patent holder or copyright owner can generally enforce their rights without taking any particular action to maintain the patent or copyright. Additionally, patent holders and copyright owners may not necessarily need to actively police their rights. However, a failure to bring a timely infringement suit or action against a known infringer may give the defendant a defence of implied consent or estoppel when suit is finally brought.

Dilution

A trademark is diluted when the use of similar or identical trademarks in other non-competing markets means that the trademark in and of itself will lose its capacity to signify a single source. In other words, unlike ordinary trademark law, dilution protection extends to trademark uses that do not confuse consumers regarding who has made a product. Instead, dilution protection law aims to protect sufficiently strong trademarks from losing their singular association in the public mind with a particular product, perhaps imagined if the trademark were to be encountered independently of any product (*e.g.*, just the word Pepsi spoken, or on a billboard). Under trademark law, dilution occurs either when unauthorized use of a mark"blurs" the"distinctive nature of the mark" or"tarnishes it." Likelihood of confusion is not required. 15 U.S.C §§ 1127, 1125(c).

Sale, Transfer and Licensing

In various jurisdictions a trademark may be sold with or without the underlying goodwill which subsists in the business associated with the mark. However, this is not the case in the United States, where the courts have held that this would"be a fraud upon the public". In the U.S., trademark registration can therefore only be sold and assigned if accompanied by the sale of an underlying asset. Examples of assets whose sale would ordinarily support the assignment of a mark include the sale of the machinery used to produce the goods that bear the mark, or the sale of the corporation that produces the trademarked goods.

Most jurisdictions provide for the use of trademarks to be licensed to third parties. The licensor (usually the trademark owner) must monitor the quality of the goods being produced by the licensee to avoid the risk of trademark being deemed abandoned by the courts. A trademark license should therefore include appropriate provisions dealing with quality control, whereby the licensee provides warranties as to quality and the licensor has rights to inspection and monitoring.

Domain Names

The advent of the domain name system has led to attempts by trademark holders to enforce their rights over domain names that are similar or identical to their existing trademarks, particularly by seeking control over the domain names at issue. As with dilution protection, enforcing trademark rights over domain name owners involves protecting a trademark outside the obvious context of its consumer market, because domain names are global and not limited by goods or service.

This conflict was more easily resolved when the domain name user actually used to compete with the trademark owner. Cybersquatting, however, involves no such competition, but instead an unlicensed user registering the trademark as a domain name to pressure a payoff from the lawful mark owner. Typosquatters-those registering common misspellings of trademarks as domain names-have also been targeted successfully in trademark infringement suits. Other types of domain name disputes include the so-called"gripe site," which use a registered trademark in a domain." There are also disputes arising from the subdomain, when a third party uses a protected mark in a web address. This clash of the new technology with preexisting trademark rights resulted in several high profile decisions as the courts of many countries tried to coherently address the issue (and not always successfully) within the framework of existing trademark law. There was no actual consumer confusion, and so initial interest confusion was a concept applied instead. Initial interest confusion refers to customer confusion that creates an initial interest in a competitor's"product". Even though initial interest confusion is dispelled by the time any actual sales occur, it allows a trademark infringer to capitalize on the goodwill associated with the original mark.

Several cases have wrestled with the concept of initial interest confusion. In Brookfield Commc'ns v. West Coast Ent'mt the court found initial interest confusion could occur when a competitor's trademarked terms were used in the HTML metatags of resulting in that site appearing in the search results when a user searches on the trademarked term. In Playboy v. Netscape, the court found initial interest confusion when users typed in Playboy's trademarks into a search engine, resulting in the display of search results alongside unlabeled banner ads, triggered by keywords that included Playboy's marks, that would take users to Playboy's competitors.

Though users might ultimately realise upon clicking on the banner ads that they were not Playboy-affiliated, the court found that the competitor advertisers could have gained customers by appropriating Playboy's goodwill since users may be perfectly happy to browse the competitor's site instead of returning the search results to find the Playboy sites. In Lamparello v. Falwell, however, the court clarified that a finding of initial interest confusion is contingent on financial profit from said confusion, such that, if a domain name confusing similar to a registered trademark is used for a non-trademark related, the site owner will not be found to have infringed where he does not seek to capitalize on the mark's goodwill for his own commercial enterprises.

In addition, courts have upheld the rights of trademark owners with regard to commercial use of domain names, even in cases where goods sold there legitimately bear the mark. In the landmark decision Creative Gifts, Inc. v. UFO, 235 F.3d 540, defendants had registered the domain name"Levitron.com" to sell goods bearing the trademark"Levitron" under an at-will license from the trademark owner. The 10th Circuit affirmed the rights of the trademark owner with regard to said domain name, despite arguments of promissory estoppel.

Most courts particularly frowned on cybersquatting, and found that it was itself a sufficiently commercial use (*i.e.*,"trafficking" in trademarks) to reach into the area of trademark infringement. Most jurisdictions have since amended their trademark laws to address domain names specifically, and to provide explicit remedies against cybersquatters. In the US, the legal situation was clarified by the Anticybersquatting Consumer Protection Act, an amendment to the Lanham Act, which explicitly prohibited cybersquatting. It defines cybersquatting as" when a person other than the trademark holder registers the domain name of a well known trademark and then attempts to profit from this by either ransoming the domain name back to the trademark holder or using the domain name to divert business from the trademark holder to the domain name holder".

The provision states that"[a] person shall be liable in a civil action by the owner of the mark... if, without regard to the goods or services of the person, that person (i) had a bad faith intent to profit from the mark...; and registers, traffics in, or uses domain name [that is confusingly similar to another's mark or dilutes another's mark]".

This international legal change has also led to the creation of ICANN Uniform Domain-Name Dispute-Resolution Policy (UDRP) and other dispute policies for specific countries (such as Nominet UK's DRS) which attempt to streamline the process of resolving who should own a domain name (without dealing with other infringement issues such as damages). This is particularly desirable to trademark owners when the domain name registrant may be in another country or even anonymous. Registrants of domain names also sometimes wish to register the domain names themselves as trademarks for perceived advantages, such as an extra bulwark against their domain being hijacked, and to avail themselves of such remedies as confusion or passing off against other domain holders with confusingly similar or intentionally misspelled domain names.

As with other trademarks, the domain name will not be subject to registration unless the proposed mark is actually used to identify the registrant's goods or services to the public, rather than simply being the location on the Internet where the applicant's web site appears. Terms which are not protectable by themselves, such as a generic term or a merely descriptive term that has not acquired secondary meaning, may become registrable when a Top-Level Domain Name is appended to it. An example of such a domain name ineligible for trademark or service mark protection as a generic term, but which currently has a registered U.S. service mark.

Among trademark practitioners there remains a great deal of debate around trademark protection under ICANN's proposed generic top-level domain name space expansion. World Trademark Review has been reporting on the at times fiery discussion between trademark owners and domainers.

International Law

It is important to note that although there are systems which facilitate the filing, registration or enforcement of trademark rights in more than one jurisdiction on a regional or global basis, it is currently not possible to file and obtain a single trademark registration which will automatically apply around the world. Like any national law, trademark laws apply only in their applicable country or jurisdiction, a quality which is sometimes known as"territoriality".

Territorial Application

The inherent limitations of the territorial application of trademark laws have been mitigated by various intellectual property treaties, foremost amongst which is the WTO Agreement on Trade-Related Aspects of Intellectual Property Rights. TRIPS establishes legal compatibility between member jurisdictions by requiring the harmonization of applicable laws. For example, Article 15(1) of TRIPS provides a definition for"sign" which is used as or forms part of the definition of"trademark" in the trademark legislation of many jurisdictions around the world.

Madrid System

The major international system for facilitating the registration of trademarks in multiple jurisdictions is commonly known as the"Madrid system". Madrid provides a centrally administered system for securing trademark registrations in member jurisdictions by extending the protection of an"international registration" obtained through the World Intellectual Property Organization. This international registration is in turn based upon an application or registration obtained by a trade mark applicant in its home jurisdiction.

The primary advantage of the Madrid system is that it allows a trademark owner to obtain trademark protection in many jurisdictions by filing one application in one jurisdiction with one set of fees, and make any changes (*e.g.* changes of name or address) and renew registration across all applicable jurisdictions through a single administrative process. Furthermore, the"coverage" of the international registration may be extended to additional member jurisdictions at any time.

Trademark Law Treaty

The Trademark Law Treaty establishes a system pursuant to which member jurisdictions agree to standardize procedural aspects of the trademark registration process. It is not necessarily respective of rules within individual countries.

Community Trade Mark system

The Community Trade Mark system is the trademark system which applies in the European Union, whereby registration of a trademark with the Office for Harmonization in the Internal Market (Trade Marks and Designs) (*i.e.* OHIM, the trademarks office of the European Union), leads to a registration which is effective throughout the EU as a whole. The CTM system is therefore said to be unitary in character, in that a CTM registration applies indivisibly across all European Union member states. However, the CTM system did not replace the national trademark registration systems; the CTM system and the national systems continue to operate in parallel to each other.

If you reside outside the EU, you must have professional representative to the procedures before the OHIM. If you are a European resident, you don't have to have professional representation to file an opposition, however, it is strongly recommended by the OHIM.

One of the tasks of a CTM owner is the monitoring of the later applications whether any of those is similar to his/her earlier trademark. Monitoring is not easy and usually requires professional expertise. To conduct a monitoring there is the so-called Trademark Watching service where it can be checked if someone tries to get registered marks that are similar to the existing marks.

Oppositions should be filed on the standard opposition form in any official language of the European Union, however, the substantive part of the opposition (*e.g.* the argumentations) can be submitted only in the language of the opposed application, that is one of the working languages of the OHIM, *e.g.* English, Spanish, German. Worth noting that in most of the cases the opponents file their oppositions in English.

Well-known Status

Well-known trade mark status is commonly granted to famous international trade marks in less-developed legal jurisdictions.

Pursuant to Article 6 bis of the Paris Convention, countries are empowered to grant this status to marks that the relevant authority considers are'well known'. In addition to the standard grounds for trade mark infringement (same/similar mark applied same/similar goods or services, and a likelihood of confusion), if the mark is deemed well known it is an infringement to apply the same or a similar mark to dissimilar goods/services where there is confusion, including where it takes unfair advantage of the well-known mark or causing detriment to it.

A well-known trademark does not have to be registered in the jurisdiction to bring a trade mark infringement action (equivalent to bringing a passing off claim without having to show goodwill and having a lesser burden of proof).

COPYRIGHT

Copyright is a set of exclusive rights granted by the law of a jurisdiction to the author or creator of an original work, including the right to copy, distribute and adapt the work. Exceptions and limitations to these rights strive to balance the public interest in the wide distribution of the material produced and to encourage creativity. Exceptions include fair dealing and fair use, and such use does not require the permission of the copyright owner. All other uses require permission and copyright owners can license or permanently transfer or assign their exclusive rights to others.

Copyright does not protect ideas, only their expression or fixation. In most jurisdictions, copyright arises upon fixation and does not need to be registered. Copyright protection applies for a specific period of time, after which the work is said to enter the public domain. The first copyright statute was the British Statute of Anne of 1709, the full title of which was:"An Act for the Encouragement of Learning, by vesting the Copies of Printed Books in the Authors or purchasers of such Copies". Copyright laws are partially standardized through international and regional agreements such as the Berne Convention and the European copyright directives.

Although there are consistencies among nations' copyright laws, each jurisdiction has separate and distinct laws and regulations covering copyright. National copyright laws on licensing, transfer and assignment of copyright still vary greatly between countries and copyrighted works are licensed on a territorial basis. Some jurisdictions also recognize moral rights of creators, such as the right to be credited for the work.

Initially copyright only applied to published books, but over time copyright was extended to other uses, such as translations and derivative works. Copyright now covers a wide range of works, including maps, dramatic works, paintings, photographs, sound recordings, motion pictures, and computer programmes.

Justification

The British Statute of Anne was the first act to directly protect the rights of authors. Under US copyright law, the justification appears in Article I, Section 8 Clause 8 of the Constitution, known as the Copyright Clause. It empowers the United States Congress"To promote the Progress of Science and useful Arts, by securing for limited Times to Authors and Inventors the exclusive Right to their respective Writings and Discoveries."

The World Intellectual Property Organisation the purpose of copyright is twofold:

- "To encourage a dynamic culture, while returning value to creators so that they can lead a dignified economic existence, and to provide widespread, affordable access to content for the public."

History

Early European Printers' Monopoly

The origin of copyright law in most European countries lies in efforts by the church and governments to regulate and control printing, which was widely established in the 15th and 16th centuries. Before the invention of the printing press a writing, once created, could only be physically multiplied by the highly laborious and error-prone process of manual copying by scribes. Printing allowed for multiple exact copies of a work, leading to a more rapid and widespread circulation of ideas and information. While governments and church encouraged printing in many ways, which allowed the dissemination of Bibles and government information, works of dissent and criticism could also circulate rapidly.

As a consequence, governments established controls over printers across Europe, requiring them to have official licences to trade and produce books. The licenses typically gave printers the exclusive right to print particular works for a fixed period of years, and enabled the printer to prevent others from printing or importing the same work during that period. The notion that the expression of dissent should be tolerated, not censured or punished by law, developed alongside the rise of printing and the press.

The Areopagitica, published in 1644 under the full title Areopagitica: A speech of Mr. John Milton for the liberty of unlicensed printing to the Parliament of England, was John Milton's response to the British parliament re-introducing government licensing of printers, hence publishers. In doing so, Milton articulated the main strands of future discussions about freedom of expression. As the"menace" of printing spread, governments established centralised control mechanism and in 1557 the British Crown thought to stem the flow of seditious and heretical books by chartering the Stationers' Company. The right to print was limited to the members of that guild, and thirty years later the Star Chamber was chartered to curtail the"greate enormities and abuses" of"dyvers contentyous and disorderlye persons professinge the arte or mystere of pryntinge or selling of books." The right to print was restricted to two universities and to the 21 existing printers in the city of London, which had 53 printing presses. The French crown also repressed printing, and printer Etienne Dolet was burned at the stake in 1546. As the British took control of type founding in 1637, printers fled to the Netherlands. Confrontation with authority made printers radical and rebellious, with 800 authors, printers and book dealers being incarcerated in the Bastille before it was stormed in 1789.

Early British Copyright Law

In England the printers, known as stationers, formed a collective organisation, known as the Stationers' Company. In the 16th century the Stationers' Company was given the power to require all lawfully printed books to be entered into its register. Only members of the Stationers' Company could enter books into the register. This meant that the Stationers' Company achieved a dominant position over publishing in 17th century England (no equivalent arrangement formed in Scotland and Ireland). The monopoly came to an end in 1694, when the English Parliament did not renew the Stationers Company's power. The newly established Parliament of Great Britain passed the first copyright statute, the Statute of Anne, full title"An Act for the Encouragement of Learning, by vesting the Copies of Printed Books in the Authors or purchasers of such Copies".

The coming into force of the Statute of Anne in April 1710 marked a historic moment in the development of copyright law. As the world's first copyright statute it granted publishers of a book legal protection of 14 years with the commencement of the statute. It also granted 21 years of protection for any book already in print. Unlike the monopoly granted to the Stationers' Company previously, the Statute of Anne was concerned with the reading public, the continued production of useful literature, and the advancement and spread of education. To encourage"learned men to compose and write useful books" the statute guaranteed the finite right to print and reprint those works. It established a pragmatic bargain involving authors, the booksellers and the public. The Statute of Anne ended the old system whereby only literature that met the censorship standards administers by the booksellers could appear in print. The statute furthermore created a public domain for literature, as previously all literature belonged to the booksellers forever.

Common Law Copyright

When the statutory copyright term provided for by the Statute of Anne began to expire in 1731 London booksellers thought to defend their dominant position by seeking injunctions from the Court of Chancery for works by authors that fell outside the statute's protection. At the same time the London booksellers lobbied parliament to extend the copyright term provided by the Statute of Anne. Eventually, in a case known as Midwinter v. Hamilton, the London booksellers turned to common law and starting a 30 year period known as the battle of the booksellers. The London booksellers argued that the Statute of Anne only supplemented and supported a pre-existing common law copyright.

The dispute was argued out in a number of notable cases, including Millar v Kincaid, Tonson v Collins, and Donaldson v Beckett (1774). Donaldson v Beckett eventually established that copyright was a"creature of statute", and that the rights and responsibilities in copyright were determined by legislation. The Lords clearly voted against perpetual copyright and by confirming that the copyright term, that is the length of time of work is in copyright, did expire just as to statute the Lords also confirmed that a large number of works and books first published in Britain were in the public domain, either because the copyright term granted by statute had expired, or because they were first published before the Statute of Anne was enacted in 1709. This opened the market for cheap reprints of works from Shakespeare, John Milton and Geoffrey Chaucer, works now considered classics. The expansion of the public domain in books broke the dominance of the London booksellers and allowed for competition, with the number of London booksellers and publishers rising threefold from 111 to 308 between 1772 and 1802.

Early French Copyright Law

In pre-revolutionary France all books needed to be approved by official censors and authors and publishers had to obtain a royal privilege before a book could be published. Royal privileges were exclusive and usually granted for six years, with the possibility of renewal. Over time it was established that the owner of a royal privilege has the sole right to obtain a renewal indefinitely. In 1761 the Royal Council awarded a royal privilege to the heirs of an author rather than the author's publisher, sparking a national debate on the nature of literary property similar to that taking place in Britain during the battle of the booksellers.

In 1777 a series of royal decrees reformed the royal privileges. The duration of privileges were set at a minimum duration of 10 years or the life of the author, which ever was longer. If the author obtained a privilege and did not transfer or sell it on, he could publish and sell copies of the book himself, and pass the privilege on to his heirs, who enjoyed an exclusive right into perpetuity. If the privilege was sold to a publisher, the exclusive right would only last the specified duration. The royal degrees prohibited the renewal of privileges and once the privilege had expired anyone could obtain a"permission simple" to print or sell copies of the work. Hence the public domain in books whose privilege had expired was expressly recognised. After the French Revolution a dispute over Comédie-Française being granted the exclusive right to the public performance of all dramatic works erupted and in 1791 the National Assembly abolished the privilege. Anyone was allowed to establish a public theatre and the National Assembly declared that the works of any author who had died more than five years ago were public property. In the same degree the National Assembly granted authors the exclusive right to authorise the public performance of their works during their lifetime, and extended that right to the authors' heirs and assignees for five years after the author's death.

The National Assembly took the view that a published work was by its nature a public property, and that an author's rights are recognised as an exception to this principle, to compensate an author for his work. In 1793 a new law was passed giving authors, composers, and artists the exclusive right to sell and distribute their works, and the right was extended to their heirs and assigns for 10 years after the author's death. The National Assembly placed this law firmly on a natural right footing, calling the law the"Declaration of the Rights of Genius" and so evoking the famous Declaration of the Rights of Man and of the Citizen. However, author's rights were subject to the condition of making depositing copies of the work with the Bibliothèque Nationale and 19th Century commentators characterised the 1793 law as utilitarian and"a charitable grant from society".

Early US Copyright Law

The Statute of Anne did not apply to the American colonies. The colonies' economy was largely agrarian, hence copyright law was not a priority, resulting in only three private copyright acts being passed in America prior to 1783. Two of the acts were limited to seven years, the other was limited to a term of five years. In 1783 several authors' petitions persuaded the Continental Congress"that nothing is more properly a man's own than the fruit of his study, and that the protection and security of literary property would greatly tends to encourage genius and to promote useful discoveries." But under the Articles of Confederation, the Continental Congress had no authority to issue copyright, instead it passed a resolution encouraging the States to"secure to the authors or publishers of any new book not hitherto printed... the copy right of such books for a certain time not less than fourteen years from the first publication; and to secure to the said authors, the copy right of such books for another term of time no less than fourteen years.

Three states had already enacted copyright statutes in 1783 prior to the Continental Congress resolution, and in the subsequent three years all of the remaining states except Delaware passed a copyright statute. Seven of the States followed the Statute of Anne and the Continental Congress' resolution by providing two fourteen year terms. The five remaining States granted copyright for single terms of fourteen, twenty and twenty one years, with no right of renewal. At the Constitutional Convention 1787 both James Madison of Virginia and Charles Pinckney of South Carolina submitted proposals that would allow Congress the power to grant copyright for a limited time. These proposals are the origin of the Copyright Clause in the United States Constitution, which allows the granting of copyright and patents for a limited time to serve a utilitarian function, namely"to promote the progress of science and useful arts".

The first federal copyright act, the Copyright Act of 1790 granted copyright for a term of"fourteen years from the time of recording the title thereof", with a right of renewal for another fourteen years if the author survived to the end of the first term. The act covered not only books, but also maps and charts. With exception of the provision on maps and charts the Copyright Act of 1790 is copied almost verbatim from the Statute of Anne.

At the time works only received protection under federal statutory copyright if the statutory formalities, such as a proper copyright notice, were satisfied. If this was not the case the work immediately entered into the public domain. In 1834 the Supreme Court ruled in Wheaton v. Peters, a case similar to the British Donaldson v Beckett of 1774, that although the author of an unpublished work had a common law right to control the first publication of that work, the author did not have a common law right to control reproduction following the first publication of the work.

Latin America

Latin American countries established national copyright laws following independence from the Spanish and Portuguese colonial powers. Latin American countries were among the first countries outside Europe to establish copyright law, with Brazil being the fourth country in the world to establish national copyright laws in 1804, after the UK, France and the United States. The foundation of Brazilian copyright law was the French Civil Code. Copyright law was initially established in Mexico following a Spanish court order in 1820 and in 1832 Mexico passed its first copyright statute. Copyright statutes had been established in eight Latin American countries by the 1850s.

Africa, Asia, and the Pacific

Copyright law was introduced in African, Asian and Pacific countries in the late 19th Century by European colonial powers, especially Britain and France. After the 1884 Congress of Berlin European colonial powers imposed new laws and institutions in their colonies, including copyright laws. The British Empire introduced copyright law in its African and Asian colonies though the Copyright Act 1911, also known as the Imperial Copyright Act of 1911. Similarly

France applied its copyright law throughout its colonies and the French National Institute for Intellectual Property (INPI) acted as the colonial intellectual property authority.

The introduction of copyright laws in colonies occurred in the context of colonial powers' desire to"civilize" their colonies and to protect the commercial interest of the colonial powers. While approaches varied, copyright laws were generally not adapted to fit local conditions.

International Copyright Law

Berne Convention for the Protection of Literary and Artistic Works

The Berne Convention was first established in 1886, and was subsequently re-negotiated in 1896, 1908, 1928 (Rome), 1948, 1967 and 1971. The convention relates to literary and artistic works, which includes films, and the convention requires its member states to provide protection for every production in the literary, scientific and artistic domain.

The Berne Convention has a number of core features, including the principle of national treatment, which holds that each member state to the Convention would give citizens of other member states the same rights of copyright that it gave to its own citizens.

Another core feature is the establishment of minimum standards of national copyright legislation in that each member state agrees to certain basic rules which their national laws must contain, though member states can if they wish increase the amount of protection given to copyright owners. One important minimum rule was that the term of copyright was to be a minimum of the author's lifetime plus 50 years. Another important minimum rule established by the Berne Convention is that copyright arises with the creation of a work and does not depend upon any formality such as a system of public registration). At the time some countries did require registration of copyright, and when Britain implemented the Berne Convention in the Copyright Act 1911 it had to abolish its system of registration at Stationers' Hall.

The Berne Convention focuses on authors as the key figure in copyright law and the stated purpose of the convention is"the protection of the rights of authors in their literary and artistic works", rather than the protection of publishers and other actors in the process of disseminating works to the public. In the 1928 revision the concept of moral rights was introduced, giving authors the right to be identified as a such and to object to derogatory treatment of their works. These rights, unlike economic rights such as preventing reproduction, could not be transferred to others.

The Berne Convention also enshrined limitations and exceptions to copyright, enabling the reproduction of literary and artistic works without the copyright owners prior permission. The detail of these exceptions was left to national copyright legislation, but the guiding principle is stated in Article 9 of the convention. The so called three-step test holds that an exception is only permitted"in certain special cases, provided that such reproduction does not conflict with a normal exploitation of the work and does not unreasonably prejudice the legitimate interests of the author". Free use of copyrighted work is expressly permitted in the case of quotations from lawfully published works, illustration for teaching purposes, and news reporting.

European Copyright Law

In the 1980s the European Community started to regard copyright as an element in the creation of a single market. Since 1991 the EU has passed a number of directives on copyright, designed to harmonise copyright laws in member states in certain key areas, such as computer programmes, databases and the internet. The directives aimed to reduce obstacles to the free movement of goods and services within the European Union, such as for example in rental rights, satellite broadcasting, copyright term and resale rights. Key directives include the 1993 Copyright Duration Directive, the 2001 InfoSoc Directive, also known as Copyright Directive, and the 2004 Directive on the enforcement of intellectual property rights.

Agreement on Trade-Related Aspects of Intellectual Property Rights

Important developments on copyright at international level in the 1990s include the 1994 Agreement on Trade-Related Aspects of Intellectual Property Rights, known as TRIPS Agreement. TRIPS was negotiated at the end of the Uruguay Round of the General Agreement on Tariffs and Trade (GATT) and contains a number of provisions on copyright. Compliance with the TRIPS Agreement is required of states wishing to be members of the World Trade Organisation (WTO). States need to be signatory of the Berne Convention and comply with all its provisions, except for the provision on moral rights). States need to bring computer programmes and databases within the scope of works covered by copyright law.

States need to provide for rental rights in at least computer programmes and films. Where copyright term, that is duration of copyright, is calculated other than by reference to the life of a natural person, States need to give a minimum term of 50 years calculated from either the date of authorised publication or the creation of the work.

Anti-Counterfeiting Trade Agreement

The Anti-Counterfeiting Trade Agreement (ACTA) is a proposed plurilateral trade agreement which is claimed by its proponents to be in response"to the increase in global trade of counterfeit goods and pirated copyright protected works." The scope of ACTA is broad, including counterfeit physical goods, as well as"internet distribution and information technology". In October 2007 the United States, the European Community, Switzerland and Japan announced that they would negotiate ACTA. Furthermore the following countries have joined the negotiations: Australia, the Republic of Korea, New Zealand, Mexico, Jordan, Morocco, Singapore, the United Arab Emirates and Canada. The ACTA negotiations have been largely conducted in secrecy, with very little information being officially disclosed. However, on 22 May 2008, a discussion about the proposed agreement was uploaded to Wikileaks, and newspaper reports about the secret negotiations quickly followed.

Copyright by Country

Copyright laws have been standardized to some extent through international conventions such as the Berne Convention. Although there are consistencies among nations' intellectual property laws, each jurisdiction has separate and distinct laws and regulations about copyright.

Obtaining Copyright

Copyright law is different from country to country, and a copyright notice is required in about 20 countries for a work to be protected under copyright. Before 1989, all published works in the US had to contain a copyright notice, the © symbol followed by the publication date and copyright owner's name, to be protected by copyright. This is no longer the case and use of a copyright notice is now optional in the US, though they are still used.

In all countries that are members of the Berne Convention, copyright is automatic and need not be obtained through official registration with any government office. Once an idea has been reduced to tangible form, for example by securing it in a fixed medium (such as a drawing, sheet music, photograph, a videotape, or a computer file), the copyright holder is entitled to enforce his or her exclusive rights. However, while registration isn't needed to exercise copyright, in jurisdictions where the laws provide for registration, it serves as prima facie evidence of a valid copyright. The original copyright owner of the copyright may be the employer of the author rather than the author himself, if the work is a"work for hire".

Copyright Term

Copyright subsists for a variety of lengths in different jurisdictions. The length of the term can depend on several factors, including the type of work (*e.g.* musical composition or novel), whether the work has been published or not, and whether the work was created by an individual or a corporation. In most of the world, the default length of copyright is the life of the author plus either 50 or 70 years. In the United States, the term for most existing works is for a term ending 70 years after the death of the author. If the work was a work for hire (*e.g.*, those created by a corporation) then copyright persists for 120 years after creation or 95 years after publication, whichever is shorter. In some countries (for example, the United States and the United Kingdom), copyrights expire at the end of the calendar year in question.

The length and requirements for copyright duration are subject to change by legislation, and since the early 20th century there have been a number of adjustments made in various countries, which can make determining the duration of a given copyright somewhat difficult. For example, the United States used to require copyrights to be renewed after 28 years to stay in force, and formerly required a copyright notice upon first publication to gain coverage. In Italy and France, there were post-wartime extensions that could increase the term by approximately 6 years in Italy and up to about 14 in France. Many countries have extended the length of their copyright terms (sometimes retroactively). International treaties establish minimum terms for copyrights, but individual countries may enforce longer terms than those.

Exclusive Rights Granted by Copyright

Copyright is literally, the right to copy, though in legal terms"the right to control copying" is more accurate. Copyright are exclusive statutory rights to exercise control over copying and other exploitation of the works for a specific period of time. The copyright owner is given two sets of rights: an exclusive, positive right to copy and exploit the copyrighted work, or license others to do so, and a negative right to prevent anyone else from doing so without consent, with the possibility of legal remedies if they do.

Copyright initially only granted the exclusive right to copy a book, allowing anybody to use the book to, for example, make a translation, adaptation or public performance. At the time print on paper was the only format in which most text based copyrighted works were distributed. Therefore, while the language of book contracts was typically very broad, the only exclusive rights that had any significant economic value were rights to distribute the work in print. The exclusive rights granted by copyright law to copyright owners have been gradually expanded over time and now uses of the work such as dramatization, translations, and derivative works such as adaptations and transformations, fall within the scope of copyright. With a few exceptions, the exclusive rights granted by copyright are strictly territorial in scope, as they are granted by copyright laws in different countries. Bilateral and multilateral treaties establish minimum exclusive rights in member states, meaning that there is some uniformity across Berne Convention member states.

The print format means that content is affixed onto the content can't be easily or conveniently manipulated by the user. Duplication of printed works is time-consuming and generally produces a copy that is of lower quality.

Developments in technology have created new formats and new means of distribution. Particularly digital formats distributed over computer networks have separated the content from its means of delivery. Users of content are now able to exercise many of the exclusive rights granted to copyright owners, such as reproduction, distribution and adaptation.

Types of Work Subject to Copyright

The types of work which are subject to copyright has been expanded over time. Initially only covering books, copyright law was revised in the 19th century to include maps, charts, engravings, prints, musical compositions, dramatic works, photographs, paintings, drawings and sculptures. In the 20th century copyright was expanded to cover motion pictures, computer programmes, sound recordings, choreography and architectural works.

Idea-expression Divide

Copyright law is typically designed to protect the fixed expression or manifestation of an idea rather than the fundamental idea itself. Copyright does not protect ideas, only their expression and in the Anglo-American law tradition the idea-expression divide is a legal concept which explains the appropriate function of copyright laws.

Related Rights and Neighboring Rights

Related rights is used to describe database rights, public lending rights, artist resale rights and performers' rights. Related rights may also refer to copyright in broadcasts and sound recordings. Related rights award copyright protection to works which are not author works, but rather technical media works which allowed author works to be communicated to a new audience in a different form. The substance of protection is usually not as great as there is for author works. In continental European copyright law, a system of neighboring rights has thus developed and the approach was reinforced by the creation of the Rome Convention for the Protection of Performers, Producers of Phonograms and Broadcasting Organizations in 1961.

First-sale Doctrine and Exhaustion of Rights

Copyright law does not restrict the owner of a copy from reselling legitimately obtained copies of copyrighted works, provided that those copies were originally produced by or with the permission of the copyright holder. It is therefore legal, for example, to resell a copyrighted book or CD. In the United States, this is known as the first-sale doctrine, and was established by the courts to clarify the legality of reselling books in second-hand bookstores. Some countries may have parallel importation restrictions that allow the copyright holder to control the resale market. This may mean for example that a copy of a book that does not infringe copyright in the country where it was printed does infringe copyright in a country into which it is imported for retailing. The first-sale doctrine is known as exhaustion of rights in other countries and is a principle that also applies, though somewhat differently, to patent and trademark rights. It is important to note that the first-sale doctrine permits the transfer of the particular legitimate copy involved. It does not permit making or distributing additional copies.

Limitations and Exceptions

The expression"limitations and exceptions" refers to situations in which the exclusive rights granted to authors, or their assignees under copyright law do not apply or are limited for public interest reasons. They generally limit use of copyrighted material to certain cases that do not require permission from the rights holders, such as for commentary, criticism, news reporting, research, teaching or scholarship, archiving, access by the visually impaired etc. They essentially create a limitation, or an exception to the monopoly exclusive rights that are granted to the creator of a copyright work by law.

Copyright theory teaches that the balance between monopoly granted to the creator, and the exceptions to this monopoly are at the heart of creativity. *i.e.* Exclusive rights stimulate investment and the production of creative works and simultaneously, exceptions to those rights create a balance that allows for the use of creative works to support innovation, creation, competition and the public interest. Limitations and exceptions have a number of important public policy goals such as market failure, freedom of speech, education and equality of access (such as by the visually impaired.)

Some view"limitations and exceptions" as"user rights" - seeing user rights provide an essential balance to the rights of copyright owners. There is no consensus amongst copyright experts as to whether they are"rights" or not. The concept of user rights has also been recognised by courts, including the Canadian Supreme Court in CCH Canadian Ltd v. Law Society of Upper Canada, which classed"fair dealing" as such a user right. These kinds of disagreements in philosophy are quite common in the philosophy of copyright, where debates about jurisprudential reasoning tend to act as proxies for more substantial disagreements about good policy.

Changing Technology and Limitations and Exceptions

The scope of copyright limitations and exceptions became a subject of significant controversy within various nations in the late 1990s and early 2000s, largely due to the impact of digital technology, the changes in national copyright legislations for compliance with TRIPS, and the enactment of anti-circumvention rules in response to the WIPO Copyright Treaty. Academics and defenders of copyright exceptions fear that technology, contract law undermining copyright law and copyright law not being amended, is reducing the scope of important exceptions and therefore harming creativity. This has resulted in a number of declarations on the importance of access to knowledge being important for creativity, such as the Adelphi Charter in 2005 and at a European level in May 2010 a declaration entitled Copyright for Creativity - A Declaration for Europe. The declaration was supported by industry, artist, education and consumer groups. The declaration states that"While exclusive rights have been adapted and harmonised to meet the challenges of the knowledge economy, copyright's exceptions are radically out of line with the needs of the modern information society. The lack of harmonisation of exceptions hinders the circulation of knowledge based goods and services across Europe. The lack of flexibility within the current European exceptions regime also prevents us from adapting to a constantly changing technological environment."

Competition Law/ Anti-Trust Law and Limitations and Exceptions

Copyright is typically thought of as a limited, legally sanctioned monopoly. Because of this, copyright licensing may sometimes interfere too much in free and competitive markets. These concerns are governed by legal doctrines such as competition law in the European Union, United States antitrust law, and anti-monopoly law in Russia and Japan. Competition issues may arise when the licensing party unfairly leverages market power, engages in price discrimination through its licensing terms, or otherwise uses a licensing agreement in a discriminatory or unfair manner. Attempts to extend the copyright term granted by law - for example, by collecting royalties for use of the work after its copyright term has expired and it has passed into the public domain - raise such competition concerns.

In April 1995, the US published"Antitrust Guidelines for the licensing of Intellectual Property" which apply to patents, copyright, and trade secrets. In January 1996, the European Union published Commission Regulation No.240/96 which applies to patents, copyright, and other intellectual property rights, especially regarding licenses. The guidelines apply mutatis mutandis to the extent possible. The interplay of copyright law and competition law is increasingly important in the digital world, as most countries laws allow private contracts to override copyright law. Given that copyright law creates a legally sanctioned monopoly, balanced by"limitations and exceptions" that allow access without the permission of the copyright holder the overriding of copyright law by private contracts can create monopoly activity.

Well known limitations and exceptions include fair dealing in the UK and Canada, as well as the fair use doctrine in the US. The undermining of copyright law, and in particular limitations and exceptions to copyright by contract law is an issue frequently raised by libraries, and library groups such as International Federation of Library Associations and Institutions. As a result of this, this issue is increasingly being looked at and discussed at a national governmental level *e.g.* UK as well as international level such as WIPO - as part of the Development Agenda.

International Legal Instruments and Limitations and Exceptions

Limitations and exceptions are also the subject of significant regulation by global treaties. These treaties have harmonized the exclusive rights which must be provided by copyright laws, and the Berne three-step test operates to constrain the kinds of copyright exceptions and limitations which individual nations can enact. On the other hand, international copyright treaties place almost no requirements on national governments to provide exemptions from exclusive rights; a notable exception to this is Article 10(1) of the Berne Convention, which guarantees a limited right to make quotations from copyrighted works.

Because of the lack of balance in international treaties in October 2004, WIPO agreed to adopt a significant proposal offered by Argentina and Brazil, the "Proposal for the Establishment of a Development Agenda for WIPO" also known simply as the "Development Agenda" - from the Geneva Declaration on the Future of the World Intellectual Property Organization. This proposal was well supported by developing countries. A number of civil society bodies have been working on a draft Access to Knowledge, or A2K.

Fair Use and Fair Dealing

Copyright does not prohibit all copying or replication. In the United States, the fair use doctrine, codified by the Copyright Act of 1976 as 17 U.S.C. § 107, permits some copying and distribution without permission of the copyright holder or payment to same. The statute does not clearly define fair use, but instead gives four non-exclusive factors to consider in a fair use analysis.

Those factors are:

1. The purpose and character of the use;
2. The nature of the copyrighted work;
3. The amount and substantialness of the portion used in relation to the copyrighted work as a whole; and
4. The effect of the use upon the potential market for or value of the copyrighted work.

In the United Kingdom and many other Commonwealth countries, a similar notion of fair dealing was established by the courts or through legislation. The concept is sometimes not well defined; however in Canada, private copying for personal use has been expressly permitted by statute since 1999. In Australia, the fair dealing exceptions under the Copyright Act 1968 (Cth) are a limited set of circumstances under which copyrighted material can be legally copied or adapted without the copyright holder's consent. Fair dealing uses are research and study; review and critique; parody and satire; news reportage and the giving of professional advice. Under current Australian law it is still a breach of copyright to copy, reproduce or adapt copyright material for personal or private use without permission from the copyright owner. Other technical exemptions from infringement may also apply, such as the temporary reproduction of a work in machine readable form for a computer. In the United States the AHRA prohibits action against consumers making noncommercial recordings of music, in return for royalties on both media and devices plus mandatory copy-control mechanisms on recorders.

Section 1008. Prohibition on certain infringement actions. No action ever may be brought under this title alleging infringement of copyright based on the manufacture, importation, or distribution of a digital audio recording device, a digital audio recording medium, an analog recording device, or an analog recording medium, or based on the noncommercial use by a consumer of such a device or medium for making digital musical recordings or analog musical recordings.

Later acts amended US Copyright law so that for certain purposes making 10 copies or more is construed to be commercial, but there is no general rule permitting such copying. Indeed making one complete copy of a work, or in many cases using a portion of it, for commercial purposes will not be considered fair use.

The Digital Millennium Copyright Act prohibits the manufacture, importation, or distribution of devices whose intended use, or only significant commercial use, is to bypass an access or copy control put in place by a copyright owner. An appellate court has held that fair use is not a defence to engaging in such distribution. Educational use is regarded as "fair use" in most jurisdictions, but the restrictions vary wildly from nation to nation. Recent Israeli District Court decision dated Sep. 2, 2009 accepted the defence of fair use for a site linking to P2P live feeds of soccer matches. The main reasoning was based on the public importance of certain sporting events, *i.e.* - the public's rights as counter weight to the copyright holders rights.

Licensing, Transfer, and Assignment

Copyright may be bought and sold much like other properties. In the individual licensing model the copyright owner authorizes the use of the work against remuneration and under the conditions specified by the license. The conditions of the license may be complex since the exclusive rights granted by copyright to the copyright owner can be split territorially or with respect to language, the sequence of uses may be fixed, the number of copies to be made and their subsequent use may also be specified. Furthermore sublicenses and representation agreements may also be made. A contractual transfer of all or some of the rights in a copyrighted work is a known as a copyright license.

A copyright assignment is an immediate and irrevocable transfer of the copyright owner's entire interest in all or some of the rights in the copyrighted work. Copyright licensing and assignment cover only the specified geographical region. There are significant differences in national copyright laws with regards to copyright licensing and assignment. Copyright licenses, as a minimum, define the copyrighted works and rights subject to the license, the territories or geographic region in which the license applies, the term or length of the license, and the consideration (such as a one of payment or royalties) for the license. The exclusive rights granted by copyright law can all be licensed, but they vary depending on local law.

Depending on how the work may be used different licenses need to be acquired. For example, the activity of distributing videocassettes of a motion picture will require the license for the right to reproduce the motion picture on a videocassette and the right to distribute the copies to the public. Because the ratio of a television screen is different from that of a wide-screen cinema, requiring the cutting of the wide-screen"ends", it may also be necessary to obtain a license for the right to modify the motion picture.

If the motion picture is to be edited or modified the copyright owner may include control over or approval of the editing process, or of the final result. Existing contractual agreements between the copyright owner and the director, may also require approval from the director to any changes made to the copyrighted work. Different types of exclusive licenses exist, such as licenses that excludes the licensor from use of the licenced copyrighted work in the relevant region and for the stated time period. Or exclusive licenses may prevent the licensor from licensing other parties in the geographic region and during the license term.

There are also various types of non-exclusive licenses, including the right of first refusal should the licensor elect to offer future licenses to third parties. If a licensing agreement does not specify that the license is exclusive it may nonetheless be deemed exclusive depending on the language of the contract. Depending on local laws the owner of an exclusive license may be deemed the"copyright owner" of that work and bring charges for copyright infringement. The term or length of the copyright license is not allowed to exceed the copyright term specified by local law. Licenses may establish various pay arrangements, such as royalties as a percentage of sales or as a stepped up or down percentage of sales, *e.g.* 5 per cent of sales up to 50,000 units, 2.5 per cent of sales in excess thereof.

The trigger for royalty payments may be sales. Minimum royalty payments are arrangements whereby a minimum up-front payment is made and then recouped against the percentage of sales. The up-front payment may be non-refundable if sales royalties do not reach the amount of the payment. Minimum royalty payment arrangements may be accompanied by marketing duties for the licensee, *e.g.* best effort and reasonable effort to market and promote the copyrighted work.

Collective Rights Management

Collective rights management is the licensing of copyright and related rights by organizations acting on behalf of rights owners. Collective management organisations, such as collecting societies, typically represent groups of copyright and related rights owners, such as authors, composers, publishers, writers, photographers, musicians and performers.

The following exclusive rights granted under copyright law are commonly collectively managed by collecting societies: the right to public performance, the right to broadcasting, the mechanical reproduction rights in recorded music, the performing rights in dramatical works, the rights of reprographic reproduction of literary and musical works, and related rights, for example the rights of performers and producers in recorded music when used in broadcasts.

The collective management of copyright and related rights is undertaken by various types of collective management organisations, most commonly collecting societies. Collecting societies act on behalf of their members, which may be authors or performers, and issue copyright licenses to users authorising the use of the works of their members. Other forms of collective management organisations include rights clearance centres and one-stop shops. One-stop shops are a coalition of collecting societies and rights clearance centres offering a centralised source for users to obtain licences. They have become popular in response to multi-media productions requiring users to obtain multiple licences for relevant copyright and related rights.

Extended Collective Licensing

The first extended collective licensing (ECL) laws were established in Denmark, Finland, Iceland, Norway and Sweden in the 1960s. ECL is a form of collective rights management whereby ECL laws allow for freely negotiated copyright licensing contracts for the exclusive rights granted by copyright. ECL laws are designed specifically for mass use, where negotiating alone will rarely allow a single right owner to fully financially benefit from their exclusive rights. Under ECL laws, collecting societies negotiate ECL agreements with users, such as a TV broadcaster, covering the types of copyrighted works for uses specified in the ECL licence.

Subject to certain conditions collecting societies can under ECL law apply to represent all rights owners on a non-exclusive basis in a specific category of copyrighted works. The collecting society can then negotiate an ECL agreement with a user for certain uses. This agreement applies to members of that collecting society, as well as non-members. ECL laws require that collecting societies treat rights owners who are non-members in the same way they treat their members. Non-members are also given the right to individual remuneration, *i.e.* royalty payment, by the collecting society, and the right to exclude their work from an ECL agreement.

Compulsory Licensing

In some countries copyright law provides for compulsory licenses of copyrighted works for specific uses. In many cases the remuneration or royalties received for a copyrighted work under compulsory license are specified by local law, but may also be subject to negotiation. Compulsory licensing may be established through negotiates licenses that provide terms within the parameters of the compulsory license. Article 11bis of the Berne Convention for the Protection of Literary and Artistic Works provide the legal basis for compulsory licenses. They state that member states are free to determine the conditions under which certain exclusive rights may be exercised in their national laws. They also provide for the minimum requirements to be set when compulsory licenses are applied, namely that they must not prejudice the author to fair compensation.

Future Rights under Pre-existing Agreements

It is commonplace in copyright licensing to license not only new uses which may be developed but also works which are not yet created. However, local law may not always recognise that the wording in licensing agreements does cover new uses permitted by subsequently developed technology. Whether a license covers future, as yet unknown, technological developments is subject to frequent disputes. Litigation over the use of a licensed copyrighted work in a medium unknown when the license was agreed is common.

Enforcement

Copyrights are generally enforced by the holder in a civil law court, but there are also criminal infringement statutes in some jurisdictions. While central registries are kept in some countries, which aid in proving claims of ownership, registering does not necessarily prove ownership, nor does the fact of copying (even without permission) necessarily prove that copyright was infringed. Criminal sanctions are generally aimed at serious counterfeiting activity, but are now becoming more commonplace as copyright collectives such as the RIAA are increasingly targeting the file sharing domestic Internet user.

Infringement

Copyright infringement, or copyright violation, is the unauthorized use of works covered by copyright law, in a way that violates one of the copyright owner's exclusive rights, such as the right to reproduce or perform the copyrighted work, or to make derivative works. For electronic and audio-visual media under copyright, unauthorized reproduction and distribution is also commonly referred to as piracy.

An early reference to piracy in the context of copyright infringement was made by Daniel Defoe in 1703 when he said of his novel The True-Born Englishman"Had I wrote it for the gain of the press, I should have been concerned at its being printed again and again by PIRATES, as they call them, and PARAGRAPHMEN: but if they do justice, and print it true, just as to the copy, they are welcome to sell it for a penny, if they please: the pence, indeed, is the end of their works.".

The practice of labeling the act of infringement as"piracy" predates statutory copyright law. Prior to the Statute of Anne 1709, the Stationers' Company of London in 1557 received a Royal Charter giving the company a monopoly on publication and tasking it with enforcing the charter. Those who violated the charter were labeled pirates as early as 1603.

Orphan Works

An orphan work is a work under copyright protection whose copyright owner is difficult or impossible to contact. The creator may be unknown, or where the creator is known it is unknown who represents them.

Public Domain

Works are in the public domain if their kind is not covered by intellectual property rights or if the intellectual property rights have expired, have been forfeited, or have never been claimed. Examples include the English language, the formulae of Newtonian physics, as well as the works of Shakespeare and the patents over powered flight.

Copyright as Property Right

Copyright as a property law was initially conceived of as a"chose in action", that is an intangible property, as opposed to tangible property. In the case of tangible property the property rights are bundled with the ownership of the property, and property rights are transferred once the property is sold. In contrast copyright law detaches the exclusive rights granted under property law to the copyright owner from ownership of the good which is regarded as a reproduction. Hence the purchase of a book buys ownership of the book as a good, but not the underlying copyright in the book's content. If a derivative work based on the content of the book is made, permission needs to be sought from the copyright owner, not all owners of a copy of the book.

The Statute of Anne specifically referred to copyright in terms of literary property that is limited in time. Many contemporaries did not believe that the statute was concerned with property"in the strict sense of the word" and the question of whether copyright is property right dates back to the Battle of the Booksellers. In 1773 Lord Gardenston commented in Hinton v. Donaldson that"the ordinary subjects of property are well known, and easily conceived... But property, when applied to ideas, or literary and intellectual compositions, is perfectly new and surprising..." It was in the 19th century that the term intellectual property began to be used as an umbrella term for patents, copyright and other laws.

The expansion of copyright and copyright term are mirrored in the rhetoric that has been employed in referring to copyright. Courts, when strengthening copyright, have characterised it as a type of property. Companies have strongly emphasised copyright as property, with leaders in the music and movie industries seeking to"protect private property from being pillaged" and making forceful assertions that copyright is absolute property right. With reference to the expanding scope of copyright, one commentator noted that"We have gone from a regime where a tiny part of creative content was controlled to a regime where most of the most useful and valuable creative content is controlled for every significant use." Graham Dutfield and Uma Suthersanen copyright is now a"class of intangible business assets", mostly owned by companies who function as"investor, employer, distributor and marketer". While copyright was conceived as personal property awarded to creators, creators now rarely own the rights in their works.

Copyright and Authors

Copyright law emerged in 18th Century Europe in relation to printed books and a new notion of authorship. In the European Renaissance and Neoclassical period the writer was regarded as an instrument, not as an independent creator. The writer was seen as using external sources to create a work of inspiration. In the 18th Century a changing concept of genius located the source of inspiration within the writer, whose special talents and giftedness was the basis for creating works of inspiration and uniqueness.

The concept of the author as original creator and owner of their work emerged partly from the new concept of property rights and John Locke's theory that individuals were"owners of themselves". Locke individuals invested their labour into natural goods, and so creating property. Authors were argued to be the owners of their work because they had invested their labour in creating it. Patterson and Livingston there remains confusion about the nature of copyright ever since Donaldson v Beckett, a case heard in 1774 by the British House of Lords about whether copyright is the natural law right of the author or the statutory grant of a limited monopoly. One theory holds that copyright's origin occurs at the creation of a work, the other that its origin exists only through the copyright statute.

Copyright and Competition Law

Copyright is typically thought of as a limited, legally sanctioned monopoly. Because of this, copyright licensing may sometimes interfere too much in free and competitive markets. These concerns are governed by legal doctrines such as competition law in the European Union, anti-trust law in the United States, and anti-monopoly law in Russia and Japan. Competition issues may arise when the licensing party unfairly leverages market power, engages in price discrimination through its licensing terms, or otherwise uses a licensing agreement in a discriminatory or unfair manner. Attempts to extend the copyright term granted by law - for example, by collecting royalties for use of the work after its copyright term has expired and it has passed into the public domain - raise such competition concerns. In April 1995, the US published"Antitrust Guidelines for the licensing of Intellectual Property" which apply to patents, copyright, and trade secrets.

In January 1996, the European Union published Commission Regulation No.240/96 which applies to patents, copyright, and other intellectual property rights, especially regarding licenses. The guidelines apply mutatis mutandis to the extent possible. The interplay of copyright law and competition law is increasingly important in the digital world, as most countries laws allow private contracts to over-ride copyright law. Given that copyright law creates a legally sanctioned monopoly, balanced by"limitations and exceptions" that allow access without the permission of the copyright holder the over-riding of copyright law by private contracts can create monopoly activity. Well known limitations and exceptions include fair dealing in the UK and Canada, as well as the fair use doctrine in the US. The undermining of copyright law, and in particular limitations and exceptions to copyright by contract law is an issue frequently raised by libraries, and library groups such as International Federation of Library Associations and Institutions. As a result of this, this issue is increasingly being looked at and discussed at a national governmental level *e.g.* UK as well as international level such as WIPO - as part of the Development Agenda.

Copyright and Economic Development

The historian Eckhard Höffner the 1710 introduction of copyright law in England and later in France acted as a barrier to economic progress for over a century, while Germany prospered in the same time frame due to the lack of copyright laws. Höffner argues that copyright laws allowed British publishers to print books in limited quantities for high prices.

ENTREPRENEURIAL MARKETING

What differentiates businesses that deliver sustained market leadership from those that don't? Michael Treacy and Fred Wiersema, as outlined in their book "The Discipline of Market Leaders," studied more than 80 companies, some acknowledged market leaders, some with less impressive results, to discover what accounted for the success of one group and the poor results of the other. To provide a framework for their findings, Treacy and Wiersema developed a concept they call "value disciplines," which identifies three fundamental ways that businesses drive their organizations to achieve leadership in their marketplaces: operational excellence, product leadership and customer intimacy.

The market leaders that Treacy and Wiersema studied exhibited high standards of performance and intense focus on one of these three disciplines, and used it to define their business. This does not mean that the other value disciplines were ignored; market leaders are competitive in all of the three values but have "honed at least one component of value to a level of excellence that puts all competitors to shame." We believe this model can be used by businesses of all sizes to develop a winning strategy and lay a foundation for competitive advantage.

OPERATIONAL EXCELLENCE

The operationally excellent organization is driven by logistical excellence, consistency, speed and quality. It typically provides lower-cost solutions than the competition. This organization is process obsessed and strives to measure and set new standards for efficiency, consistency and quality. Think of the process excellence of McDonald's in manufacturing a hamburger of consistent quality and low cost around the world, or of Dell Computer delivering a made-to-order computer from instructions received from the customer over the Internet. Wal-Mart is a pioneer in the field of retail operational excellence, using efficiency to drive its low-price promise.

Product Leadership

The product leadership organization focuses on product innovation, providing a superior product and continuously pursuing new products or enhancements. The company's products are leading edge and exhibit design or technological advancement. Intel is a prime example of a product-focused market leader that continually pushes the technology envelope; 3M also leads its markets through new product development, and Sony led the consumer electronics market through its innovative product focus for several decades.

Customer Intimacy

The customer-intimate organization provides superior customer service by providing unique or customized products or services that stem from a deep understanding of each customer's, or market segment's, needs. It consistently meets and exceeds customer expectations, providing the best total solution to the requirements of a group of customers who are prepared to pay for it, or who will reward the value proposition by entering into a long-term relationship. Four Seasons Hotels and Resorts states that its growth stemmed from a singular concept: what the global business traveller wanted most was round-theclock, personalised service. Home Depot revolutionized the retail building products industry and connected with an emerging consumer segment by hiring professional contractors to provide free, expert advice to the do-ityourself home renovator.

Applying the Model

Treacy and Wiersema found that the market leaders that they observed were focused on excelling in one of these three drivers, rather than all three. The authors put forward the notion that a business cannot become a market leader by trying to be all things to all people. After choosing a value discipline that defines what the company does best, market leaders work diligently to align all elements of their business in support of this value. When we discuss this model with business leaders, many have difficulty with the notion of losing focus on any of these key disciplines.

Using the value discipline model to develop a business strategy does not mean choosing one of the three drivers and ignoring the others. In the extreme, customer intimacy without some level of operational excellence would allow you to become close to a customer, but unable to deliver any kind of product or service to them.

It is essential to deliver satisfactory results in all three areas while striving to deliver extraordinary results in one. To apply this model to your organization, start by determining your current positioning. Where is your organization now? Are you a product leader? Are you trying to be both customer intimate and operationally excellent?

Once you determine where you are now, think about where you would like to be in the future and how your organization would look should you choose one discipline as the foundation for your business strategy.

In the safety of an internal planning session, you and your management team might think about how each of these drivers would change your business over the next three to five years if it were your focus. Which of these three best matches with your market opportunities and strengths? Defining competitive positioning and strategy is all about setting key priorities for the organization and choosing where to place your bets.

Business Strategies

Good entrepreneurs understand the role of business strategy in growing a business. Here, we discuss numerous business strategies that might work for you. It's a competitive world out there. Make sure your strategies are up to the job of outperforming the competition and helping you to achieve your business goals. A strategic alliance is a cooperative agreement with another company to combine resources in a way that is beneficial to both parties. Unlike a merger, both companies maintain their individual identities, goals, mission, etc.

The purpose of the alliance is simply to create opportunities for the two companies to work together to achieve a specified goal - promotion, purchasing, product manufacturing, or something else entirely.

Understandably, many small business owners are hesitant to partner with other businesses, particularly businesses that operate in the same industry. After all, what good could possibly come from helping the competition? But suppose you own a pizza parlor and a competitor approached you about joining forces to place a combined order that would reduce the cost of your tomato sauce by 35%.

Sure, your competitor would reduce his expenses, but so would you. More importantly, it would give both of your companies a competitive advantage over all the other pizza parlors in the area. That's the power of a strategic alliance. Both companies benefit and realise a marketplace advantage they would not have been able to achieve independently.

Setting-Up Strategic Alliance

The important thing is to make sure that both partners are aware of what they are expected to do and what they can expect to receive as a result of the alliance.

Regardless of how you decide to structure the alliance, it's important for both partners to share the risks and the benefits. If your company is left to carry all the risk for half the benefit, then you're probably being taken advantage of and need to look elsewhere for a new alliance partner. Yet many business owners fall into the rut of offering products that are nearly identical to the competition.

To stand out from the crowd, all you need is a healthy dose of creativity to take you back to your entrepreneurial roots. Here's how to get started.

Making Good or Better Product

You have a good product. But the competition has a good product, too. In fact, the market is filled with good products and the last thing your customers need is another product of average quality cluttering the buying process. More than anything else, customers are looking for a great product that leaves all the other ones in the dust.

Gather your team together and begin brainstorming about ways to improve your existing product and position yourself above the competition. Emphasize improvements that create additional features or add value - anything that will stand out from the other "been there, done that" products the industry already offers.

New Applications

Sometimes the problem isn't the product itself, but rather the product's field of use. In some industries, product use is limited to a narrow range of applications defined by the way the product has been used in the past.

However, there is a good chance that your product has applications beyond its current usage. With a little diligence and a few minor modifications, you may be able to find new applications for your product and increase demand by widening the market.

New Products

Right now, someone is wishing they had a product that doesn't exist. Yet. Innovative entrepreneurs succeed by creating new products to fill gaps in the marketplace. The way they discern those gaps is through patience and hard work.

Begin by asking your existing customers for suggestions about new products that would make their life a little easier. Then use their ideas as fodder for new product concepts, consistently returning to the customers for input throughout the development process. Before the product even hits the market it will be in demand by the customers whose input you used to produce it.

Cross-Pollinate for Ideas

Another source of ideas for new products is to cross-pollinate with other industries. For example, if your business is accounting, regularly expand your horizons by touching base with other non-related industries like healthcare, advertising, or graphic design.

Along the way, you might run across tidbits of information that spark an idea for improving your services or creating new ones altogether. You might also be able to leverage new insights and new contacts to expand your market into other industries.

Take Risks

Know why many business owners find themselves stuck in a crowd? Because they are afraid of how their business might be perceived if they stood out from the crowd. Innovation is risky business.

Successful entrepreneurs embrace a certain level of calculated risk in order to differentiate themselves from the competition. Don't let risk hold you back from acting on innovative ideas. Identify the risks ahead of time, take the necessary steps to minimize them, and step out of the crowd with confidence.

MARKET STRATEGY

Sometimes it does, but sometimes waiting for someone else to break new ground is a surer way to achieve long-term success. The key to finding the right time for the release of your product is knowing upfront the potential advantages and disadvantages associated with being the first to market.

Advantages of Being First to Market

- *Consumer Impact*: First movers enjoy the ability to make a significant impact in the minds of consumers, setting a standard for others to follow. Product characteristics, service delivery methods, price points, and other factors combine to create a level of expectation that you can progressively be refined to strengthen your brand.
- *Name Recognition*: If you are the first to bring a product to market, you will experience exclusive name recognition during the initial stages of the product's life. As long as you are able to maintain a strong market presence, your name will continue to be identified with the product even after others have entered the market.
- *Lack of Competition*: This may seem obvious, but being a first mover grants you exclusive market rights - at least for a while. By leveraging your temporary position as the sole provider, you can make significant gains in the short term and plot a strategy to remain competitive when the market gets crowded.

Disadvantages

- *Market Ignorance* - When you create a new product, you are creating a new market. As a first mover, the new market will look to your company to shoulder the burden of introducing the product to consumers and educating them about its use. This translates into time, effort, and resources that later competitors don't have to worry about.
- *Product Development* - First movers also bear the cost of developing a product to the point of marketability. For some products, research and development costs aren't a major factor. But for more complex products, it's definitely something you need to factor into your decision. Ultimately, you might be better off letting someone else work out the kinks so you can focus on creating a lasting market presence.

Cheap Knockoffs: If your product is a success, someone is inevitably going to try to steal market share by offering a cheaper alternative. Unless you can clearly articulate the value of your product compared to a cheap knockoff, you may find yourself priced out by someone who hasn't invested anything in the product's design or development. If your product doesn't stand out from the crowd, the marketplace will view it as a commodity and you'll be forced to compete on price - bad news for a business eager to boost its bottom line. The problem is that standing out is easier said than done.

Commoditization is becoming an increasingly familiar problem in some industries, leaving small business owners scrambling to price their products at a competitive level. Rather than trying to compete on price, you can beat the system and avoid the commodity trap by altering the market's perception of your product. Here are five ways to differentiate your product and avoid being lumped in with the rest of the pack.

Unique Characteristics

The first step out of the commodity trap is to examine what makes your product or service different from everyone else's. Do you have better customer support? Is your product designed better than the competition? Is your service tailored to a specific segment of the market? There's a good chance there is something that sets you apart from others who provide the same product. Finding your unique characteristics is crucial because it provides a starting point for the entire differentiation process.

Value-Added Services

Once you have identified your unique characteristics, you can begin to explore new ways to add value to your product. Use your imagination to consider how you can offer additional value while at the same time highlighting your product's strengths.

Many add-ons can be done without a substantial cost increase. In fact, some of the best ones cost very little, yet draw a significant amount of attention from the marketplace.

Target Marketing

Another effective way to differentiate your product or service is to customise it for specific industries or market niches.

Interview potential customers within a given industry to determine which features are currently missing in the marketplace and then tailor your product to meet their needs. If you play your cards right, it's possible to customise your product to the extent that it becomes a standard within the industry, safely distancing it from being perceived as a commodity.

Create a Network

An isolationist attitude in a glutted market will only make the situation worse. The businesses who rise above the competition are the ones who have created strategic relationships with vendors, consultants, and others who offer complementary products and services. The larger your network, the more likely it is that your product will find its way to the top of the heap.

Value vs. Cost

The surest way to avoid competing on price is to stop pushing price as a selling point. Instead, educate your sales staff to focus on the value of your product compared to the competition. Buyers are almost always willing to spend a little more as long as they understand the additional benefits they will receive from the more expensive product. Developing strategy can be very exciting for a business owner.

Break It Down

When you communicate a business strategy to your staff, you need to help them see how they fit into the big picture. They want to have a general idea what the big picture looks like, but more importantly they want to understand how it will impact them.

Will your new strategy affect their role in the company? Is their job still secure? What new expectations will be placed on them? These questions and many more will need to be answered before your employees can wholeheartedly commit to the strategy.

Speak their Language

It's not uncommon for business owners to immerse themselves in the language and culture of a new strategy. The problem is that employees haven't immersed themselves in the same language and culture, and may need some time to catch up. Until they do, it's important to communicate in their language, using terms and phrases they already understand.

Establish Benchmarks

Benchmarks help employees contextualize the strategy and understand the timeframe for its implementation. Each person's role in executing the strategy becomes easier to swallow when the strategy is presented in a staged format with manageable "bite-sized" goals along the way. It also becomes easier to assess progress and red flag problem areas when they arise.

Provide Updates

Once you've established strategy benchmarks, you'll need to revisit them every once in a while and communicate your progress to your employees. If you are on-schedule, your employees will want to share in your satisfaction. If you are behind schedule, your employees may be able to help you nail down the reason why and make suggestions about how to get back on track.

Avoid E-mail

One last thing about communicating strategy to your employees: If at all possible, avoid using e-mail as a communication device. E-mail is fine for everyday business correspondence. But when it comes to something as important as strategy, employees appreciate the courtesy of a face to face meeting. Meetings also have the added benefit of bringing the entire team together to brainstorm ideas and coordinate between departments. If your business is in fast-growth mode, you need to stay alert for trouble signs before it's too late. Here are five of the most common fast-growth snafus worth watching.

Growing Beyond Your Infrastructure

Infrastructure is the backbone of your business. It consists of the capital resources, systems, and processes that you use everyday to run your business effectively. If growth outpaces infrastructure, resources run thin and systems get stretched to their limits. In other words, your business becomes less effective. Planned growth buys the time you need to upgrade your infrastructure to maintain the same level of quality that made your business a success in the first place..

Losing Quality Staff

An overheated growth cycle is stressful on a business. However, quick growth is especially difficult on key employees who are typically leaned on in a pinch. Lean on them too much and you will likely lose them to competitors whose work environment reflects a more normal pace of life. Instead of losing them, engage key employees in a dialogue about how your growth is affecting the company and share your plans to remedy the situation as soon as possible.

Stretching Human Resources

Key employees aren't the only ones who are affected by rapid growth. All of your employees will be forced to deal with the reality of trying to squeeze more work into their work week. When business is booming, it's tempting to put off hiring additional staff as a way to beef up the bottom line. But the extra profits you reap will pale in comparison to the extra headaches that come with a disgruntled workforce. A more reasonable approach is to map out a schedule of new hires that is gauged to benchmarks of growth. Solicit input from department heads to determine how many additional workers you'll need and when you will need them.

Create New Products

One way to reinvent an industry is to create entirely new products that meet needs and position your business at the top of the heap. While the competition is struggling to catch up, you'll enjoy the advantages that go along with being first to market. You'll also enjoy the ability to define future expectations regarding your new product, meaning that instead of being controlled by the market, you will be in the driver's seat. Although under certain circumstances being the first to market can be a disadvantage, it's definitely an option worth considering.

Redesign Product Delivery

You don't necessarily have to create a new product to be innovative. Sometimes all it takes is a radical redesign of the manner in which your product is delivered to customers. For example, Starbucks didn't invent the coffee shop concept. However, they revolutionized the industry by transforming a simple cup of coffee into a gourmet coffee experience. With a little creativity, you can transform your industry by changing the way customers experience products you already sell.

Customise

Niche marketing has traditionally been a tool used by businesses to differentiate themselves from the competition. But you can also employ niche marketing techniques to customise your products for various segments of the market. While everyone else is offering a generic, one-size-fits-all product, you can offer an array of products designed to accommodate your customers' specific needs and applications.

Creating Strategic Partnerships

If you can't beat the competition, maybe you can join them. Strategic partnerships leverage the strengths of individual businesses to form an alliance that is beneficial to both parties. When partner companies possess complementary strengths, the result is a powerhouse that leaves other competitors scratching their heads.

Change Your Emphasis

Yet another way to turn the industry on its head is to refocus the prevailing emphasis. If the industry is focused on cost, you can focus on service. If the industry is focused on service, you can focus on cost. If it succeeds, you will soon find yourself on the cutting edge of an industry trend that you have shaped and molded to your company's strengths. Conventional wisdom says that a sure way to increase demand for a product is to slash its price.

But is that really true? Is being the lowest cost provider the best strategy for increasing sales and bumping the bottom line? On the first day of Econ 101, your professor explained a fundamental economic concept: Lower the price and demand will increase.

In a perfect world, that would always be true. The problem is that we don't live in a perfect world. Price is only one factor in determining demand for products and services. Other factors (e.g. marketing strategy) also play a significant role in attracting customers. In fact, sometimes being the lowest priced product on the market can even have a negative effect on demand.

Low Product Perception

A low-priced product is often perceived to be inferior to its higher priced counterparts, regardless of its actual quality. Think about it: If given the choice between a $10 hamburger and a $1 hamburger, chances are you will assume the $10 burger is larger, tastes better, and contains better ingredients based on nothing other than price. By choosing to compete on price, you run the risk of inviting a similar perception from your customer base. In some industries the risk may be minimal, but in others it may be a formidable obstacle to overcome.

Brand Inferiority

Another common perception that can be caused by low pricing is that your company and your brand occupy a mediocre standing within the industry. Consumers are typically willing to pay more for a brand name product. New consumers will inevitably assume lower priced products are offered by a brand that is less established or less capable of delivering quality merchandise.

Poor Service

In the mind of a typical consumer, the cost of a product doesn't just include the cost of the merchandise inside the box. It also includes the cost of back-end products such as customer service and product warranties. If your product is priced lower than everyone else's, consumers will naturally assume that it doesn't come with the same assurance of support as products that are priced higher. This perception might not be far from reality since a lower priced product may necessitate cost-cutting measures that affect the level of follow-up service you are able to provide.

It's important to remember that the price you establish for your product communicates a wide range of intangibles to potential customers. Rather than trying to offer the least expensive product, you might want to consider strategic pricing to properly position yourself within the market.

Begin to view price as a tool to communicate the quality and value of your product in relation to your competitors. Done right, this can be a powerful way to establish market presence and eliminate the need to compete on price alone. It is important to have goals for the direction of your business outside of purely monetary gain. By setting goals, you are defining a guideline for the future of your business, and if you set goals effectively, you lay the framework for making those aspirations a reality. Measuring actual performance against your goals can provide an effective barometer for the performance of your business against desired performance. Not only does goal setting provide an introspective into overall performance, but is also an effective management tool used in businesses of all sizes in all industries.

The feasibility of goals is another issue that you will encounter as a small business owner. By setting goals that are too easily attainable, you may not be pushing your business to its maximum potential, allowing for wasted potential.

This is certainly not a scenario you would want to encounter. Conversely, by setting very lofty goals, you may be fostering some unrealistic notions and setting yourself up for disappointment.

While it is important to be ambitions, striking a healthy balance between ambition and feasibility is important to the effectiveness of goals that you set for your business.

By knowing the fundamentals of effective goal setting, you can be sure that the goals you set are effective in spurring the performance of your business and inspiring confidence in your employees in their drive for continuous progress.

But growing a company takes a lot more than good intentions. You need a plan. With dozens of strategies to choose from, here are four that could put your company on the fast track to growth. Not every growth strategy is appropriate for every small business. The key to finding the right growth strategy is properly matching it to your company and its specific marketplace. Since the wrong strategy can devastate your business, it's important to determine whether you are selling new or emerging products in a new or existing market.

Diversification

Diversification is a high-risk growth strategy, largely because both the products and the market are unproven territory for the entrepreneur. Though trailblazing emerging products and markets can be exhilarating, it can also be terrifying given the fact that neither you nor anyone else can rely on prior experience for reassurance.

Market Development

A more common scenario is one in which a small business owner attempts to develop a new market for their existing products and services.

The new market can be geographical or an untapped segment of a domestic market. It's even possible to develop a new market for existing products by adjusting the product's packaging or expanding the product's distribution channels.

In any event, a market development growth strategy requires a working knowledge of existing markets and the ability to gaps in the marketplace that can be exploited to your advantage.

Product Development

A growth strategy based on product development is the mirror image of a market development strategy. Instead of pioneering a new market with existing products, you attempt to roll out a new product(s) in a market with which you are already familiar.

Many small business owners are more comfortable working in this kind of scenario because they already possess an awareness of prevailing market conditions.

However, a product development strategy can be just as challenging as a market development strategy because it often requires the business to develop new abilities and continuously adapt the products until they achieve marketplace success.

Market Penetration

Businesses that find themselves in a situation that involves neither new markets nor new products are forced to grow through a market penetration strategy, a strategy that is designed to give the business a greater percentage of market share.

This type of strategy usually seeks to gain a competitive edge through pricing, marketing, or other initiatives. Additionally, market penetration can be achieved by increasing customer usage through loyalty programs and incentives targeting your existing customer base.

Day-to-day toil shouldn't distract you from certain practices that will not only keep your business afloat, but are essential in making it thrive.

SUCCESSFUL BUS}INESS

Improve Capital Funding

Everywhere you turn there are gurus, middlemen and business development specialist who have their own "To-Do" lists readily offered up to anybody seeking capital for the start-up or expansion of a business venture.

In most every case, a business plan is as important as a loan application in the process of seeking that money. What follows is a list of 12 topics you want to address when preparing your presentation for solicitation of funding:

Be Prepared: Write a Business Plan

By going through the process of writing your business plan you will have thought through all of the issues that an investor considers when judging the viability of your business. Even if they don't look at your entire business plan on the first pass you'll be prepared to respond to important issues and concerns of the potential investor or lender.

The Executive Summary should contain the following:

- The primary objectives of your company.
- Your key personnel.
- The market you address, its needs, how those needs are currently met, and how you address its short-comings.
- Detailed description of your product or service, including how it addresses customer needs and desires.
- Financial projections for five years, profit point, break-even point, and ROI for investors.

Be Flexible to Change in Your Business Model

As you begin to implement the business plan the real world may not embrace your business model. Determine what works and doesn't work. Be willing to alter your plans accordingly. You may even find greater market potential that requires re-thinking the entire business plan.

Consider Alternatives to Product Distribution

Failing to understand how your product should be distributed is a sure way to turn away investors. Do your homework on the various distribution channels. Know their expectations and working models.

Find the channel that works with your pricing model and facilitates your growth requirements. If possible, develop partners with brand names that can provide credibility and growth potential.

Be Flexible with Investors on Issues of Control

Don't focus on retaining control of your company. Focus on what makes the company profitable. Investors need to see that you are willing to assume some level of risk and are not intent on hoarding stock.

Great businesses have been built by entrepreneurs that understood their limitations and hired executives who knew more than they did. Focusing on profits creates capital opportunities. Focusing on control creates potential barriers to investors.

Develop a Strong Management Team

A business plan is only as good as the people responsible for making the business succeed. Identify who will run the business, their achievements and ability to make the business a success. Get commitments from qualified personnel for operations, financial management, development, marketing and sales.

If not yet identified, make note of those key positions for which you must identify and recruit the appropriate individual who retains the necessary education and experience. Don't hide your weaknesses or shortcomings. Identify them and how you intend to overcome.

Give Customers a Reason to Buy from You

There must be a need and desire for your product. No longer will a clever idea, by itself, bring in the money. You need customers willing to test your product. Paying customers validate your pricing strategy.

Be Reasonable and Conservative on Near-term Revenues and Profit Projections

The biggest red flag to an investor is revenue projections that increase by the same per cent each year. You should anticipate various increase levels as your business progresses through different stages of growth. Your engineering, sales and marketing expenses will also change with these growth stages. Conduct the research of your industry to determine expected ratios for expenses and revenue per employee. Investors will take you seriously when they see that you have a clear understanding of the financial implications.

Give Investors Alternative Exit Strategies

Understand what motivates an investor, their expectations, exit strategy, and their minimally acceptable return on investment (ROI). The investor has many alternative investment opportunities. If the investor is going to take a risk on your concept he or she has to "BELIEVE". Demonstrate your potential for profitability with thorough descriptions of the market, your personnel and your product concept.

Don't Ignore the Competition

Customers always have a choice. They can either choose to do things the way they have always done them, find alternative solutions, or purchase your product. Identify your competitors, their strengths, and weaknesses and emerging technologies. Without this knowledge you will not be able to plan on how to respond to their retaliation.

Accurately and Honestly Define Your Market

Do your market research. Investors can easily discern between substantive and superficial data. Define and locate your market niche then determine its TAM and SAM (Served Available Market). Through the use of surveys and secondary data you can calculate the approximate percentage of the SAM your company can penetrate, and how much to increase the SAM. Stating that you will capture the entire TAM is a clear indicator you don't understand the market and your potential in that market.

Don't Ignore Requirements of Incorporation, Patents, Trademarks and Copyrights

In some industries it is critical that competition be dissuaded through the use of patents, which protect your research and development investments and provide a window of opportunity to realise a share of revenues before competitive offerings arrive in the marketplace.

Trademarks, copyrights, non-disclosure agreements, employee agreements, etc. are a necessary part of the protection of a company's intellectual assets and branding. Incorporation will help to protect the investors and company assets in the event of legal proceedings against your company.

Identify the Methods and Costs of Getting Your Message to the Marketplace

Investors want to know what methods will be employed to gain customer attention, customer acquisition costs, average and target per-customer revenues, customer breakeven milestones and product life cycles. They also want to see your future plans for retaining existing customers. In most every business sector the returning customer represents the most reliable source of near and long-term revenues and profits.

STEPS TO A GREAT BUSINESS PLAN

A business plan serves two purposes:

- It provides a road map for your business.
- It helps you obtain outside financing.

If you're going into business for yourself, you must have a business plan - period. Numerous studies have shown that one of the major reasons new businesses fail is poor planning.

- Are you an entrepreneur?
- Start your own small business

The good news is that developing a business plan is not as hard as it seems. In order to develop a solid business plan, you need to have a thorough understanding of the business you're entering.

Next, you need to determine how you'll use the plan and who your target audience is. Finally, you should create a complete a business plan that is comprehensive and concisely written. We'll explore each of these steps in detail.

Step 1: Know Your Business

In order to prepare a business plan, you must know the business you are entering inside and out. This means lots of research. Research comes in two forms: reading everything you can about the industry and talking to those who are already in it. Learn everything you can about your business and industry.

Step 2: Determine your Purposes for the Plan

A business plan serves to crystallize your business vision and guide you in fulfilling that vision; it is also frequently used to entice potential investors.

- 6 steps to a better business budget
- Can you handle a home-based business?

If you are self-financing your business, you design the plan mostly for your benefit, but if you're seeking outside investors, you'll need to target them. As such, before you create your plan, determine whether you will solicit outside investors.

Step 3: Determine your Audience

If you plan to recruit investors, you need to build a plan to suit them. Outside investors, who range from friends and family members to banks and venture capitalists, will invest through either loaning you the money, buying shares in your company or some combination of the two.

Determine their level of sophistication and what they are looking for in a potential business investment.

Remember that regardless of their level of sophistication, they are all looking for four things:

Financial Confidence

Clearly articulate the risks of investing in your business. Also, show investors how they can recoup their money - whether your venture succeeds or fails.

A good return on investment - Over the period of 1928-2007, the geometric return for stocks was 9.8 per cent, while for 10-year Treasury bonds, it was 5 per cent.

Historical private-equity returns are more difficult to measure, but, in general, investors will expect a premium of anywhere from 2-5 per cent over public-equity market returns.

The return on equity for your new business must be in the private-equity range. Typically, investors will look to beat a certain internal rate of return. Your job is to make sure your projected returns are in line with those of similar industries.

Step 4: Create your Business Plan

First, develop an outline of your business plan. Consider every aspect of your business and how it will affect your business plan. Remember, this business plan is a road map. It must guide you. It must also communicate to investors what you're doing and why they should invest with you.

The order in which your plan is presented should be something like the following:

- Mission Statement
- Executive Summary
- Product or Service Offerings
- Target Market
- Marketing Plan
- Industry and Competitive Analysis
- Pro-Forma Financials
- Resumes of the Company Principals
- Your Offering (what type of financing you're seeking)

Mission Statement

The mission statement is a concise, one- to three-paragraph description of your business objectives, or your business's guiding principles.

In this section, you should state your unique selling point, or what separates your company from all the others in the industry that are otherwise just like it.

This is a one- to two-page summary of your business. Potential investors will read this to decide whether they want to look at the rest of your plan.

Product or Service Offering

Create a section describing your product or service offerings in detail, as well as how much you'll charge for what you're selling.

Target Market

Present your primary and secondary target markets, along with any research that demonstrates how your target market will benefit from and consequently purchase what you're offering.

Marketing Plan

Present your marketing plan, which should show in detail how you'll reach your target market. This part of the plan will include advertising and promotional strategies.

Industry and Competitive Analysis

Include a complete and thorough industry and competitive analysis that includes all stakeholders in your business. Don't forget to include governmental and regulatory agencies.

Financial Statements

These must be complete, accurate and thorough. Each number on your spreadsheets must mean something. Don't estimate payroll, for instance; determine what it will actually be. Your income statement must reconcile to your cash flow statement, which reconciles to your balance sheet. Your balance sheet must balance at the end of every period. You must have supporting schedules (e.g. depreciation and amortisation schedules) to back up your projections.

If you are having trouble building your pro-forma financial models, which should project out for at least five years, seek outside help from a qualified professional.

Use realistic projections. In estimating the growth of your business, you will make certain assumptions, which should be based on thorough industry research combined with a strategy for how you'll compete.

Also, analyse how quickly you'll achieve positive cash flow. Investors vary in their standards, but most like to see positive cash flow within the first year of operation, particularly if this if your first venture. In order for your projections to be accurate, you must know your business. If you've built an accurate and realistic model, but still project negative cash flow for more than 12 months, rethink your business model.

Resumes of Company Principals

Include the bios and professional backgrounds of all significant employees of your business. You will want to emphasize how their backgrounds have prepared them to take on the challenge of running your new startup. Also, if an employee's business background is in a significantly different industry, you might want to emphasize how this can be an advantage instead of a detriment.

Your Offering

Present what level of investment you're seeking and for what purposes you will use the funds. If you're selling business units, state the individual price per unit. Once you've put together all of this key information, make sure to present your plan professionally.

It should be typed, margin aligned and neatly bound. Use colour graphics and pictures where possible. Do not handwrite changes or corrections. The inside of your business plan should be near book or magazine quality.

After you've finished your plan, have a professional you trust, such as a Certified Public Accountant or attorney, look it over. This person may catch details, errors or omissions you've made. They also will be able to give you a more objective opinion of the viability of your business.

MARKET EXPANSION STRATEGIES

The Quarterly global survey of business executives reports that 84 per cent of executives consider growing number of consumers in emerging markets as an important trend but a lesser number of executives view these consumers as a future source of profits and a still lesser number of executives say that their companies have pursued this opportunity. Real challenge lies in converting non-customers of an industry into customers. However, traditionally, strategy researchers and practitioners have focused their attention on the problem of dealing with competition and how to get and keep market share.

Kim and Mauborgne conceptualize a "blue ocean" strategy framework for creation of demand in an untapped market. They visualize it as an alternative strategy to market share growth.

However, not every one agrees that market expansion and market share growth are mutually exclusive strategies. Some of the strategies suggested in this framework do not lead to market expansion in the same sense as we define it in this paper.

A "blue ocean" strategy framework provides tools and techniques for dealing with competition at different levels. But it does not pay enough attention to the exogenous factors affecting market demand such as the purchasing and consumption abilities of potential customers.

Prahalad with other scholars like Hammond and Lieberthal has developed a "bottom of the pyramid (BOP) marketing framework" as a means of expanding low income markets. In the context of developing countries, a BOP framework is more relevant than a "blue ocean strategy" framework.

Although a "BOP" framework is useful for development of a general framework for market expansion, conceptually expansions of markets do not necessarily mean expansion of "bottom of the pyramid" markets.

A "BOP" framework puts strong emphasis on the creation of consumption capacity among the poor. However, like a "blue ocean strategy" framework, it does not adequately address a very important consumer behaviour related issue of how to bring an unwilling customer into the market. "BOP" framework also ignores the competitive dimension in the formulation of strategy.

Much before the writings on "blue ocean strategy" and "bottom of the pyramid marketing," Kotler wrote about demand creation activities. He had identified specific situations in which a company needs to undertake demand creation efforts.

Although he wrote about marketing tasks in each such situation, these tasks do not constitute a holistic framework, especially in the context of developing countries. Moreover he did not write specifically about demand for a product as against demand for a brand.

The objective of this paper is to conceptualize a market expansion strategy in such a way that a generic framework can be developed which should be useful for the expansion of markets of any type, including the bottom of the pyramid markets in developing countries.

METHODOLOGY

We develop a framework without making any assumption as to whether market expansion is a strategic alternative to market share or not. We look into the fundamental issues such as: what is a market and what is market expansion. We synthesize some significant contributions to the market expansion-related strategy literature with relevant concepts and theories from literature in other areas. On the basis of the survey of the literature, we first clarify the domain of the market expansion construct and market expansion strategy. Then we identify the antecedent conditions that drive market expansion.

We also identify the moderating conditions under which the effect of antecedents is enhanced or ameliorated. On the basis of the identified antecedents and moderators, we develop a process-based framework for implementation and measurement of market expansion strategy. We also present a series of research propositions in the spirit of propositional inventories such as those developed by scholars like Kohli and Jaworski.

In the marketing literature the term "market" is referred to a set of actual and potential buyers of a product. Size of the market is measured in terms of demand. Demand for a product category as a whole is termed as primary demand while demand for a particular brand of a product is called selective demand. The upper limit of market demand is called market potential. In the marketing and strategy literature, primary demand creation and selective demand creation have been identified as distinct strategic options. Companies selling in mature markets often take primary demand as given.

They concentrate their marketing resources on building selective demand. However in countries which are characterized by huge but largely untapped market potential, some companies attempt to build primary demand as well as preference for their brands.

Demand for a product category can be expressed in terms of volume (i.e. quantity or number of units) or value. Whether the growth in the sales volume or value of a product category can be considered as market expansion or not depends on the source of the demand's growth.

We can visualize three sources of the growth in the demand for a product category:

- Demand from the first time buyers i.e. existing non-customers of the industry,
- Increase in the usage rate of existing customers of the industry,
- Value growth because of some customers upgrading to higher priced products.

Besides this, most products have replacement demand. We define a market expansion strategy as a strategy of increasing primary demand for a product category by converting non-customers into customers of an industry and/or by increasing the usage rate of industry's existing customers.

Focus on increasing the usage rate is especially relevant in case of products with high penetration levels but low per capita consumption.

For example, expansion of market of consumer non durables (i.e. toilet soaps and detergent cakes/powders) in India, can take place through increase in its usage rate.

"Expansion" and other similar terms used in the business and corporate strategy literature do not always mean market expansion.

For instance, Glueck and Jauch suggest concen-tration, integration, diversification, cooperation, and interna-tionalization as different routes to expansion. But these strategies do not necessarily lead to expansion of market for a particular product category.

Similarly, Ansoff in his product-market growth matrix talks about "market extension strategy" and "market penetration strategy." But extension of a market by reaching out to new market segments in present geographic markets is not the same as regional, national, or international geographic expansion of the company's sales.

The former option leads to an increase in primary demand for the product category. But in the latter case, a company might grow its sales by gaining market share from existing competitors in new geographic markets. Similarly, if market penetration is sought by converting non-customers into the customers of the industry's products, it leads to increase in the primary demand. But if market penetration is brought about by attracting competitor's customers, it leads to increases in the selective demand. This paper is concerned with market expansion for a particular product category and not corporate level expansion of overall sales revenue.

In order to measure market potential, it is necessary to define boundaries of a market. For defining market boundaries, Brooks conceptualizes "market" as a set of customers served by a set of suppliers, where both sets are defined in terms of products and services and in terms of geographic locations.

This means for each of its products in a chosen geographical area, a company can have different estimates of market potential depending on the definition of respective product's market boundaries in terms of competition.There exist two approaches to the definition of competition.

Demand-oriented approaches define competitors with respect to customer needs and wants, while supply-oriented approaches focus on physical product and manufacturing processes.

Levitt highlights the importance of demand side perspective in his article on 'Marketing Myopia' wherein he asks companies to focus on customer needs rather than the products that they sell. Marketing strategists generally define competitors from a consumer behaviour perspective.

By using four levels of competition as a framework, we can conceptualize different levels of market expansion. We can measure market potential for a product form (i.e. low cost airlines/motorbikes/herbal shampoo) or for a product category (i.e. airlines/two wheelers/shampoos) or for a generic need (i.e. travel/personal transport/hair care). At one extreme end, a firm may try to increase sales of its specific brand without attempting to increase the market potential of the product form to which the brand belongs. Resultant increase in the sales of that brand can not be termed as market expansion. A company can make efforts to increase the sales of a product form within a product category. For example, Air Deccan popularized the low cost air travel format in Indian domestic air travel market.

3

Role of Entrepreneurship in Economic Development

ENTREPRENEUR

An entrepreneur can be regarded as a person who has the initiative skill and motivation to set up a business or enterprise of his own and who always look for high achievements. He is the catalyst for social change and works for the common good. They looks for opportunities, identifies them and seizes them mainly for economic gains. An action oriented entrepreneur is a highly calculative individual who is always willing to undertake risks in order to achieve their goals.

NEED FOR ENTREPRENEURSHIP DEVELOPMENT

Economic development essentially means a process of upward change whereby the real pr capita income of a country increases over a period of time.Entrepreneurship has an important role to play in the development of a country. It is one of the most important inputs in economic development. The number and competence of entrepreneurs affect the economic growth of the country.

The economic history of the presently advanced countries like USA, Russia and Japan supports the fact that economic development is the outcome for which entrepreneurship is an inevitable cause. The crucial and significant role played by the entrepreneurs in the economic development of advanced countries has made the people of developing and under developed countries conscious of the importance of entrepreneurship for economic development.

It is now a widely accepted fact that active and enthusiastic entrepreneurs can only explore the potentials of the countries availability of recourses such as labour, capital and technology. The role of entrepreneurs is not identical in the various economies. Depending on the material resources, industry climate and responsiveness of the political system, it varies from economy to economy. The contribution of entrepreneurs may be more in favourable opportunity conditions than in economies with relatively less favourable opportunity conditions.

ENTREPRENEURSHIP AND ECONOMIC DEVELOPMENT

Entrepreneurship helps in the process of economic development in the following ways:

- *Employment Generation*: Growing unemployment particularly educated unemployment is the problem of the nation. The available employment opportunities can cater only 5 to 10% of the unemployed. Entrepreneurs generate employment both directly and indirectly. Directly, self employment as an entrepreneur and indirectly by starting many industrial units they offer jobs to millions. Thus entrepreneurship is the best way to fight the evil of unemployment.
- *National Income*: National Income consists of the goods and services produced in the country and imported. The goods and services produced are for consumption within the country as well as to meet the demand of exports. The domestic demand increases with increase in population and increase in standard of living. The export demand also increases to meet the needs of growing imports due to various reasons. An increasing number of entrepreneurs are required to meet this increasing demand for goods and services. Thus entrepreneurship increases the national income.
- *Balanced Regional Development*: The growth of Industry and business leads to a lot of Public benefits like transport facilities, health, education, entertainment etc. When the industries are concentrated in selected cities, development gets limited to these cities. A rapid development. When the new entrepreneur grow at a faster rate, in view of increasing competition in and around cities, they are forced to set up their enterprises in the smaller towns away from big cities. This helps in the development of backward regions.
- *Dispersal of economic power*: Industrial development normally may lead to concentration of economic powers in a few hands. This concentration of power in a few hands has its own evils in the form of monopolies. Developing a large number of entrepreneur helps in dispersing the economic power amongst the population. Thus it helps in weakening the harmful effects of monopoly.
- *Better standards of living*: Entrepreneur plays a vital role in achieving a higher rate of economic growth. Entrepreneurs are able to produce goods at lower cost and supply quality goods at lower price to the community just as to their requirements. When the price of the comedies decreases the consumers get the power to buy more goods

for their satisfaction. In this way they can increase the standard of living of the people.

- *Creating innovation*: An entrepreneur is a person who always looks for changes. Apart from combining the factors of production, he also introduces new ideas and new combination of factors. He always try to introduce newer and newer technique of production of goods and services. An entrepreneur brings economic development through innovation.

Entrepreneurship also helps in increasing productivity and capital formation of a nation. In short, the development of the entrepreneurship is inevitable in the economic development of the country.

The Role played by the entrepreneurship development can be expressed in the following words:

" *Economic development is the effect for which entrepreneurship is a cause*"

WOMEN ENTREPRENEURSHIP: GROWTH AND DEVELOPMENT

WOMEN ENTREPRENEURSHIP

Description

Historically, women have experienced special problems as entrepreneurs or aspiring entrepreneurs. It probable is still true in some locales that women cannot get business loans without a husband's or father's co-signature. For this sort of reason, specially focused programmes for women can be important for a community to obtain the full benefit of this important sector for business development, quite apart from questions of equity.

Programmes in women entrepreneurship may, but ordinarily do not also serve men, although much of the content of such programmes would be no different if they happened to be organized for a group of men. For example, there are, of course, no gender differences in the processes of feasibility studies or market analyses. However, an emphasis, for example, on networking among solely women entrepreneurs provides a significant support for sharing experiences with gender-related obstacles and techniques or dealing with them. Moreover, seminars and other training sessions restricted to women probable offer a greater opportunity for the participants to gain from them than if the usual pattern of male-dominated interactions in the school and other training settings must otherwise be countered.

In rural communities, families on farms must seek supplementary income, and the woman who considers a side-business is particularly a potential client for an entrepreneurship programme. Similarly, women dependent upon welfare supplements are another client base when these seek some means of self-employment in a very restricted labour market. A women entrepreneurship programme should not be limited to working with individuals or groups of entrepreneurs. An important function for such a programme is to act as a collective advocate for women in business in the local community or in wider venues, including the province and the nation.

For example, WRED (Women and Rural Economic Development) has been especially active in advocacy at the provincial and national level. It as also addressed the problem of credit for women business by getting a credit union to establish a loan programme. It this instance, WRED offered to guarantee loans so as to encourage the credit union's participation. Through WRED's advocacy efforts the lenders are also making some financial contribution by offering the loans at minimal rates.

Benefits

All too often the ideas, energy, and effort of women have been denied by and to a community's business development activities. This onerous handicap can be overcome by the techniques considered here. Thus today's national trend in which most new businesses are being started by women can be capitalized on in a CED strategy that promotes women entrepreneurship.

Major Challenges

The biggest problem to address is the need for comprehensiveness in programming, especially in rural areas. It is not enough to simply encourage women to start their businesses; they will need a variety of supportive services to sustain the businesses, including access to capital. And probable most important is access to continuing consultation as they try to grow their businesses. These, of course, are the needs of all new businesses, but in rural areas, the infrastructure of support is so sparse.

Thus a women entrepreneurship programme, to be most effective, has to step in to do a variety of tasks that in urban settings are being addressed by other agencies or groups – *e.g.*, basic numeracy and literacy training. Or failing that, the programme would have to restrict its clients to those who do not need the full range of supportive services and preparatory training. In that case, the programme neglects those who most need aid in moving into self-employment, particularly considering that they are least able to access any government programmes.

WOMEN AS ENTREPRENEURS IN INDIA

Women owned businesses are highly increasing in the economies of almost all countries. The hidden entrepreneurial potentials of women have gradually been changing with the growing sensitivity to the role and economic status in the society. Skill, knowledge and adaptability in business are the main reasons for women to emerge into business ventures.

'Women Entrepreneur' is a person who accepts challenging role to meet her personal needs and become economically independent. A strong desire to do something positive is an inbuilt quality of entrepreneurial women, who is capable of contributing values in both family and social life.

With the advent of media, women are aware of their own traits, rights and also the work situations. The glass ceilings are shattered and women are found indulged in every line of business from pappad to power cables.

The challenges and opportunities provided to the women of digital era are growing rapidly that the job seekers are turning into job creators. They are flourishing as designers, interior decorators, exporters, publishers, garment manufacturers and still exploring new avenues of economic participation.In India, although women constitute the majority of the total population, the entrepreneurial world is still a male dominated one. Women in advanced nations are recognized and are more prominent in the business world.

But the Indian women entrepreneurs are facing some major constraints like:

- *Lack of confidence*: In general, women lack confidence in their strength and competence. The family members and the society are reluctant to stand beside their entrepreneurial growth. To a certain extent, this situation is changing among Indian women and yet to face a tremendous change to increase the rate of growth in entrepreneurship.
- *Socio-cultural barriers*: Women's family and personal obligations are sometimes a great barrier for succeeding in business career. Only few women are able to manage both home and business efficiently, devoting enough time to perform all their responsibilities in priority.
- *Market-oriented risks*: Stiff competition in the market and lack of mobility of women make the dependence of women entrepreneurs on middleman indispensable. Many business women find it difficult to capture the market and make their products popular. They are not fully aware of the changing market conditions and hence can effectively utilize the services of media and internet.
- *Motivational factors*: Self motivation can be realised through a mind set for a successful business, attitude to take up risk and behaviour towards the business society by shouldering the social responsibilities. Other factors are family support, Government policies, financial assistance from public and private institutions and also the environment suitable for women to establish business units.
- *Knowledge in Business Administration*: Women must be educated and trained constantly to acquire the skills and knowledge in all the functional areas of business management. This can facilitate women

to excel in decision making process and develop a good business network.

- *Awareness about the financial assistance*: Various institutions in the financial sector extend their maximum support in the form of incentives, loans, schemes etc. Even then every woman entrepreneur may not be aware of all the assistance provided by the institutions. So the sincere efforts taken towards women entrepreneurs may not reach the entrepreneurs in rural and backward areas.
- *Exposed to the training programmes*: Training programmes and workshops for every type of entrepreneur is available through the social and welfare associations, based on duration, skill and the purpose of the training programme. Such programmes are really useful to new, rural and young entrepreneurs who want to set up a small and medium scale unit on their own.
- *Identifying the available resources*: Women are hesitant to find out the access to cater their needs in the financial and marketing areas. In spite of the mushrooming growth of associations, institutions, and the schemes from the government side, women are not enterprising and dynamic to optimize the resources in the form of reserves, assets mankind or business volunteers.

Highly educated, technically sound and professionally qualified women should be encouraged for managing their own business, rather than dependent on wage employment outlets. The unexplored talents of young women can be identified, trained and used for various types of industries to increase the productivity in the industrial sector. A desirable environment is necessary for every woman to inculcate entre-preneurial values and involve greatly in business dealings.

The additional business opportunities that are recently approaching for women entrepreneurs are:

- Eco-friendly technology
- Bio-technology
- IT enabled enterprises
- Event Management
- Tourism industry
- Telecommunication
- Plastic materials
- Vermiculture
- Mineral water

- Sericulture
- Floriculture
- Herbal and health care
- Food, fruits and vegetable processing

Empowering women entrepreneurs is essential for achieving the goals of sustainable development and the bottlenecks hindering their growth must be eradicated to entitle full participation in the business. Apart from training programmes, Newsletters, mentoring, trade fairs and exhibitions also can be a source for entrepreneurial development. As a result, the desired outcomes of the business are quickly achieved and more of remunerative business opportunities are found. Henceforth, promoting entrepreneurship among women is certainly a short-cut to rapid economic growth and development. Let us try to eliminate all forms of gender discrimination and thus allow 'women' to be an entrepreneur at par with men.

RURAL ENTREPRENEURSHIP: MEANING, NEED/OBJECTIVE

ENTREPRENEURSHIP AS AN ECONOMIC FORCE IN RURAL DEVELOPMENT

Rural development is more than ever before linked to entrepreneurship. Institutions and individuals promoting rural development now see entrepreneurship as a strategic development intervention that could accelerate the rural development process. Furthermore, institutions and individuals seem to agree on the urgent need to promote rural enterprises: development agencies see rural entrepreneurship as an enormous employment potential; politicians see it as the key strategy to prevent rural unrest; farmers see it as an instrument for improving farm earnings; and women see it as an employment possibility near their homes which provides autonomy, independence and a reduced need for social support.

To all these groups, however, entrepreneurship stands as a vehicle to improve the quality of life for individuals, families and communities and to sustain a healthy economy and environment. The entrepreneurial orientation to rural development accepts entrepreneurship as the central force of economic growth and development, without it other factors of development will be wasted or frittered away. However, the acceptance of entrepreneurship as a central development force by itself will not lead to rural development and the advancement of rural enterprises. What is needed in addition is an environment enabling entrepreneurship in rural areas. The existence of such an environment largely depends on policies promoting rural entrepreneurship. The effectiveness of such policies in turn depends on a conceptual framework about entrepreneurship, *i.e.*, what it is and where it comes from. This deals with the following three issues: firstly, it sets out the reasons why promoting entrepreneurship is a force of economic change that must take place if many rural communities are to survive; secondly, it deals with what policies are necessary in order to create an environment in rural areas conducive to entrepreneurship; and thirdly, it considers women and entrepreneurship.

Entrepreneurship Concept

The entrepreneurship concept, what it means and where it comes from, is the foundation for policies promoting entrepreneurship and the key to understanding the role of entrepreneurship in development.

What, Who and Why?

Defining entrepreneurship is not an easy task. There are almost as many definitions of entrepreneurship as there are scholar books on the subjects. To some, entrepreneurship means primarily innovation, to others it means risk-taking? to others a market stabilising force and to others still it means starting, owning and managing a small business. The entrepreneur is then viewed as a person who either creates new combinations of production factors such as new methods of production, new products, new markets, finds new sources of supply and new organizational forms; or as a person who is willing to take risks; or a person who, by exploiting market opportunities, eliminates disequilibrium between aggregate supply and aggregate demand, or as one who owns and operates a business. To choose the definition of entrepreneurship most appropriate for the rural area context, it is important to bear in mind the entreprencurial skills that will be needed to improve the quality of life for individuals, families and communities and to sustain a healthy economy and environment.

Taking this into consideration, as suggested, find that each of the traditional definitions has its own weakness. The first definition leaves little room for innovations that are not on the technological or organizational cutting edge, such as, adaptation of older technologies to a developing-country context, or entering into export markets already tapped by other firms. Defining entrepreneurship as risk-taking neglects other major elements of what we usually think of as entrepreneurship, such as a well-developed ability to recognise unexploited market opportunities. Entrepreneurship as a stabilising force limits entrepreneurship to reading markets disequilibria, while entrepreneurship defined as owning and operating a business, denies the possibility of entrepreneurial behaviour by non-owners, employees and managers who have no equity stake in the business.

Therefore, the most appropriate definition of entrepreneurship that would fit into the rural development context, argued here, is the broader one, the one which defines entrepreneurship as: "a force that mobilises other resources to meet unmet market demand", "the ability to create and build something from practically nothing", "the process of creating value by pulling together a unique package of resources to exploit an opportunity" It combines definitions of entrepreneurship by Jones and Sakong, 1980; Timmons, 1989; Stevenson, *et al.*, 1985. Entrepreneurship so defined, pertains to any new organization of productive factors and not exclusively to innovations that are on the technological or organizational cutting edge, it pertains to entrepreneurial activities both within and outside the organization.

Entrepreneurship need not involve anything new from a global or even national perspective, but rather the adoption of new forms of business organizations, new technologies and new enterprises producing goods not previously available at a location. This is why entrepreneurship is considered to be a prime mover in development and why nations, regions and communities that actively promote entrepreneurship development, demonstrate much higher growth rates and consequently higher levels of development than nations, regions and communities whose institutions, politics and culture hinder entrepreneurship.

An entrepreneurial economy, whether on the national, regional or community level, differs significantly from a non-entrepreneurial economy in many respects, not only by its economic structure and its economic vigourousness, but also by the social vitality and quality of life which it offers with a consequent attractiveness to people.

Economic structure is very dynamic and extremely competitive due to the rapid creation of new firms and the exit of 'old' stagnant and declining firms. It is populated with rapidly growing firms, gazelles as they are called in the literature of entrepreneurship. Gazelles are the key to economic development. As described by Twaalfhoven and Indivers, they are run by dynamic entrepreneurs, who manage and lead their companies not only to remain in the business but to expand it. Dynamic entrepreneurs look for growth, they do not have only a vision but are also capable of making it happen.

They think and act globally, look for expansion, rely on external resources, seek professional advice or they work with professional teams. They challenge competitors instead of avoiding them and take and share risks in a way that leads to success. In this way economic vitality of a country largely depends on the overall level of entrepreneurial capacity, *i.e.*, on its ability to create rapidly growing companies, gazelles. Equally important is the speed by which new small companies are created.

These phenomena explain why countries, regions and communities with a similar number of large and small firms show a completely different economic vitality. Economic vitality of a country is no doubt a necessary condition for social vitality. Without it other important factors that make living attractive in certain areas, such as education, health, social services, housing, transport facilities, flow of information and so on, cannot be developed and sustained in the area in the long run.

As evidence suggests, it is false to assume that socially and economically depressed areas will transform into fast growing areas by injection of external investment funds and external expertise. Without entrepreneurial capabilities which are well developed or potentially available, external funds will be wasted on projects that will not provide long term economic growth. Consequently instead of becoming more and more integrated into other economically and socially rich areas, such areas will become increasingly isolated, depopulated, poorer and therefore less and less capable of attracting people who, given other available resources, would make an impact from a development standpoint.

Entrepreneurial, orientation to rural development, contrary to development based on bringing in human capital and investment from outside, is based on stimulating local entrepreneurial talent and subsequent growth of indigenous companies. This in turn would create jobs and add economic value to a region and community and at the same time keep scarce resources within the community.

To accelerate economic development in rural areas, it is necessary to increase the supply of entrepreneurs, thus building up the critical mass of first generation entrepreneurs, who will take risks and engage in the uncertainties of a new venture creation, create something from practically nothing and create values by pulling together a unique package of resources to exploit an opportunity. By their example they will stimulate an autonomous entrepreneurial process, as well as a dynamic entrepreneurship, thereby ensuring continuous rural development. It is important to stress that rural entrepreneurship in its substance does not differ from entrepreneurship in urban areas.

Entrepreneurship in rural areas is finding a unique blend of resources, either inside or outside of agriculture. This can be achieved by widening the base of a farm business to include all the non-agricultural uses that available resources can be put to or through any major changes in land use or level of production other than those related solely to agriculture. Thus, a rural entrepreneur is someone who is prepared to stay in the rural area and contribute to the creation of local wealth. To some degree, however, the economic goals of an entrepreneur and the social goals of rural development are more strongly interlinked than in urban areas. For this reason entrepreneurship in rural areas is usually community based, has strong extended family linkages and a relatively large impact on a rural community.

Sources of Entrepreneurship

From the policy viewpoint? the promotion of entrepreneurship, the understanding where entrepreneurship comes from is as equally important as understanding the concept of entrepreneurship. It indicates where the governments, national, regional or local, should target their promotional efforts. If entrepreneurial skills, for example, are innate, active promotion policies have a small role to play. If instead, only certain entrepreneurial characteristics are innate, then active promotion policies can contribute to entrepreneurship development in the community in the region and in the nation, since entrepreneurial skills can be acquired through training. Empirical research on the sources of entrepreneurship is extensive, particularly within the discipline of psychology and sociology.

The standard perception is that entrepreneurship is a special personal feature, either a person is, or is not an entrepreneur. This perception entrepreneurial traits, such as the need to achieve, risk taking propensity, self-esteem and internal locus of control, creativity and innovative behaviour, the need for independence, occupational primacy, fixation upon goals and dominance, are all inborn. Therefore, policies directed specifically towards promoting the development of entrepreneurship would not help much since chose characteristics cannot be acquired by training. Risk talking propensity here is understood as the perceived probability of receiving rewards as opposed to the perceived probability of incurring a failure. Another perception is that some cultures or some social groups are more conducive to entrepreneurial behaviour than others.

The factors that contribute to the supply of entrepreneurs are an inheritance of entrepreneurial tradition, family position, social status, educational background and the level of education. Based on research into the origins of business owners, it is believed that persons who come from small business owner families, are more likely to become entrepreneurs than others. Studies of family position of existing entrepreneurs demonstrate that entrepreneurs are often found among elder children, since just as to the explanation, they are pressed to take more authority and responsibility at earlier stages than younger members of the family. The outsider group, ethnic minority, or the outsider individual, the marginal person, who are by a combination of different factors rendered outsiders in relation to the social groups with whom they normally interact, are both viewed as a significant source of entrepreneurship.

It is claimed that to minorities small business ownership means escape form marginality. Whether educational background influences potential entrepreneurs or not is a matter of debate. The popular idea of an entrepreneur is that of a totally self-made man, lacking in formal qualifications. This of course is not in conflict with findings that entrepreneurs who are better educated are more successful than the less educated ones. Apparently two things are involved simultaneously: propensity to start an entrepreneurial venture and skills to run the venture successfully. The research which tries to explain, by personal traits and/or other social aspects, why certain individuals become entrepreneurs, has not yet produced convincing results. Consequently, a widely accepted view is the following: while personal characteristics as well as social aspects clearly play some role, entrepreneurship and entrepreneurs can also be developed through conscious action.

Development of entrepreneurs and of entrepreneurship can be stimulated through a set of supporting institutions and through deliberate innovative action which stimulates changes and fully supports capable individuals or groups. It is argued, that controllable variables such as a stable system of property rights and freedom of action in the economic sphere, availability of other inputs in the economy as well as education and training, contribute significantly to the development of entrepreneurship. Therefore, policies and programmes designed specifically for entrepreneurship promotion, can greatly affect the supply of entrepreneurs and thus indirectly represent an important source of entrepreneurship. This view has important implications for entrepreneurship development in rural areas. If currently entrepreneurial activities in a given rural area are not thriving? one should not jump to the entrepreneurship is something inherently alien to rural areas.

While this feeling could have some legacy due to the slower pace of changes occurring in rural areas compared to urban ones, proper action can make a lot of difference with respect to entrepreneurial behaviour of people living in rural areas. Many examples of successful entrepreneurship confirm this statement and there is no reason why there should not be plenty of them. By bringing together different capabilities and different experiences in entrepreneurship development, everyone could enhance his/her own capabilities, motivation and determination in achieving the goal: attaining a sustainable and healthy rural economy and environment in order to ensure a high quality of life for individuals, families and communities.

Rural Entrepreneurship

Many examples of successful rural entrepreneurship can already be found in literature. Diversification into non-agricultural uses of available resources such as catering for tourists, blacksmithing, carpentry, spinning, etc. as well as diversification into activities other than those solely related to agricultural usage, for example, the use of resources other than land such as water, woodlands, buildings, available skills and local features, all fit into rural entrepreneurship. The entrepreneurial combinations of these resources are, for example: tourism, sport and recreation facilities, professional and technical training, retailing and wholesaling, industrial applications, servicing, value added and the possibility of off-farm work. Equally entrepreneurial, are new uses of land that enable a reduction in the intensity of agricultural production, for example, organic production. Dynamic rural entrepreneurs can also be found.

They are expanding their activities and markets and they find new markets for their products and services beyond the local boundaries.

To leave general examples of rural entrepreneurship behind, let us look at the real cases. All illustrating entrepreneurial initiatives, individuals and local communities from Great Britain. The names of entrepreneurs I have chosen to present here are not globally known but are no less important because of that. They are very well known to the communities to which they belong and their initiatives are highly appreciated by the community members. One of them is Graham-Probin owner of a 110 acre farm in Malpas, Cheshire, England. By converting a two-storey building into four workshop units, he created employment opportunities within the community.

Another one is John Anderson from Kirkwhelpington, who created employment opportunities in the local area by restoring traditional stables into business premises and renting them out to a blacksmith who shoes horses and does light engineering work for farmers. Another is the McNamara family from Canaston Bridge. They responded to the dairy quotas imposed by the Government by diversification of their land for non-agricultural usage. The family converted 80 acres of land into an adventure and leisure complex. After three years of investment, amounting to £800 000, the adventure and leisure facilities were opened in 1987, boasting a range of attractions entirely unconnected with agriculture, such as: a bobsleigh run, a miniature railway, a pitch and putt golf course, a natural history centre, go-kart tracks, assault courses, a restaurant and various shops.

This entrepreneurial venture is an example of a straightforward entrepreneurship and not so much an example of on-farm diversification. It is an example of how seeing and seizing the opportunity are vital ingredients of entrepren eurial success. Let me turn now to illustrations related to social entrepreneurship, to examples of when people have changed things, acting in the interest of their communities while playing the same role as an individual entrepreneur. East Cleveland Training and Enterprise Group from Loftus, Small Industries Groups in Somerset and Antur Teifi from West Wales, are all real examples of social entrepreneurship. The East Cleveland Training and Enterprise Group began as a group of four people in Loftus who were angry and frustrated at the lack of action by statutory bodies to tackle the area's unemployment.

The Group developed a large programme of activities, such as employment training, youth training, initiating the establishment of a training and enterprise centre, improving environmental and property acquisition to benefit the community. The Small Industries Group Somerset, West Somerset, started with the objective of helping to create local jobs. The founding group consisted of a dairy farmer, a sub-postmaster, an insurance broker, a lecturer, a youth worker and the manager of a field studies centre. For ten years the Group greatly fostered the development of the community and contributed to the change of attitudes of farmers as well as local communities, to favour self employment and business expansion.

Antur Teifi, from the Teifi Valley, the enterprise agency, was started by a group of local volunteers who were concerned with the high level of unemployment and unbalanced structure of the local population. The group set the objectives as follows: to identify and support community initiatives, to establish new permanent jobs and to initiate activities to prevent the area's economic and cultural decline. The group has more than achieved these objectives. Among the case studies presented here, there is no woman's name. Although the evidence shows that there are many activities in rural areas pursued by female entrepreneurs such as: trade, food processing, handicrafts, production of basic consumer articles, catering, running tourist establishments, and bed and breakfast arrangements.

However, compared to male entrepreneurs, female entrepreneurs in rural areas still tend to be limited to what have traditionally been viewed as women's activities. Also the scale of their entrepreneurial operation tends to be smaller when compared with male entrepreneurs. Although agriculture today still provides income to rural communities, rural development is increasingly linked to enterprise development. Since national economies are more and more globalized and competition is intensifying at an unprecedented pace, affecting not only industry but any economic activity including agriculture, it is not surprising that rural entrepreneurship is gaining in its importance as a force of economic change that must take place if many rural communities are to survive. However, entrepreneurship demands an enabling environment in order to flourish.

Environment Conducive to Entrepreneurship

Behind each of the success stories of rural entrepreneurship there is usually some sort of institutional support. Besides individual or group entrepreneurial initiative the enabling environment supporting these initiatives is of utmost importance. The creation of such an environment starts already at the national level with the foundation policies for macro-economic stability and for well-defined property rights as well as international orientation. Protection of the domestic economy hinders instead of fosters entrepreneurship. National agricultural policies such as price subsidies to guarantee minimum farm incomes and the keeping of land in production when over-production already exists are definitely counter-productive to entrepreneurship. The long run solution for sustainable agricultural development is only one, *i.e.*' competitive agriculture. While prices can set the direction, entrepreneurs who will meet the challenge of increasingly demanding international markets and who will find profitable alternative uses of land, alternative business opportunities and so on are needed. Therefore, policies and programmes targeted more specifically at the development and channelling of entrepreneurial talent, are needed. Policies to increase the supply of entrepreneurs, policies developing the market for other inputs into successful entrepreneurship, policies for increasing the effectiveness of entrepreneurs and policies for increasing demand for entrepreneurship can significantly speed up entrepreneurial activities at national, regional and community levels. The policies and programmes targeted specifically to the development of entrepreneurship do not differ much with respect to location.

From the perspective of the process of entrepreneurship, whether the location is urban, semi-rural or rural, is not important in itself. For example, the needs of a would be entrepreneur or an existing small business do not differ much from those in an urban area. To realise their entrepreneurial ideas or to grow and sustain in business, they all need access to capital, labour, markets and good management skills. What differs is the availability of markets for other inputs.

The inputs into an entrepreneurial process, capital, management, technology, buildings, communications and transportation infrastructure, distribution channels and skilled labour, tend to be easier to find in urban areas. Professional advice is also hard to come by. Consequently, entrepreneurial behaviour, the ability to spot unconventional market opportunities, is most lacking in those rural areas where it is most needed *i.e.*, where the scarcity of 'these other inputs' is the highest.

These are the reasons why rural entrepreneurship is more likely to flourish in those rural areas where the two approaches to rural development, the 'bottom up. and the 'top down', complement each other. Developing entrepreneurs requires a much more complex approach to rural development than is many times the case in practice. It requires not only the development of local entrepreneurial capabilities but also a coherent regional/local strategy. Evidence shows that where this is the case, individual and social entrepreneurship play an important role in rural economic, social and community development. The top down approach gains effectiveness when it is tailored to the local environment that it intends to support. The second prerequisite for its success is that ownership of the initiative remains in the hands of members of the local community.

The regional development agencies that fit both criteria can contribute much to rural development through entrepreneurship. Other institutions that can make a difference to rural development based on entrepreneurship are agricultural extension services. However, to be able to act in this direction, they too must be entrepreneurially minded. They must see agricultural activities as one of many possible activities that contribute to rural development. They must seek new entrepreneurial uses of land and support local initiative in this respect. While tradition is important it is nevertheless dangerous to be over-occupied with the past, otherwise the rural community may turn into a nostalgia-driven society.

Networking between different agencies involved in the promotion of rural development through entrepreneurship, by pooling together different sources and skills, by reaching a greater number of would be entrepreneurs and by assisting a greater number of local entrepreneurial initiatives, can have a much more positive effect on rural development than when each agency is working on its own. Entrepreneurship in rural areas can benefit a lot from the so called strategic development alliances, *i.e.*, partnership among governments or nonprofit seeking organizations, universities and the private sector.

To summarise, policy implications for rural entrepreneurship development are:

- Sound national economic policy with respect to agriculture, including recognition of the vital contribution of entrepreneurship to rural economic development;
- Policies and special programmes for the development and channelling of entrepreneurial talent;
- Entrepreneurial thinking about rural development, not only by farmers but also by everyone and every rural development organization; and
- Institutions supporting the development of rural entrepreneurship as well as strategic development alliances.

Women Entrepreneurs

Is there still a need to talk specifically about women entrepreneurs. on top of everything that has been already said'? Yes and no. No, because all that has been said about entrepreneurship is directly applicable to women, the concept, characteristics, sources' etc. Women entrepreneurs, as research demonstrates, may do things differently. For example, in comparison to male entrepreneurs, women tend to work more in teams, are less self-centred and personal ego to them is less important than success of the organization or business idea they are pursuing.

However, there is no difference in characteristics such as achievement, autonomy, aggression, independence and benevolence between female and male entrepreneurs. Also, no differences were found in risk taking propensity of male and female entrepreneurs.

However, we do need to talk explicitly about women entrepreneurs. It should be stressed that rural women can encounter many constraints when trying to take part in the transformation process. Rural areas tend to be more traditional in regard to the gender issue.

In rural areas, the gender issue is usually a much stronger hindering factor to potential female entrepreneurs than it is in urban areas, their self-esteem and managerial skills being lower when compared to urban women and access to external financial resources more difficult than in urban areas. Therefore, special programmes of assistance to overcome these constraints should be developed and designed to meet the needs of rural women in order to be able to take an active part in entrepreneurial restructuring of their communities, to start to develop their own ventures, to expand their already existing businesses, or to function as social entrepreneurs since their number today is still below the potential one.

To this end, based on my own experience as well as on the experiences of so many entrepreneurial women I have met across the world in my profession and in business, I very much agree with Juliana Schwager-Jebbink's comment: "Nowadays, reflecting on the phenomenon of the successful female manager read entrepreneur), it is the individuality which must stand out and there are no general recipes to be presented. After my years as President of the Swiss Federation of Business and Professional Women, going all over the country and abroad to speak on development programmes for women, I firmly believe that quotas, positive discrimination and equal opportunity' politics do not help the female manager: it is she herself who must do the managing of her life. This is true for all of Europe... " This belief is the one for which we as trainers are responsible to bring to rural women in addition to trying to put in place all factors crucial for rural women to enter into entrepreneurial activities. Without it, entrepreneurial opportunities will not be seen, they will be lost and then the role of women in rural development will be much below their potential.

ENTREPRENEURSHIP AND ECONOMIC GROWTH

The idea that entrepreneurship and economic growth are very closely and positively linked together has undoubtedly made its way since the early works of Schumpeter. An increase in the number of entrepreneurs leads to an increase in economic growth. This effect is a result of the concrete expression of their skills, and more precisely, their propensity to innovate.

Schumpeter has already described this innovative activity, "the carrying out of new combinations", by distinguishing five cases:"

1. The introduction of a new good - that is one with which consumers are not yet familiar - or of a new quality of a good.
2. The introduction of a new method of production, that is one not yet tested by experience in the branch of manufacture concerned, which need by no means be founded upon a discovery scientifically new, and can also exist in a new way of handling a commodity commercially.

3. The opening of a new market, that is a market into which the particular branch of manufacture of the country in question has not previously entered, whether or not this market has existed before.
4. The conquest of a new source of supply of raw materials or halfmanufactured goods, again irrespective of whether this source already exists or whether it has first to be created.
5. The carrying out of the new organisation of any industry, like the creation of a monopoly position or the breaking up of a monopoly position".

Through his innovative activity, the Schumpeterian entrepreneur seeks to create new profit opportunities. These opportunities can result from productivity increases, in which case, their relationship to economic growth appears quite clearly. Moreover, the disequilibrium created by the entrepreneur can be propitious for additional innovations and profit opportunities. Therefore, more entrepreneurs means more growth, which in turn leads to more entrepreneurs... The phenomena seem to be self-feeding. Although in some way relatively limited in regards to the interaction between entrepreneurship and economic growth, economic theory is not without enlightening arguments on the subject.

As suggested, use some of these arguments in our examination of two fundamental questions, which have already received some treatment in the economic literature. The first of these questions is the assessment, by means of a non-formalised discussion, of the interdependent nature of entrepreneurship and growth. This assessment will permit us to set certain limits on this relationship. As suggested, grant special attention to particular concepts, as well as to the description of entrepreneurial supply, by referring to individual decisions to undertake economic activities.

These decisions can appear as the result of an arbitrage between different professional occupations based on relative expected rewards just as to the specific abilities of the agent. As suggested, then suggest the endogenous relationship between entrepreneurship and growth and how labour market reactions operate to create some boundaries on their symbiotic interactions. The second question that is examined is in fact threefold.

It deals with the types of activities to which the entrepreneur directs his talents. These activities will be distinguished just as to the social productivity of their character. As suggested, introduce, at this time, rent-seeking behaviour, followed by an examination of factors explaining the allocation of entrepreneurial skill. Finally, respective to this allocation, as suggested, see that an assessment of its impact in terms of economic growth must be appreciated not only in a static framework - the importance of positive effects for the society as a whole depends upon the proportion of productive projects

-, but must also take into account the interactions between entrepreneurship and rent-seeking behaviour.

OCCUPATIONAL ARBITRAGE AND ECONOMIC GROWTH

This part is articulated as follows: first, as suggested, reappraise, from the introduction, the relationship between entrepreneurship and economic growth by going a step further into conceptualisation. As suggested, point out skills that are generally associated with the entrepreneur. The individual arbitrage between different professional occupations will then be sketched. An entrepreneurial supply will be defined. Finally, taking into account the aggregated impact of individual choices on expected pay-offs, will allow us to underscore the endogeneity of growth and entrepreneurial decisions.

Innovative Entrepreneurship and Economic Growth

Among the possible sources of economic growth and development, innovation has received a special treatment in the economic literature because it has been more or less linked with the figure of the individual entrepreneur. Relatively to this question, the early Schumpeter appears to be particularly original and pervasive.

Since the beginning of the twentieth century however, the way in which economic theory brings together economic and innovative processes through entrepreneurship, must certainly be revised. In fact, this has been in that economic analysis has undoubtedly reduced the"noise" between the articulation of simple concepts and recent observations. Schumpeter himself predicted that, due to irresistible trend of concentration in the capitalist system, innovation could no longer be the realm of the entrepreneur, but would in fact primarily be the job of innovation professionals and laboratories controlled by big companies, themselves being directed by managers.

If indeed there still remains a place for innovative entrepreneurship, embodied by the action of individuals, it can no longer be seen as the sole vector of innovation. In a recent and comprehensive survey of the literature, Wennekers and Thurik emphasise the decomposition of the concept of entrepreneurship in order to gain a better understanding of the links between entrepreneurship and economic growth. Although their"pragmatic distinctions" are formulated for operational and not theoretical purposes, they remain helpful in grasping the question at hand.

Table. Three Type of Entrepreneurs

Employee	Self-employed
Entrepreneurial Intrapreneurs Managerial Executive managers	Schumpeterian Entrepreneurs Managerial business owners

Associating, on the one hand, entrepreneurial with"the manifest ability and willingness of individuals, on their own, in teams, within and outside existing organisations, to perceive and create new economic opportunities and to introduce their ideas in the market, in the face of uncertainty and other obstacles, by making decisions on location, form and the use of resources and institutions", and, on the other hand, managerial with"organising and coordinating", Wennekers and Thurik cross these definitions with the distinction between self-employed and employee. Thus, the authors are able to define four different types of situations. Three of these are types of entrepreneurs: Schumpeterian entrepreneurs (entrepreneurial and self- employed), entrepreneurs (entrepreneurial and employee) and managerial business owners (managerial and self-employed).

Both Schumpeterian entrepreneurs and intrapreneurs contribute actively to feed a creative destruction process. Although managerial business owners play an important role in the economy for the achievement of production and trade, and can even reveal themselves as entrepreneurial and develop innovative projects, their activities are more closely tied to routine work. So,"(t)hey include many franchisees, shopkeepers and people in professional occupations" and generally represent the great majority of the self-employed. By introducing new ideas, new processes, new products and services, Schumpeterian entrepreneurs and intrapreneurs affect and ultimately renew the economic activities: the activities not only of the firms and industries, but also those of the region in which they are situated. When these entrepreneurial initiatives are aggregated and evaluated in terms of economic impacts at a territorial level, it could mean economic growth.

This process tends to be a diverse one."At the aggregate level of industries, regions and national economies, the many individual entrepreneurial actions compose a mosaic of new experiments. In evolutionary terms this can be called variety. A process of competition between these various ideas and initiatives takes place continuously, leading to the selection of the most viable firms and industries. Variety, competition, selection and also imitation (...) expand and transform the productive potential of a regional or national economy (by replacement or displacement of obsolete firms, by higher productivity and by expansion of new niches and industries)".

Greater productivity, as well as firm exits, allow for the possibility of resource reallocation into new combinations. When particular to a given territory, this greater productivity could mean an increase in competitive advantages and localised economic growth. However, this process should be globally followed by a positive net effect. In other words, the competition case that we describe is not a zero-sum game. From entrepreneurial initiatives to economic growth, a number of conditions and multiple effects, at different levels, ultimately determine the impact of one phenomenon in regards to another.

However, a working assumption will be: the larger the share of innovative entrepreneurs in the workforce, the more elevated the rhythm of economic growth.

Towards the Definition of an Entrepreneurial Supply

A simple approach in determining the share of innovative entrepreneurs in the active population is to begin by considering each individual as a potential entrepreneur, characterised by the specific capacity to become one. That is, we recognise the heterogeneity of the population. These individuals are then confronted with heterogeneous career opportunities with different expected pay-offs. The individual choice is finally an arbitrage between pairs of project and pay-offs, for given skill sets. These projects include the choice of a career as an employee. What then, briefly, are the individual characteristics that determine the entrepreneurial potentialities? Knight introduces a distinction between risk and uncertainty. Risk enters into computations with known probabilities.

On the contrary, uncertainty although it takes into account the notion of risk, refers also to non-foreseeable events. In other words, events whose probabilities are at this time unknown. Estimating the degree, to which a particular event is weighted with uncertainty, depends upon individual judgement expressed in terms of subjective probabilities. This understood, an entrepreneurial candidate is the one who, taking into account his judgement, would accept to bear the uncertainty of production and trade. Expected profits would be payment for this specific activity. We note, by the way, that, within a Schumpeterian framework, what characterises an entrepreneur is not a particular ability to bear the consequences of unforeseeable events. The capitalist plays this role. Undertaking economic activities and innovating require skills that make the entrepreneur a person of exception. One of his motives continues to be profit-seeking.

Lucas, Murphy, Shleifer and Vishny, Jovanovic come closer to a Schumpeterian concept of entrepreneurship in the sense that, in their models, individuals are not different in their attitude towards risk, but in their competence, intelligence, creative capacities... It is in fact possible to see in the enumeration, a wide range of skills that are corresponding to "talents", valuable traits in an entrepreneurial project. A synthesis of the different approaches runs through the tight definition of an entrepreneur offer curve. This offer sums up, amongst other arguments, the previously evoked traits of the working population. It meets an entrepreneurial demand that represents a variety of profit opportunities. What can be considered as the advantageous aspects of the offer-demand synthesis, at the same time comprises some of its weaknesses. The general framework on which it is based, can disguise heterogeneous situations that each previous model translates, although only in part. We must recognise that what is following an individual arbitrage is in fact rather coming out of a black box.

More Entrepreneurs, more Growth, more Entrepreneurs

We can consider an individual's career as a chain of individual arbitrages between pairs of project and pay-offs given individual abilities. Aggregating individual situations at a given time t, reveals the share of entrepreneurs in the working population. However, for the purposes of assessing more carefully the links between entrepreneurship and economic growth, this is not a sufficient result. Time must be reintroduced as a period, allowing in that case interactions between each term By fostering economic growth, entrepreneurship affects the whole economy. Particularly hard to ignore are its effects on labour markets. More growth might, on one hand, signify an increase in profit opportunities for potential entrepreneurs. On the other hand, it could lead to inflationary pressures on wages.

It must be noted that raises in wage cannot necessarily be derived as the result of disequilibrium on the labour markets. In fact, raises in wage may indeed be the consequence of the application of profit-sharing schemes within the firms. It follows that growth in turn can seriously affect the individual arbitrage that we have discussed. So, appears the problem of endogeneity by way of markets and pay-offs adjustments.

ENTREPRENEURSHIP VERSUS RENT-SEEKING

Different rhythms of growth between nations, that have been theoretically associated with entrepreneurship, are not fully explained by different entrepreneurial supply, measured in quantitative terms. The allocation of this supply between more and less socially productive projects must also be taken into account. This question introduces the idea of rent-seeking behaviour. After having briefly defined the general framework and the employed concepts, as suggested, discuss the allocation of entrepreneurs between different types of economic projects, as well as the explicative factors of this allocation. A dynamic set-up will follow, where as suggested, examine interactions between project categories and their relations to growth.

Definitions

To this point, the individual arbitrage between different remunerative occupations ended up, in all cases, in the development of socially productive activities. Therefore, the described economy has been a strict income economy. Individuals were exploiting, as best they could, their skills entrepreneurial or otherwise and given the exercised occupations, private interests and social benefits were successfully coinciding. As suggested, introduce another type of activity, which is remunerated by transfers. We may note that, by definition, transfers do not imply a productive counterpart. This assumption will result in the possibility that a distortion between private and collective interests may occur. This distortion becomes undoubtedly effective when rent-seeking is involved. The rent-seeking refers to "the socially costly pursuit of wealth transfers". In other words, rent-seeking is manifested when the bottom-line of its social consequences is negative.

The fact that this definition allows for an expression of the social opportunity cost that represents a diversion of resources towards this type of activity should be emphasised. Examples of rentseeking are: corruption, stealing, bribery, as well as seeking abusive judicial compensation or protection-seeking with the express purpose of limiting economic competition and promoting particular interest… Rent-seeking can originate both from the public or private sector.

In regards to the connection between entrepreneurship and growth, the occurrence of unproductive but yet remunerated activities means not only that projects with socially positive or negative impacts are in competition, but also that there is a direct potential diversion of entrepreneurial talents. For this diversion to take place, we need indeed to assume that the skills and abilities required by entrepreneurship and by rent-seeking correspond. Following these considerations, at least two remarks can be formulated. The first one refers to public services.

These are generally financed by transfers, but are not included in rent-seeking, given their productive contribution. We note furthermore that discussing the redistribution role of the state is outside the framework. This is different, however, as soon as we look at legal institutions that organise productive activities, as they might, by limiting competition for example, create rent-seeking situations. The second remark concerns the entrepreneurial initiatives.

Through innovation, the entrepreneur seeks to create a monopoly position, from which he will assume overprofit. In the Schumpeterian model, this position is necessary fore it motivates the innovation activity. It is however temporary, as competition will quickly reduce this position to zero in favour of a new monopoly position created by a new innovation… The institutional framework, that of competition, is then of primary importance. In this case, a dynamic assessment of events will justify the existence of an abnormal profit, as it will distinguish its positive net contribution to the social benefit. Rent-seeking behaviour thus being defined, as suggested, address in the remaining discussion the allocation of talents and its links to growth.

Explaining the Allocation of Talents

The allocation of talents between socially productive and unproductive projects and its impact on economic growth have already been subject to theoretical studies. The static results of these studies scarcely elicit further commentary, when we take into account the preceding arguments. Indeed it appears quite easily that the diversion of entrepreneurial talents towards unproductive activities will have a negative impact on growth rate. However, the explicative factors of the allocation deserve greater consideration. Attempting to explain the allocation of talents implies both reconsidering the arguments that have been exposed with regard to the individual arbitrage between remunerative activities and considering the non-pecuniary factors that may also have some impact. Murphy, Shleifer and Vishny, the point is the following: "talent goes into activities with the highest private returns, which need not have the highest social returns". These authors assume increasing returns on talent.

In other words, the greater the ability of an individual, the greater his private benefits will be. Because the exercise of talent is physically limited, talented individuals tend to invest themselves and their abilities into reward maximising occupations. It follows that their occupational choice will be determined by the size of the market, the compensation contract and the technology. Furthermore, the allocation of talent can be linked both with institutional context, as well as non-pecuniary explicative factors. The legal framework and its effective use define a propitious environment for entrepreneurship and, contrarily, for rent-seeking behaviour. Property rights, the conditions of their application, and the respect of these rights, appear to be crucial factors. They contribute particularly and decisively to precise the compensation circumstances that have already been quoted, as well as the fiscal organisation.

Information is also important as it determines the efficiency of allocation and the possibility of linking the application of talent and its results. Social esteem might play a role. The question becomes therefore how much entrepreneurship is socially valuable and valorised, over another less socially productive occupation. Finally, entrepreneurs or rent-seekers might influence, by voting or lobbying, political organisation and political decisions. The idea is that the political equilibrium, replying to one or another group's interests, will make decisions that favour its maintenance.

Entrepreneurship and Rent-seeking in Motion

The interaction between entrepreneurship and rent-seeking is without doubt an interesting question to examine. Formalised models show that multiple equilibria – an equilibrium being defined by an entrepreneur share in the population and a rate of growth – may exist. As suggested, not insist on model developments. The interested reader may consult the references we provide. However, briefly, we note that the results are grounded on the specification of two functions, both with negative slopes, and consequently a potential for multiple intersections. Because it places burdens on entrepreneurial rewards, rent-seeking negatively affects entrepreneurship. Moreover, given competition in the rent-seeking sector itself, rent-seeking rewards will depend negatively on the number of rent-seekers. Baland and Francois formalise as well the effect of entrepreneurial activities on rent-seeking. Their model can apply to an economy with import license. The production of direct substitutes by local entrepreneurs tends to turn off the rents obtained by importers. Here also, results suggest the existence of multiple equilibria. Murphy, Shleifer and Vishny deal with rent-seeking affecting the innovation sector. The rent-seeking, whether from private or public origins, can undoubtedly burden the profits of established productive sectors. The innovation sector, however, might be described the reserved hunting ground, for the most part, of public rent-seeking. Their arguments rely particularly on the nature of innovation. In his project developments, the innovative entrepreneur is confronted with legal and environmental constraints. Innovation can imply indeed production permits, licenses, dispensations, as well as amending the local zoning regulations.

This results in demand for government intervention and it provides opportunities for corruption. Moreover, the socially unproductive transfers that corruption implies, might have some inhibitive effects on innovation activity, given that innovators may not have equal lobbying power compared to that of established firms, or the same financial resources to pay bribes. Important funds may then be consumed instead of being invested, to avoid expropriation. The ex post existence of rent-seeking should raise the project risk and effective cost. The authors mention, following these arguments, that the negative effects of rent-seeking could be limited if the rent-seeker himself becomes a stakeholder in the innovation project. In the long run, he would find his interest in such an involvement.

We note moreover that this idea can be generalised as: rent-seeking, by burdening current entrepreneurial profits, limits its future transfer opportunities. Thus, the interaction between entrepreneurship and rent-seeking can generate multiple equilibria that correspond to an allocation of talents and an economic growth rate. Starting from a dynamic extension of his basic model, Acemoglu discusses the history dependence of an economy. Past and current allocations of talents influence the future structure of rewards. Given historical circumstances, the economy can be locked in low or high steady state equilibrium. Under these circumstances, only a shock will have any positive and sustainable effect.

FACTORS EFFECTING ENTREPRENEURIAL GROWTH

Following are the factors of environment affecting entrepreneurial growth. These conditions are grouped under two categories:

1. Economic conditions
2. Non-economic conditions

ECONOMIC FACTORS

Economic conditions includes the capital, labour, raw material and market.

Capital

It is the essence of enterprise. Availability of capital facilitates mobility of land, material etc., is required to produce goods. Therefore, capital is a lubricant which smoothens the working of vehicle called enterprise. Increases capital investment, capital output ratio results in profit, which ultimately goes up to capital formation.

Labour

Quality and quantity of labour influence the entrepreneurship mobility, dexterity and immobility.

Low cost labour and capital intensive technology oriented enterprises influence entrepreneurship.

Raw Material

Availability of raw material, nature of industrial establishment, technology innovation and mobility of raw material encourages or curbs the development of entrepreneurship.

Market

The potential of the market constitutes the major department of probable rewards from entrepreneurial function. The size and composition of market monopoly in a particular product influence entrepreneurship.

NON-ECONOMIC FACTORS (WITH REFERENCE TO CLASS STUDY)

Non-economic conditions are as follows: social conditions, psychological conditions and political or governmental action.

Sociologists and psychologists view that the influence of economic factors on entrepreneurial emergence largely depend upon the existence of non-economic factors.

Social conditions are as follow:

- Socio-cultural norms and values
- Degree of approval or disapproval of entrepreneurial behaviour.
- Family background, standard of education, technical knowledge and information.
- Financial stability, caste and religious affiliation.

Psychological conditions are as follow:

- David Mcdellond's theory of need achievement—A constellation of personality characteristics, and high need achievement is the major determinant of entrepreneurship.
- Individual works in the society but remains different.
- Impact of achievement motivation and training programmes influence development of entrepreneurship.

GOVERNMENT ACTIONS:- (WITH REFERENCE TO SPECIAL LEGISLATIONS AND COURT CASES)

- Government encourage entrepreneurship by creating basic facilities, utilities and services and by providing incentives and concessions.
- Government provides the prospective entrepreneurships a facilitative socio-economic setting.
- Entrepreneurship development is based on the government interest in economic development of the society.

The emergence of entrepreneurship. These factors are interlocking, mutually dependent and mutually reinforcing.

ENTREPRENEURIAL MOTIVATION—MEANING

It is often said that a person cannot win a game that they do not play. In the context of entrepreneurship, this statement suggests that success depends on people's willingness to become entrepreneurs. Moreover, because the pursuit of entrepreneurial opportunity is an evolutionary process in which people select out at many steps along the way, decisions made after the discovery of opportunities—to positively evaluate opportunities, to pursue resources, and to design the mechanisms of exploitation—also depend on the willingness of people to "play" the game.

We argue that human motivations influence these decisions, and that variance across people in these motivations will influence who pursues entrepreneurial opportunities, who assembles resources, and how people undertake the entrepreneurial process. In recent years, entrepreneurship research has focused largely on the environmental characteristics influencing firm foundings and the characteristics of entrepreneurial opportunities. Although this focus has greatly enhanced our understanding of the entrepreneurial phenomenon, it ignores the role of human agency. Entrepreneurship depends on the decisions that people make about how to undertake that process.

We argue that the attributes of people making decisions about the entrepreneurial process influence the decisions that they make. Although previous researchers have rightly criticized much of the existing empirical research on the role of human motivation in entrepreneurship, we argue that inadequate empirical work does not negate the importance of understanding the role of human motivation in the entrepreneurial process. In fact, even sociologists who have argued strongly against the usefulness of trait-based research in entrepreneurship implicitly acknowledge that motivation must matter to this process.

Aldrich and Zimmer, for example, write, entrepreneurial activity "can be conceptualized as a function of opportunity structures and motivated entrepreneurs with access to resources". We also believe that these criticisms have resulted in insufficient consideration of the role of the human motivation in the entrepreneurial process in recent entrepreneurship research. Consequently, we are left with theories of entrepreneurship that do not consider variation in the motivations of different people.

We believe that such an omission is problematic because, as Baumol eloquently argued, the study of entrepreneurship that does not explicitly consider entrepreneurs is like the analysis of Shakespeare in which "the Prince of Denmark has been expunged from the discussion of Hamlet." We identify several human motivations that influence the entrepreneurial process. In our arguments, we explicitly assume that all human action is the result of both motivational and cognitive factors, the latter including ability, intelligence, and skills. We also assume that entrepreneurship is not solely the result of human action; external factors also play a role. However, environmental factors being held constant, we argue that human motivation plays a critical role in the entrepreneurial process.

To this end, we suggest ways that researchers could develop more realistic explanations for how human motivation influences the entrepreneurial process than is the norm in the literature to date. We believe that this approach could overcome many of the criticisms of prior research on person-centric explanations for entrepreneurship. Finally, we offer suggestions on how empirical researchers should test these arguments in ways that overcome many of the criticisms of extant research on this topic.

Our object proceeds as follows: We define entrepreneurship and present several arguments for why the study of entrepreneurship in general and consideration of the role of human motivation in the process in particular are important.

We discuss opposing views of how opportunities may affect the relationship between motivation and entrepreneurship. We summarize the major mechanisms by which previous researchers believe motivation influences entrepreneurship. We identify what we believe are the major problems with prior research on motivation and entrepreneurship. We provide some recommendations for researchers conducting empirical research in this area.

WHAT IS ENTREPRENEURSHIP AND WHY STUDY IT FROM THE POINT OF VIEW OF HUMAN MOTIVATION?

We believe that the study of the entrepreneurial process is important for several reasons. First, entrepreneurship drives innovation and technical change, and therefore generates economic growth. Second, as the Austrian economists have explained, entrepreneurial action is the process through which supply and demand are equilibrated.

Third, entrepreneurship is an important process by which new knowledge is converted into products and services. Fourth, entrepreneurship has become an important vocation and we need to understand its role in the development of human and intellectual capital. We adopt Shane and Venkataraman's definition of entrepreneurship as the process by which "opportunities to create future goods and services are discovered, evaluated, and exploited." As these authors have explained, this definition does not require viewing entrepreneurs as the founders of new organizations. An options trader can be an entrepreneur, as can a corporate salesman who discovers and pursues opportunities for the creation of new products. Moreover, this definition shows that entrepreneurship is a creative process.

By rearranging resources in a new way, entrepreneurs engage in creative activity. However, the degree of creativity involved in entrepreneurship varies across the types of resource recombination that occurs. For example, the creation of business to undertake space tourism may be more creative than the creation of a new restaurant in a strip mall. Entrepreneurship involves human agency. The entrepreneurial process occurs because people act to pursue opportunities. People differ in their willingness and abilities to act on these opportunities because they are different from each other. We argue that the variation among people in their willingness and ability to act has important effects on the entrepreneurial process.

Recent research has been relatively accepting of arguments that people vary in their willingness and ability to engage in the entrepreneurial process because of nonmotivational individual differences. Researchers have shown that the willingness of people to pursue entrepreneurial opportunities depends on such things as their opportunity cost, their stocks of financial capital, their social ties to investors, and their career experience. We argue that motivational differences also influence the entrepreneurial process. For example, such things as variation across people in their perceptions of risk and opportunity influence entrepreneurial decisions.

People vary in how they view the risk of expending resources before knowing the distribution of outcomes. Similarly, the probability of success at the entrepreneurial process is low, and those people who are willing to proceed despite these odds might be more optimistic or higher in self-efficacy than people deterred by these odds. We consider the incorporation of this individual-level variation in motivation to be important to the entrepreneurial process.

To isolate the effects of entrepreneurial motivation, other factors that could have a causal effect on the process and outcome of entrepreneurship need to be controlled. One category of control variables is the external environment. *These would include such things as*:

- Political factors (*e.g.*, legal restrictions, quality of law enforcement, political stability, and currency stability);
- Market forces (*e.g.*, structure of the industry, technology regime, potential barriers to entry, market size, and population demographics);
- Resources (*e.g.*, availability of investment capital, labour market including skill availability, transportation infrastructure, and complementary technology).

Most researchers either explicitly or implicitly agree that these categories of factors influence the entrepreneurial process and need to be controlled to measure the effect of motivations on the entrepreneurial process. While it is clear why the factors need to be controlled if we are to fully understand how motivation is related to entrepreneurship, it is less clear how opportunities affect this relationship. Because the first two authors were unable to agree on the concept of opportunities, we present two versions of the relationship between opportunities and motivation. First, as suggested, present the view shared by Shane and Collins, then as suggested, present Locke's view.

ENTREPRENEURS, OPPORTUNITIES, AND THE EFFECTS OF MOTIVATION

Opportunities are aspects of the environment that represent potentialities for profit making. We follow Shane and Venkataraman to define entrepreneurial opportunities as "situations in which new goods, services, raw materials, and organizing methods can be introduced and sold at greater than the cost of their production." Since potentialities are not yet actual, measuring them objectively and prospectively at the level of an individual entrepreneur poses daunting challenges. Entrepreneurs can pursue opportunities in any industry at any time. For example, some entrepreneurs build successful new companies by contributing to the founding of a new industry, such as Robert Swanson in biotechnology. Other entrepreneurs build new companies in old and mature industries such as Sam Walton in retailing. Aggregate statistics show us that the general category of opportunities to which Sam Walton and Bob Swanson responded was not equal.

The average value of new businesses created in retail is lower than the average value of new businesses created in biotechnology. Because human motivations are likely widely distributed across industry categories at the aggregate level, statistically significant differences in the mean value of businesses created in different industry categories suggest that the value of opportunities varies across industry. This does not mean that entrepreneurs cannot successfully pursue opportunities in lowopportunity industries. Rather it means that the opportunities in these industries are simply less attractive to the average person.

The value of opportunities also varies within industries. Because the opportunities that entrepreneurs identify and pursue have different economic value, the opportunities themselves influence entrepreneurial behaviour. We believe that it is important for behaviourally oriented entrepreneurship researchers to consider and measure the economic value of these opportunities in research about the motivations of entrepreneurs. For example, in the early 1970s, Butler Lampson and Chuck Thacker, researchers at Xerox Parc, invented the Alto—the first personal computer.

However, their design would have cost over US$10,000 to build. When Steve Jobs and Steve Wozniak came up with the design for the Apple computer, their design cost less than US$3000 to build. Because the number of people who would pay more than US$10,000 for a PC was much smaller than number of people who would pay US$3000, the financial value of the Jobs and Wozniak opportunity was greater than the value of the Xerox opportunity. One would expect that differences in the estimates of the value of the PC opportunity that resulted from the different solutions influenced the decisions of the different parties about their opportunities. Of course, although it is possible that Jobs and Wozniak possessed more of the relevant motives to pursue entrepreneurial opportunities than did Lampson and Thacker, researchers can only estimate the effect of these motives if they account for the differences in the two opportunities.

Although we argue that opportunities influence entrepreneurial behaviour, we do not argue that opportunities fully determine the process. Entrepreneurs are people and may make different decisions when confronted with similar opportunities. In addition to being influenced by the opportunity that Steve Jobs pursued at the time of founding, the development of Apple was likely influenced by Steve Jobs' motivations. Empirically, the objective and subjective parts of opportunity are difficult to separate.

The mechanism for actualizing an opportunity often initially exists mainly in the entrepreneur's mind, making the entrepreneur's idea for how to exploit the opportunity a personal interpretation of the opportunity. This idea is basically what we would call vision. Such judgements may be mistaken; entrepreneurs sometimes believe that they have identified valuable opportunities when, in fact, no valuable opportunities actually existed, at least in the form in which they were conceptualized. Also, entrepreneurs may differ in how they interpret opportunities. For example, the development of the

Internet has allowed entrepreneurs to develop new organizing methods, such as "e-tailing," that were never before possible. Although a wide variety of entrepreneurs have responded to the opportunities to develop new organizing methods that the Internet has generated, these entrepreneurs have developed approaches of different value in response to this organizing opportunity.

Some entrepreneurs have developed opportunities to compete with established retailers through e-tailing, while others have sought only to design web sites. Even though the way that opportunities are manifested in the entrepreneur's plans for exploitation are personal, the variance in their estimated value likely influences the decisions that people make in the entrepreneurial process and can confound attempts to measure the effects of motivation on this process. This is true even if the value is partially a function of the other decisions that the entrepreneur has made and partially a function of external forces.

MOTIVATION AND ENTREPRENEURSHIP: IMPORTANT MOTIVATIONAL CONCEPTS FROM PRIOR QUANTITATIVE RESEARCH

Previous research has explored several motivations and their effects on entrepreneurship. We discuss several of these concepts. However, we do not provide a complete review of prior empirical research for two reasons. First, the definitions of entrepreneurship used in previous empirical research on motivation and entrepreneurship are inconsistent with our definition, making it impossible to draw direct implications of prior work for research using our definition. Second, prior research has suffered from significant methodological problems, making prior findings suggestive rather than conclusive, even for research that employs the same definition of entrepreneurship as was used in those studies. Therefore, we discuss empirical research only to show the ways in which motivation can influence different aspects of the entrepreneurial process.

Need for Achievement

Within the research domain of personality traits and entrepreneurship, the concept of need for achievement has received much attention. McClelland argued that individuals who are high in nAch are more likely than those who are low in nAch to engage in activities or tasks that have a high degree of individual responsibility for outcomes, require individual skill and effort, have a moderate degree of risk, and include clear feedback on performance.

Further, McClelland argued that entrepreneurial roles are characterized as having a greater degree of these task attributes than other careers; thus, it is likely that people high in nAch will be more likely to pursue entrepreneurial jobs than other types of roles. Johnson conducted a traditional review of 23 studies, which varied regarding samples, measurement of nAch,, and definitions of entrepreneurship. Based on this group of studies, Johnson concluded that there is a relationship between nAch and entrepreneurial activity—in this case, nAch distinguished firm founders from other members of society. In a similar review of 19 studies, Fineman concluded that both projective and questionnaire measures of nAch significantly predict firm founding. Collins, Locke, and Hanges conducted the first and only meta-analysis of nAch and entrepreneurship studies, examining 63 nAch and entrepreneurship studies.

The overall finding of the meta-analysis is that nAch is significantly related to founding a company. The nAch both differentiated between entrepreneurs and others and predicted the performance of the founders' firms. Further, they found no significant differences in the predictive validity of three different measures of nAch. Moreover, Collins found that the relationship between nAch and entrepreneurial activity was moderated by several factors. First, nAch was a more robust predictor of group-level effects (*e.g.*, mean differences between firm founders and another profession, mean differences between high-performing and low-performing founders) than individuallevel effects (*e.g.*, predicting the performance of individuals). Second, they found that while nAch is a strong differentiator between firm founders and nonmanagerial employees, it is not a strong differentiator between firm founders and managers.

Based on these results, Collins concluded that nAch is an effective tool for differentiating between firm founders and the general population but less so for differentiating between firm founders and managers. Further, they concluded that nAch might be particularly effective at differentiating between successful and unsuccessful groups of firm founders. Thus, nAch could play a very useful role in explaining entrepreneurial activity.

Risk Taking

Risk-taking propensity is another motivation of interest, which emerged from McClelland's original research on entrepreneurs. McClelland claimed that individuals with high achievement needs would have moderate propensities to take risk. This claim by McClelland is especially interesting for entrepreneurship research because the entrepreneurial process involves acting in the face of uncertainty. Liles argued that entrepreneurs often must accept uncertainty with respect to financial well-being, psychic well-being, career security, and family relations.

Moreover, several theories of entrepreneurship view the entrepreneur as bearing residual uncertainty. Atkinson argued that individuals who have higher achievement motivation should prefer activities of intermediate risk because these types of activities will provide a challenge, yet appear to be attainable. On the other hand, individuals who score high on the motive to avoid failure will avoid intermediate risks. Instead, they will prefer easy and safe undertakings or extremely difficult and risky ones. Following the lead of Atkinson, risk-taking propensity has been defined in the entrepreneurship literature as the willingness to take moderate risks. Despite these theoretical claims, previous research suggests that firm owners do not differ significantly from managers or even the general population in risk taking. For example, Litzinger failed to find any difference between motel owners and motel managers on risk preference.

Kogan and Wallach found that firm founders clustered around the mean risk-taking score of the general population. In comparisons of firm founders and managers, neither Babb and Babb nor Palich and Bagby found significant differences between the two groups in terms of risk-taking propensity. However, moderate, or high risk-takers.

Only Brockhaus tested for the actual level of risk taking, and he found that firm founders did prefer moderate risk but did not differ from managers in this regard. Only one study found a difference between firm founders and managers in this motivation. In a study of 239 New England business executives, Begley found that risk-taking propensity was the only trait on which founders and nonfounders differed. Begley failed to identify whether the level of entrepreneurial risk taking was low, moderate, or high.

While these empirical findings suggest that risk taking may or may not be an entrepreneurial motivation, self-efficacy may be confounding the findings. Several recent evaluative studies using interviews and expert evaluations showed that firm founders objectively have a higher propensity for risk than do members of the general population, but that firm founders do not perceive their actions as risky. Similarly, Sarasvathy, Simon, and Lave found that when expert firm founders were asked to evaluate the same entrepreneurial simulations as bankers, the firm founders saw opportunities in information that the bankers thought indicated risk. Thus, the measurement of risk-taking propensity may be confounded with high self-efficacy.

Tolerance for Ambiguity

Schere argued that tolerance for ambiguity is an important trait for entrepreneurs because the challenges and potential for success associated with business start-ups are by nature unpredictable. Budner defined tolerance for ambiguity as the propensity to view situations without clear outcomes as attractive rather than threatening. Because entrepreneurs continually face more uncertainty in their everyday environment than do managers of established organizations, entrepreneurs who remain in their jobs are likely to score high on tests for this trait than would managers. There is mixed support for this prediction. Begley and Boyd found that firm founders scored significantly higher in tolerance for ambiguity than did managers, defined as nonfounders working in business.

In smaller sample studies, both Schere and Miller and Drodge found that firm founders were significantly higher in tolerance for ambiguity than were managers. Finally, based on a review of four additional studies, Sexton and Bowman identified tolerance for ambiguity as a distinguishing psychological characteristic between firm founders and managers. However, several studies did not match these findings. Babb and Babb found no significant difference in tolerance for ambiguity between founders and nonfounders of rural businesses in Northern Florida. Similarly, Begley found no significant differences between New England firm founders and managers on their tolerance for ambiguity. This inconsistency in findings and potential methodological problems in the research that provides support for the tolerance of ambiguity proposition suggests that we do not yet know if tolerance of ambiguity is a motivation that affects any part of the entrepreneurial process.

Locus of Control

Another motivational trait that has received attention is locus of control—the belief in the extent to which individuals believe that their actions or personal characteristics affect outcomes. Individuals who have an external locus of control believe that the outcome of an extent is out of their control, whereas individuals with an internal locus of control believe that their personal actions directly affect the outcome of an event.

As McClelland discussed earlier, individuals who are high in nAch prefer situations in which they feel that they have direct control over outcomes or in which they feel that they can directly see how their effort affects outcomes of a given event. This point was extended by Rotter who argued that individuals with an internal locus of control would be likely to seek entrepreneurial roles because they desire positions in which their actions have a direct impact on results. The research on locus of control suggests that firm founders differ from the general population in terms of locus of control.

Shapero found that firm founders from Texas and Italy were more "internal" than other groups of professions reported by Rotter. This same pattern holds with female firm founders versus the general female population and with Black firm founders versus the general Black population. While locus of control orientation differs between firm founders and the general public, most studies have not found a difference between firm founders and managers on locus of control, a result similar to the situation with studies on nAch. For example, Babb and Babb found no differences in locus of control between founders and managers in small businesses in Northern Florida. Similarly, Brockhaus found that managers and owners of new businesses did not differ on locus of control. In a longitudinal study of students, Hull, Bosley, and Udell found that locus of control did not differentiate between students who went on to work in managerial positions and those who started their own business.

Finally, in the studies of New England entrepreneurs, Begley and Begley and Boyd found that locus of control did not distinguish between founders and managers. We suspect that one reason for the difference between firm founder and the general population, but not between founders and managers, is the similarity between founding a company and managing. Defining entrepreneurial situations as starting a company rather than working for others might not capture the real differences between entrepreneurial and nonentrepreneurial situations. For example, serving as a manager in a rapidly growing high-technology company might demand greater entrepreneurial motivations than starting a corner grocery store.

Self-efficacy

Self-efficacy is the belief in one's ability to muster and implement the necessary personal resources, skills, and competencies to attain a certain level of achievement on a given task. In other words, self-efficacy can be seen as task-specific self-confidence.

Self-efficacy for a specific task has been shown to be a robust predictor of an individual's performance in that task and helps to explain why people of equal ability can perform differently. An individual with high self-efficacy for a given task will exert more effort for a greater length of time, persist through set backs, set and accept higher goals, and develop better plans and strategies for the task.

A person with high self-efficacy will also take negative feedback in a more positive manner and use that feedback to improve their performance. These attributes of self-efficacy may be important to the entrepreneurial process because these situations are often ambiguous ones in which effort, persistence, and planning are important. One study directly assessed the effect of self-efficacy on some dimension of the entrepreneurial process. Baum assessed firm founders in the architectural woodworking industry on a number of variables including general traits and motives, specific skills and competencies, situation-specific motivation, vision, and strategic action. In a LISREL model, Baum found that self-efficacy had a strong positive relationship with realised growth. In fact, it was the single best predictor in the entire array of variables.

Goal Setting

Tracy, Locke, and Renard conducted a study of the owners of small printing firms. Both concurrent and longitudinal measures of four aspects of performance were obtained: financial performance, growth, and innovation. The quantitative goals the entrepreneurs had for each outcome were significantly related to their corresponding outcomes, both concurrently and longitudinally. Baum, Locke, and Smith also found that growth goals were significantly related to the subsequent growth of architectural woodworking firms. Although there have been other studies of entrepreneurial goals, to our knowledge, only these two have related quantitative measures of goal difficulty to performance.

PROBLEMS WITH PREVIOUS RESEARCH ON HUMAN MOTIVATION AND ENTREPRENEURSHIP AND SUGGESTED SOLUTIONS TO THESE PROBLEMS

Despite the importance of including individual-level factors in a comprehensive explanation for the entrepreneurial process, previous studies of entrepreneurial motivation have often led to disappointing results. However, we believe that researchers should not conclude from this failure that human motivation is irrelevant to the entrepreneurial process. Rather, we suggest that there are specific reasons for the limited results obtained in previous research.

Controls for Opportunities

Previous research has suffered from a lack of control for the variation in the opportunities that different entrepreneurs pursue. To accurately measure the effects of motivation on entrepreneurial decisions, researchers need to control the effects of opportunities. As Venkataraman argued, a valuable opportunity for an individual is one that generates a level of profit that exceeds the entrepreneur's opportunity cost, a premium for the illiquidity of money, time, and effort expended, and a premium for bearing risk and uncertainty. Because some opportunities will exceed this threshold by a greater amount than will others, the nature of the opportunity will influence entrepreneurial decisions.

Researchers need to know the magnitude of the force exerted by the opportunities themselves to accurately estimate the effect of the individual motivations on entrepreneurial decisions. In the absence of such controls, one cannot know if the effects observed represent the effects of individual motivations or are artifacts of unobserved correlation between the opportunities and the people who pursue them.

Prior research has generally failed to control the effect of opportunities by examining entrepreneurs pursuing different opportunities without explicitly modeling the value of the different opportunities pursued. In addition, prior studies have generally compared managers with firm founders. However, human motivations can influence the tendency of people to engage in entrepreneurial activities only if those activities are possible. If people have not discovered entrepreneurial opportunities or have discovered opportunities but cannot act on those discoveries, it is impossible to determine if their individual motivations make them more or less likely than others to act on entrepreneurial opportunities.

Therefore, one cannot tell from studies that compare managers to firm founders whether certain motivations influence people to make entrepreneurial decisions unless researchers have ensured that the managers have discovered opportunities and have measured the value of those opportunities. Otherwise, researchers might only capture the fact that some managers have all of the right motivations, but no opportunities in which to use them. We offer four suggestions to researchers interested in examining the effect of motivations on entrepreneurial decisions about how to deal with variation in opportunities. First, researchers could explore settings in which potential entrepreneurs pursue reasonably identical opportunities. For example, every year, many potential entrepreneurs evaluate and pursue opportunities to purchase McDonald's franchises.

When a person applies to be a McDonald's franchisee or company-owned outlet manager, one applies only to be part of the system rather than to select a particular outlet. Therefore, the opportunities to which people respond in this setting are identical. By comparing the motivations of a sample of people seek to be McDonald's franchisees with people who seek to be McDonald's company-owned outlet managers, researchers can determine the contributions of particular motivations on the decision to entrepreneur. Second, as a variety of researchers are beginning to do, scholars could employ experimental designs in which potential entrepreneurs are asked to make a series of entrepreneurial decisions in a controlled simulation.

By measuring the motivations of potential entrepreneurs and examining the correlation between the motivations and the decisions made in these simulations, researchers could determine how motivations influence entrepreneurial decisions. Third, the most obvious means of controlling opportunity are to use a sample of entrepreneurs within the same industry and country and to measure aspects of the environment that might vary within industry and region.

We recommend these approaches to limiting other sources of variance than motivations from studies of motivation and entrepreneurship. Fourth, as some researchers are beginning to do, scholars could employ third parties to code the value of potential opportunities. For example, researchers could explore the propensity of inventors to found companies based on their inventions. Because all inventors are at risk of exploiting their inventions through firm formation, this setting provides a useful context in which to explore the decision to entrepreneur. By partialing out the externally evaluated value of the opportunities, researchers could determine whether motivations influence the decision to entrepreneur, net of the effects of the value of the opportunity.

Entrepreneurship as a Process

Much of the prior research has looked at entrepreneurship as a profession that certain types of people adopt, rather than as a process that occurs over time. This approach is problematic because the appropriate conceptual lens through which to look at entrepreneurship is as a dynamic process. Because entrepreneurship is episodic and much entrepreneurial action is not long lasting, it is unrealistic to model motivation as dividing entrepreneurs and other members of society into two groups. In fact, relatively little of the motivation research on entrepreneurship has considered the effects of motivation on specific steps in the entrepreneurial process. Most studies on motivation and entrepreneurship adopt static designs that seek to determine if firm founders are different from each other, managers, or the general population at the moment the two groups are measured.

This approach makes two problematic assumptions. First, it assumes that a given motivation influences all steps in the entrepreneurial process equally, and that the effects of a given motivation do not select out some people at earlier stages in the process. Second, it assumes that, at the moment in which the founders are compared to the others, the founders who are still in charge of the organizations that they founded represent the population of people who engage in entrepreneurial activity.

Because entrepreneurship is a process, with tremendous selection at each step, we believe that these assumptions are quite faulty. The motivations that allow progression from opportunity recognition to resource assembly might not lead from financial assembly to first sales. For example, to assemble resources, a person might need to be highly confident. Those people lacking sufficient overconfidence to assemble resources are selected out of the entrepreneurial process. If there is very little variation in overconfidence among the people who have resources and seek to reach first sales, overconfidence will have no effect on achieving first sales.

For these reasons, we believe that it may not be possible to examine the direct effects of a lead entrepreneur's motivations on the financial performance of a new company that the individual founds. The effects of motivation might be captured by the intervening variables in any causal model of the effects of motivation on firm performance.

For example, those higher in nAch might be more likely to obtain venture capital financing. However, once venture capital financing is measured, there is no effect of nAch on firm performance.

We offer several specific suggestions for how researchers could better think about how motivations influence the entrepreneurial process. First, researchers could incorporate motivations into a dynamic evolutionary perspective on entrepreneurship by using motivations to distinguish those individuals who select out at different steps in the entrepreneurial process. For example, motivations could separate those individuals who positively evaluate opportunities from those who do not, those who obtain outside funding from those who do not, those who continue to pursue opportunities from those who abandon the effort, or those who pursue rapid rather than slow growth.

The pursuit of opportunity provides a good example. As Aldrich and Zimmer explain, "opportunities are irrelevant unless taken advantage of, and people vary widely in their ability to seize opportunities". We agree, but would argue that people also differ widely in their motivation to seize opportunities. It would be interesting to know if certain motivations predispose people to take action in response to the discovery of opportunities. One might argue, for example, that people higher in self-efficacy will be more likely to seek financing to exploit opportunities than will people lower in self-efficacy. Because the process of financing exposes a person's entrepreneurial ideas to the scrutiny of skeptical others, those people willing to expose their ideas to scrutiny might have to be more confident than those who will not.

Second, researchers could theorize more deeply about how motivation might impact entrepreneurial decisions. Rather than falling back on the stock idea that firm founders must be fundamentally different types of people from other members of society, we suggest researchers consider how motivations might influence some people to make different decisions from others in the entrepreneurial process.

For example, inventors higher in selfefficacy might found firms to exploit their inventions while inventors lower in self-efficacy might license their technology to others. Similarly, entrepreneurs with a greater need for independence might self-finance new firms, whereas those with a lesser need for independence might seek venture capital.

We also suggest that it is not necessarily important for entrepreneurship researchers to show that specific motivations influence the financial performance of new firms. If financial performance of a new firm is conditional on the ability of an entrepreneur to create the firm, and that act of creation depends heavily on human motivation, then human motivation matters to entrepreneurship even if motivation has no direct effect on the performance of the newly founded firm. In fact, we would expect that the more significant a firm that an entrepreneur founds, the less their motivations influence the firm formation process. For example, the more significant the new firm that an entrepreneur builds, the less influence they will have personally on day-to-day operations, and the less that we would expect the financial performance of the firm to be affected by their personal motivations.

Meta-analysis

The third criticism of previous research is the failure to use meta-analysis. The ability to combine the results of scores or hundreds of individual studies into a single statistic was not always available to researchers. This sometimes led people who conducted narrative reviews to underestimate the effect of the variable being considered; for example, nonsignificant results in single studies may be due to sampling error rather than invalidity. Although metaanalytic results are not available for all the motivations we discuss, such data, where available, throw new light on some motivations.

Wrong Motives

A fourth criticism of extant research is its tendency to study the wrong motives. Some motives are more relevant to entrepreneurial activity than others. For example, risk-taking propensity as measured by self-perception and tolerance for ambiguity has long been assumed to be an entrepreneurial motive, but the evidence so far is only equivocal. Regarding risk, perhaps the problem has been that people cannot perceive the riskiness of their own actions, or that what is risky to one person is not risky to another. For example, several recent studies using interviews and expert evaluations showed that entrepreneurs objectively have a higher propensity for risk than either entrepreneurs or the general population but that entrepreneurs do not perceive their actions as risky.

Thus, the effects of risk-taking propensity may be confounded with the high self-efficacy of entrepreneurs. We suggest that researchers better define the motives that they think are important and focus on more precise measures of them. One way to do that would be for researchers to go back to the underlying psychological literature and examine how researchers have dealt with the nuances of theorizing about and measuring the same motives in other settings. If psychologists have figured a way around the problems of using self-perceptions in the measurement of risky behaviour, like drug usage, those same techniques can be brought to bear on the measurement of risky behaviour in entrepreneurial settings. We believe that another important step for research on motivation and entrepreneurship would be for researchers to develop more complete models of the entrepreneurial process before examining the effects of particular motives on particular activities.

A fuller understanding of the role of motivations in the overall process would require consideration of factors other than motives. We suggest that researchers develop explanations that include the variety of such influences.

Indirect Effects

A fifth criticism has been the failure to look for indirect effects of motivational traits. Most, though not all, researchers have assumed that traits and motives have direct effects on outcomes and this may be true to some extent. However, an increasing body of literature is revealing that traits affect action indirectly through other mechanisms. For example, in the general realm of work, conscientiousness is a reliable predictor of performance, but there is considerable evidence that the effects of conscientiousness on work performance are mediated by situation-specific factors such as goal setting and goal commitment. Similarly, Bandura has argued that locus of control is not a strong, direct predictor of performance in a task; and studies have shown that the effects of self-efficacy mediate the effects of locus of control when self-efficacy is added to the equation.

Therefore, locus of control effects reported in the entrepreneurship literature might be proxying unobserved self-efficacy. One recent study to have taken the approach of considering indirect effects of motivation in the setting of entrepreneurial action is that of Baum, who studied the growth of small companies in the architectural woodworking industry. They included variables from five separate domains: traits and motives, skills and abilities, situation-specific motivation, business strategies, and environmental factors.

They combined the measures within each domain into single indexes and related these indexes to each other and to venture growth. All the domains played a role in venture growth but the effects of motives were all indirect. Motives worked through skills, situation-specific motivation, and strategies to affect growth. Given the indirect effects observed in this study, we suggest that researchers consider such indirect patterns in their explanations for the effect of motivation on entrepreneurial action.

Definitions

A sixth criticism has stemmed from a lack of consistent definitions of entrepreneurship. In general, the definition of what constitutes entrepreneurial activity varies significantly across studies. For example, McClelland viewed managerial positions of certain types such as sales as one that demanded entrepreneurial skills, whereas much of the recent work in the applied field of management has sought to compare entrepreneurs to managers. Therefore, it is unclear if the samples from these different studies are comparable, or even represent entrepreneurship in a meaningful way. This point, of course, brings us back to the importance of a common definition of entrepreneurship. As we indicated earlier, we advocate the definition proposed by Shane and Venkataraman. Whether researchers adopt this particular definition, however, is less important than the existence of a common definition. Without a common definition, it will not be possible to accumulate findings that are comparable from study to study.

HOW MOTIVATIONS INFLUENCE ENTREPRENEURSHIP

We suggest how human motivations might influence the entrepreneurial process. We offer this example to help future researchers design empirical tests of the role of motivation in entrepreneurship. Our example is shown graphically in Fig.

We begin with the set of human motivations that psychologists have shown to influence many aspects of human behaviour. These include the motivations that we described earlier in the study, in particular, nAch, locus of control, desire for independence, passion, and drive. We propose that entrepreneurship is a process that begins with the recognition of an entrepreneurial opportunity and is followed by the development of an idea for how to pursue that opportunity, the evaluation of the feasibility of the opportunity, the development of the product or service that will be provided to customers, assembly of human and financial resources, organizational design, and the pursuit of customers. We suggest that some or all of the motivations influence the transition of individuals from one stage of the entrepreneurial process to another. In some cases, all of the motivations might matter. In other cases, only some of the motivations might matter.

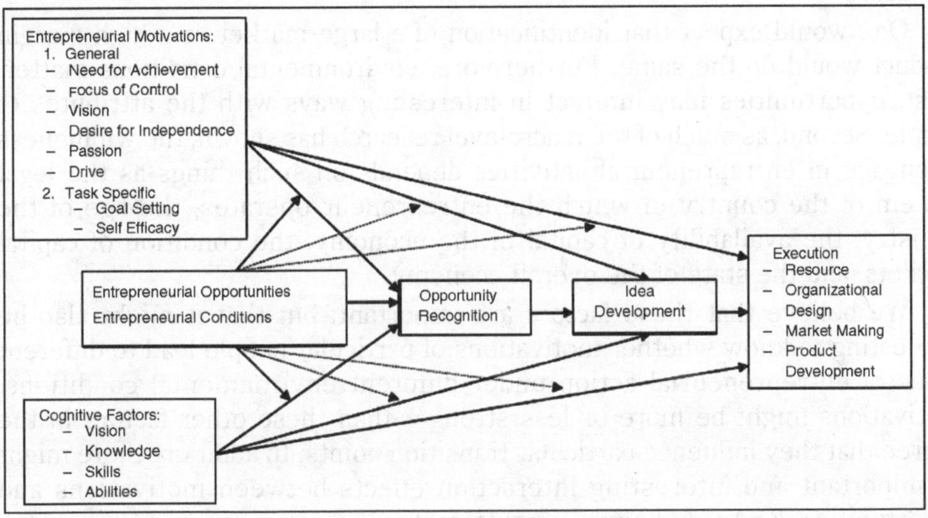

The relative magnitudes of how much each motivation matters will likely vary, depending on the part of the process under investigation. In fact, it is quite plausible that motivations that influence one part of the process have all of their effects at that stage in the process and have no effects on later stages in the process. In this example, motivations are not the only things that influence these transitions. Cognitive factors, including knowledge, skills, and abilities, certainly matter. All action is the result of the combination or integration of motivation and cognition. First, the entrepreneurs need to have some knowledge, especially of the industry and of any relevant technology that is critical to success.

They can hire people with certain specialized skills that they lack, but they must possess enough expertise to know that they are doing the right thing. Second, the entrepreneur must have skills. The necessary skills will depend on the circumstances, but they may include such factors as selling and bargaining, leadership, planning, decision making, problem solving, team building, communication, and conflict management. Third, the entrepreneur needs to have the requisite abilities, including intelligence. Possessing the necessary KSAs enables the entrepreneurs to develop a viable vision, including a strategy for the organization and to carry it out successfully. Motivation helps the entrepreneur to acquire such KSAs in the first place and provide the impetus and energy to implement the needed actions.

The human capital literature in entrepreneurship has begun to show the effect of certain types of knowledge and skills on the start-up and resource assembly parts of this process. The opportunities themselves certainly matter. Prior research has shown that such things as the possession of a patented technology make individuals more likely to engage in the entrepreneurial process.

One would expect that identification of a large market or a high margin product would do the same. Furthermore, environmental conditions matter. First, opportunities may interact in interesting ways with the attributes of people. Second, as much of the macrolevel research has shown, the willingness to engage in entrepreneurial activities depends on such things as the legal system of the country in which the entrepreneur operates, the age of the industry, the availability of capital in the economy, the condition of capital markets, and the state of the overall economy.

We believe that these factors are important, but that it might also be interesting to know whether motivations of particular people lead to different types of entrepreneurial action under different environmental conditions. Motivations might be more or less stronger than these other factors in the degree that they influence particular transition points. In addition, there might be important and interesting interaction effects between motivations and opportunities, KSAs, and environmental factors.

The relative importance of different categories of factors, their independent and combined effects, and their relative importance at different stages of the entrepreneurial process are clearly important theoretical and empirical questions that remain largely unexplored. We hope that researchers will begin to explore them because they appear to us to be central issues in the field of entrepreneurship.

MOTIVATION FACTORS AND THEORIES

MOTIVATION FACTORS

When we look at the psychology of human behaviour we can begin to understand certain baseline motivations which draw adults to on line social networks. Abraham Maslow published his theory of human motivation in 1943. Its popularity continues unabated. Like his colleague Carl Rogers, Maslow believed that actualization was the driving force of human personality, a concept he captures in his 1954 book, Motivation and PersonalityMaslow's great insight was to place actualization into a hierarchy of motivation. Self actualization, as he called it, is the highest drive, but before a person can turn to it, he or she must satisfy other, lower motivations like hunger, safety and belonging.

The hierarchy has five levels:

1. Physiological (hunger, thirst, shelter, sex, etc.)
2. Safety (security, protection from physical and emotional harm)
3. Social (affection, belonging, acceptance, friendship)
4. Esteem. The internal ones are self respect, autonomy, achievement and the external ones are status, recognition, and attention.
5. Self actualization

Maslow points out that the hierarchy is dynamic; the dominant need is always shifting. The hierarchy does not exist by itself, but is affected by the situation and the general culture. Satisfaction is relative. Douglas McGregor makes it the building block for his Theory X and Theory Y. Mihalyi Csikszentmihalyi continues the tradition in his concept of"flow." A 1990s example of self actualization may be surfing the Internet. Empirical research has confirmed the first three levels, but has not done so for the fourth and fifth levels of esteem and self actualization. Some have noted that Maslow's hierarchy follows the life cycle. A newborn baby's needs are almost entirely physiological.

As the baby grows, it needs safety, then love. Toddlers are eager for social interaction. Teenagers are anxious about social needs; young adults are concerned with esteem and only more mature people transcend the first four levels to spend much time self actualizing.

Based on the observations across numerous networking platforms and reflect on the past definitions of human motivation we can see that social networks on line provide a primary motivation for adults in the category of self actualization, or doing things. Maslow defines self actualization as growth-motivated rather than deficiency-motivated.

What Things are Adults doing within Social Networks than Enhance Individual Growth

Based on observations and interview as suggested, provide a general categorization of the factors that enhance individual growth for adults participating in on line social networks.

The Learning Factor

With all the hype, craze and media coverage of social networking platforms, *i.e.*, Facebook and Linkedin, many adults are drawn to the medium to learn what the hype is all about.

The Connection Factor

Once adults enter networks and learn the"tools of the trade" many are amazed to find the presence of other adults they know and many they don't already engaged with the medium.

The Affinity Factor

Adults begin to find association with groups, causes, forums, media and other affinities which relate to their interest both personally and professionally. The predominant business segment using social networks today is employment recruiters. However, as the medium and adult participation has grown there is an exponential growth of business opportunities that adults are learning to facilitate using social networks as the medium.

The Creative Factor

Adults, and their businesses, are applying creative ways to use the technology behind social computing to extend its value to both personal and professional needs.

The Expectation Factor

When you consider the creative possibilities of social networks adults expect to the formation of some economic and social value to be derived from their participation whether currently or in the future. The expectation of individual growth and satisfaction is high.These factors combined with the media hype over social networking are the motivating issues which are driving millions of adults to the medium at annual growth rates of 70% and more. The opportunity to capitalize economically is emerging quickly. Word of mouth will fuel growth rates faster than any other technological medium in our past. The growth and related factors will usher in The Relationship Economy.

THEORIES OF MOTIVATION

Contribution of Robert Owen

Though Owen is considered to be paternalistic in his view, his contribution is of a considerable significance in the theories of Motivation. During the early years of the nineteenth century, Owen's textile mill at New Lanark in Scotland was the scene of some novel ways of treating people. His view was that people were similar to machines.

A machine that is looked after properly, cared for and maintained well, performs efficiently, reliably and lastingly, similarly people are likely to be more efficient if they are taken care of. Robert Owen practiced what he preached and introduced such things as employee housing and company shop. His ideas on this and other matters were considered to be too revolutionary for that time.

Jeremy Bentham's "The Carrot and the Stick Approach"

Possibly the essence of the traditional view of people at work can be best appreciated by a brief look at the work of this English philosopher, whose ideas were also developed in the early years of the Industrial Revolution, around 1800. Bentham's view was that all people are self-interested and are motivated by the desire to avoid pain and find pleasure. Any worker will work only if the reward is big enough, or the punishment sufficiently unpleasant. This view - the 'carrot and stick' approach - was built into the philosophies of the age and is still to be found, especially in the older, more traditional sectors of industry.

The various leading theories of motivation and motivators seldom make reference to the carrot and the stick. This metaphor relates, of course, to the use of rewards and penalties in order to induce desired behaviour. It comes from the old story that to make a donkey move, one must put a carrot in front of him or dab him with a stick from behind. Despite all the research on the theories of motivation, reward and punishment are still considered strong motivators. For centuries, however, they were too often thought of as the only forces that could motivate people.

At the same time, in all theories of motivation, the inducements of some kind of 'carrot' are recognized. Often this is money in the form of pay or bonuses. Even though money is not the only motivating force, it has been and will continue to be an important one. The trouble with the money 'carrot' approach is that too often everyone gets a carrot, regardless of performance through such practices as salary increase and promotion by seniority, automatic 'merit' increases, and executive bonuses not based on individual manager performance. It is as simple as this: If a person put a donkey in a pen full of carrots and then stood outside with a carrot, would the donkey be encouraged to come out of the pen? The 'stick', in the form of fear–fear of loss of job, loss of income, reduction of bonus, demotion, or some other penalty–has been and continues to be a strong motivator.

Yet it is admittedly not the best kind. It often gives rise to defensive or retaliatory behaviour, such as union organization, poor-quality work, executive indifference, failure of a manager to take any risks in decision making or even dishonesty. But fear of penalty cannot be overlooked. Whether managers are first-level supervisors or chief executives, the power of their position to give or with hold rewards or impose penalties of various kinds gives them an ability to control, to a very great extent, the economic and social well-being of their subordinates.

Abraham Maslow's "Need Hierarchy Theory"

One of the most widely theories of motivation is the hierarchy of needs theory put forth by psychologist Abraham Maslow. Maslow saw human needs in the form of a hierarchy, ascending from the lowest to the highest, and he concluded that when one set of needs is satisfied, this kind of need ceases to be a motivator. As per his theory this needs are:

Physiological Needs

These are important needs for sustaining the human life. Food, water, warmth, shelter, sleep, medicine and education are the basic physiological needs which fall in the primary list of need satisfaction. Maslow was of an opinion that until these needs were satisfied to a degree to maintain life, no other motivating factors can work.

Security or Safety Needs

These are the needs to be free of physical danger and of the fear of losing a job, property, food or shelter. It also includes protection against any emotional harm.

Social Needs

Since people are social beings, they need to belong and be accepted by others. People try to satisfy their need for affection, acceptance and friendship.

Esteem Needs

Maslow, once people begin to satisfy their need to belong, they tend to want to be held in esteem both by themselves and by others. This kind of need produces such satisfaction as power, prestige status and self-confidence. It includes both internal esteem factors like self-respect, autonomy and achievements and external esteem factors such as states, recognition and attention.

Need for Self-actualization

Maslow regards this as the highest need in his hierarchy. It is the drive to become what one is capable of becoming, it includes growth, achieving one's potential and self-fulfillment. It is to maximize one's potential and to accomplish something.

As each of these needs are substantially satisfied, the next need becomes dominant. From the standpoint of motivation, the theory would say that although no need is ever fully gratified, a substantially satisfied need no longer motivates. So if you want to motivate someone, you need to understand what level of the hierarchy that person is on and focus on satisfying those needs or needs above that level. Maslow's need theory has received wide recognition, particularly among practicing managers.

This can be attributed to the theory's intuitive logic and ease of understanding. However, research does not validate these theory. Maslow provided no empirical evidence and other several studies that sought to validate the theory found no support for it.

"Theory X and Theory Y" of Douglas McGregor

McGregor, "The Human side of Enterprise" states that people inside the organization can be managed in two ways. The first is basically negative, which falls under the category X and the other is basically positive, which falls under the category Y. After viewing the way in which the manager dealt with employees, McGregor concluded that a manager's view of the nature of human beings is based on a certain grouping of assumptions and that he or she tends to mold his or her behaviour towards subordinates just as to these assumptions.

Under the assumptions of theory X:

- Employees inherently do not like work and whenever possible, will attempt to avoid it.
- Because employees dislike work, they have to be forced, coerced or threatened with punishment to achieve goals.
- Employees avoid responsibilities and do not work fill formal directions are issued.
- Most workers place a greater importance on security over all other factors and display little ambition.

In contrast under the assumptions of theory Y:

- Physical and mental effort at work is as natural as rest or play.
- People do exercise self-control and self-direction and if they are committed to those goals.
- Average human beings are willing to take responsibility and exercise imagination, ingenuity and creativity in solving the problems of the organization.
- That the way the things are organized, the average human being's brain power is only partly used.

On analysis of the assumptions it can be detected that theory X assumes that lower-order needs dominate individuals and theory Y assumes that higher-order needs dominate individuals. An organization that is run on Theory X lines tends to be authoritarian in nature, the word "authoritarian" suggests such ideas as the "power to enforce obedience" and the "right to command." In contrast Theory Y organizations can be described as "participative", where the aims of the organization and of the individuals in it are integrated; individuals can achieve their own goals best by directing their efforts towards the success of the organization. However, this theory has been criticized widely for generalization of work and human behaviour.

Contribution of Rensis Likert

Likert developed a refined classification, breaking down organizations into four management systems.

- 1st System – Primitive authoritarian
- 2nd System – Benevolent authoritarian
- 3rd System – Consultative
- 4th System – Participative

As per the opinion of Likert, the 4th system is the best, not only for profit organizations, but also for non-profit firms.

Frederick Herzberg's Motivation-hygiene Theory

Frederick has tried to modify Maslow's need Hierarchy theory. His theory is also known as two-factor theory or Hygiene theory. He stated that there are certain satisfiers and dissatisfiers for employees at work. Intrinsic factors are related to job satisfaction, while extrinsic factors are associated with dissatisfaction. He devised his theory on the question: "What do people want from their jobs ?" From the responses that he received, he concluded that opposite of satisfaction is not dissatisfaction.

Removing dissatisfying characteristics from a job does not necessarily make the job satisfying. He states that presence of certain factors in the organization is natural and the presence of the same does not lead to motivation. However, their nonpresence leads to demotivation. In similar manner there are certain factors, the absence of which causes no dissatisfaction, but their presence has motivational impact.

Examples of Hygiene factors are:

- Security, status, relationship with subordinates, personal life, salary, work conditions, relationship with supervisor and company policy and administration.

Examples of Motivational factors are:

- Growth prospectus job advancement, responsibility, challenges, recognition and achievements.

Contributions of Elton Mayo

The work of Elton Mayo is famously known as "Hawthorne Experiments." He conducted behavioural experiments at the Hawthorne Works of the American Western Electric Company in Chicago. He made some illumination experiments, introduced breaks in between the work performance and also introduced refreshments during the pause's. It was not only about pay, work condition and morale but also included psychological and social factors.

Although this research has been criticized from many angles:

- People are motivated by more than pay and conditions.

- The need for recognition and a sense of belonging are very important.
- Attitudes towards work are strongly influenced by the group.

Vroom's Valence x Expectancy Theory

The most widely accepted explanations of motivation has been propounded by Victor Vroom. His theory is commonly known as expectancy theory. The theory argues that the strength of a tendency to act in a specific way depends on the strength of an expectation that the act will be followed by a given outcome and on the attractiveness of that outcome to the individual to make this simple, expectancy theory says that an employee can be motivated to perform better when their is a belief that the better performance will lead to good performance appraisal and that this shall result into realisation of personal goal in form of some reward.

Therefore an employee is:

- Motivation = Valence x Expectancy.

The theory focuses on three things:

- Efforts and performance relationship
- Performance and reward relationship
- Rewards and personal goal relationship

This leads us to a conclusion that:

The Porter and Lawler Model

Lyman W. Porter and Edward E. Lawler developed a more complete version of motivation depending upon expectancy theory.

Actual performance in a job is primarily determined by the effort spent. But it is also affected by the person's ability to do the job and also by individual's perception of what the required task is. So performance is the responsible factor that leads to intrinsic as well as extrinsic rewards. These rewards, along with the equity of individual leads to satisfaction. Hence, satisfaction of the individual depends upon the fairness of the reward.

Clayton Alderfer's ERG Theory

Alderfer has tried to rebuild the hierarchy of needs of Maslow into another model named ERG *i.e.* Existence – Relatedness – Growth.

The existence group is concerned mainly with providing basic material existence. The second group is the individuals need to maintain interpersonal relationship with other members in the group. The final group is the intrinsic desire to grow and develop personally.

The major of this theory are:

- In an individual, more than one need may be operative at the same time.
- If a higher need goes unsatisfied than the desire to satisfy a lower need intensifies.
- It also contains the frustration-regression dimension.

McClelland's Theory of Needs

David McClelland has developed a theory on three types of motivating needs:

1. Need for Power
2. Need for Affiliation
3. Need for Achievement

Basically people for high need for power are inclined towards influence and control. They like to be at the centre and are good orators. They are demanding in nature, forceful in manners and ambitious in life. They can be motivated to perform if they are given key positions or power positions. In the second category are the people who are social in nature. They try to affiliate themselves with individuals and groups.

They are driven by love and faith. They like to build a friendly environment around themselves. Social recognition and affiliation with others provides them motivation. People in the third area are driven by the challenge of success and the fear of failure.

Their need for achievement is moderate and they set for themselves moderately difficult tasks. They are analytical in nature and take calculated risks. Such people are motivated to perform when they see atleast some chances of success. McClelland observed that with the advancement in hierarchy the need for power and achievement increased rather than Affiliation. He also observed that people who were at the top, later ceased to be motivated by this drives.

Equity Theory

As per the equity theory of J. Stacey Adams, people are motivated by their beliefs about the reward structure as being fair or unfair, relative to the inputs. People have a tendency to use subjective judgment to balance the outcomes and inputs in the relationship for comparisons between different individuals. Accordingly:

If people feel that they are not equally rewarded they either reduce the quantity or quality of work or migrate to some other organization. However, if people perceive that they are rewarded higher, they may be motivated to work harder.

Reinforcement Theory

B.F. Skinner, who propounded the reinforcement theory, holds that by designing the environment properly, individuals can be motivated. Instead of considering internal factors like impressions, feelings, attitudes and other cognitive behaviour, individuals are directed by what happens in the environment external to them. Skinner states that work environment should be made suitable to the individuals and that punishments actually leads to frustration and de-motivation. Hence, the only way to motivate is to keep on making positive changes in the external environment of the organization.

Goal Setting Theory of Edwin Locke

Instead of giving vague tasks to people, specific and pronounced objectives, help in achieving them faster. As the clarity is high, a goal orientation also avoids any misunderstandings in the work of the employees. The goal setting theory states that when the goals to be achieved are set at a higher standard than in that case employees are motivated to perform better and put in maximum effort. It revolves around the concept of "Self-efficacy" *i.e.* individual's belief that he or she is capable of performing a hard task.

Cognitive Evaluation Theory

As per this theory a shift from external rewards to internal rewards results into motivation. It believes that even after the stoppage of external stimulus, internal stimulus survives.

It relates to the pay structure in the organization. Instead of treating external factors like pay, incentives, promotion etc and internal factors like interests, drives, responsibility etc, separately, they should be treated as contemporary to each other.

The cognition is to be such that even when external motivators are not there the internal motivation continues. However, practically extrinsic rewards are given much more weightage.

OBJECTIVES AND ACHIEVEMENTS OF MOTIVATION

MAIN OBJECTIVES OF MOTIVATION

Self preservation, whether this is pointed directly to survivial or towards our image of ourselves painted by our beliefs and ideals. What I mean by this is that we have in our mind a view point of who we are and we trive to accomplish this in either advancement or a continuation of our currant state. This personal view point might look down upon theft, and so seeing a theft we might feel "motivated" to call police, in order to up keep our currant view of what kind of person we see ourselves as.

ACHIEVEMENT

Over the years, behavioural scientists have noticed that some people have an intense desire to achieve something, while others may not seem that concerned about their achievements. This phenomenon has attracted a lot of discussions and debates. Scientists have observed that people with a high level of achievement motivation exhibit certain characteristics. Achievement motivation is the tendency to endeavor for success and to choose goal oriented success or failure activities.

Achievement motivation forms to be the basic for a good life. People who are oriented towards achievement, in general, enjoy life and feel in control. Being motivated keeps people dynamic and gives them self-respect. They set moderately difficult but easily achievable targets, which help them, achieve their objectives. They do not set up extremely difficult or extremely easy targets. By doing this they ensure that they only undertake tasks that can be achieved by them.

Achievement motivated people prefer to work on a problem rather than leaving the outcome to chance. It is also seen that achievement motivated people seem to be more concerned with their personal achievement rather than the rewards of success. It is generally seen that achievement motivated people evidenced a significantly higher rate of advancement in their company compared to others. Programmes and courses designed, involves seven "training inputs." The first step refers to the process through which achievement motivation thinking is taught to the person.

The second step helps participants understand their own individuality and goals. The third assist participants in practicing achievement-related actions in cases, role-plays, and real life. A fourth refers to practicing of achievement-related actions in business and other games. A fifth input encourages participants to relate the achievement behaviour model to their own behaviour, self-image, and goals.

The sixth programme facilitates participants to develop a personal plan of action. Finally, the course provides participants with feedback on their progress towards achieving objectives and targets. Achievement motivation as a branch of study has greatly established its prominence. A number of companies are now training their employees in the same.

ENTREPRENEURIAL COMPETENCIES—MEANING

Every career draws on the competencies of an individual. Some of these competencies may be general and some peculiar to the chosen career. You may understand competencies to mean abilities and skills. However, we would desist from calling these as personality traits as such a conceptualization only reinforces the mistaken belief that entrepreneurs are born rather than made.

We believe that recognition of these competencies as abilities and skills makes entrepreneurship as a teachable and learnable behaviour. We orient you towards a set of entrepreneurial competencies developed by the Entrepreneurship Development Institute of India Ahemdabad. These competencies were identified by a thorough research procedure based on critical analysis of the case studies of the successful entrepreneurs.

ENTREPRENEURIAL COMPETENCIES IDENTIFIED BY THE EDI

- *Initiative*: Acting out of choice rather than compulsion, taking the lead rather than waiting for others to start.
- *Sees and Acts on Opportunities*: A mindset where one is trained to look for business opportunities from everyday experiences.
- *Persistence*: A 'never say die' attitude, not giving up easily, striving Information seeking continuously until success is achieved.
- *Knowing*: Knowing who knows, consulting experts, reading relevant material and an overall openness to ideas and information.
- *Concern for High Quality of Work*: Attention to details and observance of established standards and norms.
- *Commitment to Work Contract*: Taking personal pains to complete a task as scheduled.
- *Efficiency Orientation*: Concern for conservation of time, money and effort.
- *Systematic Planning*: Breaking up the complex whole into parts, close examination of the parts and inferring about the whole; *e.g.* simultaneously attending to production, marketing and financial aspects of the overall business strategy.
- *Problem solving*: Observing the symptoms, diagnosing and curing.
- *Self-confidence*: Not being afraid of the risks associated with business and relying on one's capabilities to successfully manage these.
- *Assertiveness*: Conveying emphatically one's vision and convincing others of its value.
- *Persuasion*: Eliciting support of others in the venture.
- *Use of Influence Strategies*: Providing leadership.
- *Monitoring*: Ensuring the progress of the venture as planned.
- *Concern for Employee Welfare*: Believing in employee well being as the key to competitiveness and success and initiating programmes of employee welfare.

These competencies matter in entrepreneurial success. EDI estimates that development of these competencies can substantially bring down incidence of business failures/industrial sickness.

DEVELOPING COMPETENCIES

'Awareness,' they say, is the first step towards 'improvement' and 'success.' Now that you are aware of the critical competencies for entrepreneurial success and also have a measure of your scores on these, it is appropriate that you also think in terms of how to improve your scores. Suppose, you find yourself lacking in the competency- 'opportunity spotting,' you may start practicing to think like an entrepreneur. With just a little change in perspective, the world changes for you. Similarly you may work on the other competencies as well.

4

Tax

INTRODUCTION

To tax is to impose a financial charge or other levy upon a taxpayer by a state or the functional equivalent of a state such that failure to pay is punishable by law. Taxes are also imposed by many subnational entities. Taxes consist of direct tax or indirect tax, and may be paid in money or as its labour equivalent. A tax may be defined as a "pecuniary burden laid upon individuals or property owners to support the government [...] a payment exacted by legislative authority." A tax "is not a voluntary payment or donation, but an enforced contribution, exacted pursuant to legislative authority" and is "any contribution imposed by government [...] whether under the name of toll, tribute, tallage, gabel, impost, duty, custom, excise, subsidy, aid, supply, or other name."

The legal definition and the economic definition of taxes differ in that economists do not consider many transfers to governments to be taxes. For example, some transfers to the public sector are comparable to prices. Examples include tuition at public universities and fees for utilities provided by local governments.

Governments also obtain resources by creating money, through voluntary gifts, by imposing penalties, by borrowing, and by confiscating wealth. From the view of economists, a tax is a non-penal, yet compulsory transfer of resources from the private to the public sector levied on a basis of predetermined criteria and without reference to specific benefit received.

In modern taxation systems, taxes are levied in money, but in-kind and corvée taxation are characteristic of traditional or pre-capitalist states and their functional equivalents. The method of taxation and the government expenditure of taxes raised is often highly debated in politics and economics. Tax collection is performed by a government agency such as Canada Revenue Agency, the Internal Revenue Service in the United States, or Her Majesty's Revenue and Customs in the UK. When taxes are not fully paid, civil penalties or criminal penalties may be imposed on the non-paying entity or individual.

PURPOSES AND EFFECTS OF TAXATION

The funds raised by taxation have customarily been used by different states and their functional equivalents throughout history to carry out the functions such as:

- Upkeep of public property
- Economic infrastructure - roads, legal tender, enforcement of contracts, etc.
- Enforcement of law and public ordero Protection of propertyo Military defenceo Redistribution of wealth
- The operational costs involved in the running of the government itself
- Any work in favour of public interest

So also, most modern day governments also use taxes to fund welfare and public services, such as:

- Pensions for the elderly
- Unemployment benefits
- Education systems
- Health care systems
- Energy, water and waste management systems
- Public transportation

States that were colonies of bigger super power nations which are on the road to modernization have also used cash taxes to draw or force reluctant subsistence producers into cash economies.

Various government bodies use different kinds of taxes and vary the tax rates with the following intentions in mind:

- In order to redistribute resources between individuals or classes within the population. In olden times, the nobility were supported by the taxes paid by the poor, however, in modern social security systems, taxes are intended to support the poor, the disabled or those retired from service, by taxes on those who are still working
- In order to distribute the tax burden between individuals or strata of the population involved in taxable activities, with high turn over of income such as businesses
- In order to modify patterns of consumption or employment within an economy, by making some types of transactions more or less attractive
- In order to influence the macro-economic performance of the economy

The resources taken from the common man through taxation is always more or less greater than the amount that can be used by the government. This difference is called the compliance cost, and includes, for example, the labour cost and other expenses incurred while executing compliance with tax laws and rules. The collection of a tax in order to spend it on a particular purpose, for instance, collection of taxes on alcohol to pay directly to maintain alcoholism rehabilitation centres, is called hypothecation.

This practice is seldom liked by finance ministers, since it greatly hampers their freedom of action. Some economic theorists consider this concept to be morally dishonest, since in reality the money is generated by a means that further eats into society. Furthermore, it also often occurs that taxes or excises initially levied to fund a specific government programme are later diverted to the government's general fund. In some cases, such taxes are collected in fundamentally inefficient ways, exemplified by highway tolls.

Some economists, especially neo-classical ones argue that all types of taxation result in distortion of the market and economic inefficiency. They have therefore sought to identify and develop a system of taxation that would minimize this distortion. One of the theories is that the most economically neutral tax is the tax on land. A government's primary duty must be to maintain and defend the title to land, and therefore it must collect most of its revenues in order to provide for this unique service.

Since governments also play a role in resolving commercial disputes, especially in countries where a common law is executed, this doctrine is often used to justify a sales tax or a value added tax. Other libertarians argue that almost all forms of taxes are immoral due to their involuntary and therefore eventually coercive or violent nature. The most extreme anti-tax view is that of anarcho-capitalism, in which the provision of the state interfering with an individual's earnings or demanding a share of it to facilitate salvaging downtrodden classes of society is looked upon with intense scorn.

PROPORTIONAL TAX

A proportional tax could also be called a flat tax rate. It is a system under which the percentage of tax taken from income, or charged to individuals, remains the same no matter how much is made or how much is spent. The US does not have a proportional tax on income, and instead employs a progressive tax system, where higher incomes are taxed at higher amounts than are lower incomes.

The reasoning behind this is that people with less money have a more difficult time paying taxes. A person making just slightly above the poverty rate will pay a much lower percentage of their income in taxes because they need that income in order to survive.The US does have some proportional tax types. Sales tax for instance is a constant where it is applied, though the percentage can vary if cities add additional taxes to sales tax. Person A, who lives in City B will pay the same rate in City B for all items considered taxable. He might pay more or less in another city or in another state if he travels or moves.

Some argue that the proportional taxes on most goods are most difficult to pay for those who are poor. Rich or poor pay the same taxes on a box of detergent, but it hurts the poor man or woman's pocket more when they have little money to spare. These arguments tend to suggest that a proportional tax on sales goods really represents a regressive tax. Poorer people will use more of their income than will rich people to pay for same goods.

A regressive tax in general can be defined as a tax that tends to impact the poorest people the most. Whereas, the wealthiest people tend to pay the least amount of their income under such a situation. There has been some discussion in the US of converting to a flat tax rate or a proportional tax. Yet again, those who argue against such a tax claim it is regressive. Even though the tax rate remains constant, those least able to afford the tax have to pay it, with no exceptions.

Consider a proportional tax of 10% on income. The person who makes $200,000 US Dollars (USD) a year would pay $20,000 USD a year in taxes. That seems like a lot, but it still leaves this consumer with $180,000 USD of income. In contrast, the person making $10,000 USD a year pays $1000 USD in taxes, leaving him or her with $9000 a year to meet all expenses. Those who argue against a flat tax or proportional tax say that an inflexible rate would make it that much harder for the poor to survive. The wealthy might be able to afford to lose $20,000 USD, but can a poor person really afford to lose $1000 USD? It's pretty difficult to attempt to live on $9000 USD a year, especially if sales tax for most items remains in place too.

In order to keep sales taxes from becoming burdensome, many states do not tax items like food. However, many other goods, like toilet paper or dish detergent are taxed. Moreover, proportional taxes exist on many utilities, though the working poor may be able to qualify for reduced rates on certain utilities like telephone and gas and electric service. This helps reduce the overall effect of the proportional tax, making it less regressive in nature.

PROGRESSIVE TAX

A progressive tax is a tax rate applied to either income or profits, or spending, that increases as income/profits, or spending increases. This is the tax system used in the US, and in many other countries. Those who make the least amount of money tend to pay the lowest percentage of their income in taxes. People who make larger amounts of money are taxed at a higher percentage.

Taxation in most countries, including the US, is slightly more difficult to compute. Many misunderstand the progressive tax rate as the following formula: Mr. X who makes $20,000 US Dollars (USD) will pay 10% of his income in taxes. Mr. Y makes $40,000 USD and will pay 15% of his income. Ms. Z makes $60,000 USD and will pay 20% of her income in taxes.

Instead, taxes on amounts made increase progressively. My. Y would pay 10% on the first $20,000 USD he makes, and 15% on the second $20,000. Ms. Z would pay 10% on the first $20,000, 15% on the second, and 20% on the third.

There are also a number of things that can reduce taxation percentage. If you are marrying and filing a joint tax return, or if you have a number of dependents to support, progressive tax percentages would diminish because less of your money would be actually considered taxable income. The lowest incomes, especially those below the poverty level would owe very little in actual taxes. Businesses that lose money during a year instead of making profits would probably not owe taxes either.

The progressive tax may be applied to certain types of spending. Any sales tax may remain at a stable amount, but a person who spends more of their income on taxable goods will be proportionately be spending a higher amount of their income on sales tax, even though the sales tax percentage is the same for everyone. Further, some items, like yachts and luxury cars, are subject to luxury taxes, which are much higher percentages of tax for these items.

There are many people who support progressive tax, since they feel it is only fair that those who make more should contribute more to the government. Those who make the least, and can't really afford to lose their income to taxes shouldn't be spending much to fund government programmes. Not all people agree with progressive tax, since it means that people who make more money are "punished" for their success or wealth. Some propose a flat tax rate instead of a progressive tax, or a tax on spending instead of on income.

Others favour a regressive tax, where percentage of taxes decreases when income increases. This would mean people who make the most would pay a much lower percentage in taxes, but since their income is high, they'd still pay quite a bit in taxes. People who make the least would pay the highest percentages, though allowances might still be made for those under the poverty level. This system would purportedly mean everyone would pay about the same amount in taxes each year. Critics of the regressive tax system suggest this would be an unfair burden on those least able to afford taxes.

MEASURING PROGRESSIVITY

Models such as the Suits index, Gini coefficient, Theil index, Atkinson index, and Robin Hood index are sometimes used to factor progressivity through measures of inequality of income distribution or inequality of wealth distribution.

Effective Progression

An effective progression can be computed from inequality measures. *The following example uses the Gini coefficient*:

Inflation and Tax Brackets

Many tax laws are not accurately indexed to inflation. Either they ignore inflation completely, or they are indexed to the Consumer Price Index (CPI), which tends to understate real inflation. In a progressive tax system, failure to index the brackets to inflation will eventually result in effective tax increases, as inflation in wages will increase individual income and move individuals into higher tax brackets with higher percentage rate. One example is the United States Alternative Minimum Tax; since it is not indexed to inflation, an increasing number of upper-middle-income taxpayers have been finding themselves subject to this tax.

Marginal and Effective Tax Rates

The rate of tax can be expressed in two different ways, the marginal rate expressed as the rate on each additional piece of income or expenditure and the effective rate expressed as the total tax paid divided by total income or expenditure. In most progressive tax systems, both rates will rise as amount subject to taxation rises, though there may be ranges where the marginal rate will be constant.

With a system of negative income tax, refundable tax credits, or income-tested welfare benefits, it is possible for marginal rates to fall as amount subject to taxation rises: this can still be seen as progressive providing that the marginal rate is higher than the average rate at any particular level, since the average rate will rise; high marginal rates for those with low means can lead to a poverty trap within a progressive system, even if they face negative average rates.

BASE OF TAXATION

Income

The key concept of progressive income taxation is that income is considered in different steps, where income earned between certain points will be taxed at a certain rate. This is done to avoid creating incentive traps, where earning more might actually decrease your income. The size and severity of the different steps varies a great deal and the differences inside the term "progressive" can be enormous. In this sense, it is not surprising that most economists support progressive taxation to some degree - the primary differences come when looking at the maximum income taxes that the highest earners might have to pay.

Expenditure

While a tax on expenditures can be structured like a pure sales tax, many proposals make adjustments to decrease regressive effects. Using exemptions, graduated rates, deductions, credits or rebates, a consumption tax can be made less regressive or progressive, while allowing savings to accumulate tax-free. A sales tax on luxury goods or the exemption of basic necessities may be described as having progressive effects as it increases a tax burden on high end consumption or decreases a tax burden on low end consumption respectively. Economist Alan J. Auerbach of University of California, Berkeley states that "annual income is not an especially accurate measure of one's ability to pay.

A household's consumption tends to fluctuate less from year to year than its income does, and in some respects offers a better measure of a family's sustainable standard of living. Averaged over periods longer than one year, which smoothes out fluctuations in annual income, consumption taxes look less regressive relative to income than they look on an annual basis." Tax reform proposals that transition from an income tax to a consumption tax would be more equitable because consumption requires a balance between known and complex social costs.

IMPLEMENTATION

There are two ways that a progressive income tax can be implemented:

- *Increasing percentage rates*: When implementing a progressive tax with increasing percentage rates, the percentage of tax of each dollar increases as the total revenue increases. For example, a tax of 15% on all income earned up to $50,000, plus a tax of 25% on each dollar earned between $50,001 and $100,000, plus a tax of 34% of all income earned above $100,000. The United States currently uses increasing percentage rates.
- *Single tax rate*: A progressive tax rate can also be achieved by combining a single flat rate with a threshold. For example, all income up to $100,000 is earned tax free; income above $100,000 is taxed at 35%.

REGRESSIVE TAX

A regressive tax can be defined as a tax that tends to increase the total percentage of income paid on those who must pay the tax. In contrast, those who have a higher income pay less of their total income on items taxed. A tax can also be considered regressive when poorer folks must purchase more of the items taxed than do richer folks. An example of regressive tax can occur when people who are poorer live, as they tend to do in poorly insulated homes.

Due to poor insulation, they may pay more money to heat or cool their homes, and pay a higher tax on the purchase of electricity and gas. Similarly a person with an old car that is a gas-guzzler may have to consume more gas and thus pay a higher proportion of their income on gas taxes, than does a person who is able to afford to purchase an energy efficient car or a hybrid vehicle.

The wealthier person gets something of a tax advantage in these situations, making taxes on energy or fuel regressive in nature. The wealthier person may live in a better insulated home, be able to increase energy efficiency by investing in double-paned windows or newer appliances, and can purchase a hybrid or at least newer vehicle. Thus their energy bills may be less, and the taxes are less.

In simpler terms, the person who makes $30,000 US Dollars (USD) per year and drives an old car might need to purchase more gas. Say they need 20 gallons of gas per week, and the tax is $1.00 USD per gallon. In a years time the person pays slightly over $1000 USD on gas taxes alone, about 3% of total income.

Let's say a similar person who makes $60,000 USD has a fuel-efficient car. He purchases 10 gallons of gas a week and pays just over $500 USD a year in total gas taxes. The percentage of income spent on gas tax each year is less than 1%, approximately 0.83%. You can see how this system is regressive tax in nature. The poorer person pays three times the amount of income as the richer person.

Even if a person with greater income chooses to purchase a car with less fuel efficiency, chances are the gas tax will still consume less of his/her income than it does for the poorer person. The person earning $60,000 USD per year does buy 20 gallons of gas a week, he or she is still only paying 1.6% of total income on gas taxes per year, about half of what the poorer person pays.

In order to prevent regressive tax on items purchased, many states make certain types of things non-taxable, especially food. This means the poorer person is not paying taxes when he or she is already consuming a large portion of their income on food expenses. Yet many items considered staples in a home are still taxed, like cleaners or paper products. Another way in which regressive tax can hit people hard is when it comes time to pay things like vehicle registration each year, which can really be difficult for many people to pay.

The litmus test then, for defining regressive tax is the percentage of income a person must pay on a tax. Few countries have regressive tax systems in place. However it has been noted that people who make especially high incomes may have access to certain tax shelters unavailable to those with low to moderate incomes. Even though such a system is progressive, tax loopholes can ultimately mean that those who make more pay less of their income in taxes than those who make less, resulting in regressive taxation.

DIFFERENCE BETWEEN PROGRESSIVE AND REGRESSIVE TAX

Progressive taxation refers to a form of taxation where the percentage of income paid by an individual, increases with increasing income. People with higher income pay more total taxes imposed at a higher rate. Thus, a person with an income of $200,000 may pay a tax of $20,000, whereas a person with an income of $50,000 may pay a tax of $4,000. In case of regressive taxation, the proportion of income which is paid in taxes, decreases with an increase in income.

This is in direct contrast to progressive tax, where the proportion paid as taxes, rises as the income increases. Sales tax on grocery products is also considered to be a form of regressive taxation because of the fact that a poor individual pays the same amount of tax as a wealthy person. The U.S. Taxation system contains a mixture of both progressive and regressive taxes.

A regressive tax system also includes the taxes imposed on essentials, like, transport, housing and clothing.

This is because the income elasticity of the demand for these essentials is less, thus increasing the percentage of a lowly paid individual's budget which is taken as tax. Taxes on alcohol and tobacco are also a form of regressive taxation because both the lowly paid and highly paid individuals consume these products.

Taxation on property is also sometimes considered as regressive taxation because the property taxes take up a higher percentage of an individual's budget who has a low income, than it does for an individual with a higher income.

COMMON EXAMPLES

- A value-added tax or other sales tax on food and other essentials such as clothing, transport, and residential rents can be regressive. Since the income elasticity of demand of food is usually less than 1, it tends to take up a higher percentage of the budget of a person or family with a lower income.
- A poll tax is a fixed tax for each person. Since each person pays the same amount of money, it is a lower proportion for people with higher incomes.
- Television licences that are implemented in many countries, especially in Europe, are considered regressive taxes and in most cases consist of a flat annual payment for the use of a television.
- The so called sin taxes are also criticized for being regressive, since the products taxed "are often consumed more by the lower classes".

DIRECT TAXES

A Direct tax is a kind of charge, which is imposed directly on the taxpayer. The examples of direct tax include property tax and income tax. Alternatively, it can be said that a direct tax is one that is taken away from one's salary or wages. When the tax is imposed by the government upon the property, then it is called property tax, which is also a direct tax.

MEANING OF DIRECT TAX: DIFFERENT VIEWS

The term direct tax can be defined from two different perspectives. One is from Colloquial point and the other is from U.S. constitutional law point. Certain taxes may fall under indirect tax categories in the constitutional sense, but fall under direct tax category in the colloquial sense.

DIRECT TAX: COLLOQUIAL SENSE

From the Colloquial point of view, a direct tax is the charge levied directly to the taxpayers by the government. Examples include corporate taxes, income taxes and transfer taxes. The transfer taxes include estate tax and gift tax.

DIRECT TAXATION IN INDIA

Direct taxation in India is taken care by the Central Board of Direct Taxes; it is a division of Department of revenue under Ministry of Finance. CBDT is governed by the revenue act 1963.CBDT is given the authority to create and control direct taxes in India. The most important function of CBDT is to manage direct tax law followed by Income Tax department.

In India the tax structure is divided amongst the central government and state government.

The central government levies taxes on income, custom duties, central excise and service tax. While the state government levies tax like state excise, stamp duty, VAT, land revenue and professional tax.

LOCAL CIVIC BODIES LEVY TAX ON PROPERTIES, OCTROI ETC

Capital gains tax, personal income tax, tax on corporate income and tax incentives all come under the purview of direct tax.

Direct taxes are charged on the basis of residential status and not on the basis of citizenship.

The assessee are charged based upon the following factors:

- Resident
- Resident but not ordinary resident.
- Nonresident.

DIRECT TAXES BEFORE REFORM

They had a major impact on economic policies, creation of savings and the trend of investment. There was no proportion in terms of the impact of direct taxes on the economy and there relative share in total tax revenues. The system of direct taxes was very much complex and inefficient because of the combination of high marginal rates of personal income and wealth taxation and high rates of corporate profits. The corporate tax was pretty high. It leads to large scale evasion.

Members of Parliament and Central Government Ministers get comparatively low salaries, but they are given a sitting allowance which is not taxable. Ministers, MP's and other high ranking government officials get government allocated accommodation, where the charges are pretty less in comparison to the prevailing market rate.

GROWTH IN DIRECT TAX COLLECTION DURING THE FINANCIAL YEAR 2008-09

Net direct tax collection during the fiscal 2008-09 stands at Rs.338, 212 crore, up from Rs.312, 202 crore during 2007-08, registering a growth of 8.33 per cent. Growth in Corporate Taxes was 10.84 per cent, while Personal Income Tax grew at 9.09%. Despite economic slow-down and substantial relief to non-corporate taxpayers, direct tax collections exceeded the previous year's collection by about Rs.26, 000 crore.

GROWTH IN DIRECT TAX COLLECTION DURING THE FINANCIAL YEAR 2009-2010

The net direct tax collections grew by 5.77 per cent during the first two months of the current fiscal. It was Rs 24,158 crore compared to Rs 22,840 crore at the same time last year. Corporate tax grew at5.56 per cent (Rs 8578 crore against Rs 8126 crore), while personal income tax (including FBT, STT and BCTT) grew at 5.92 per cent (Rs 15,559 crore as against Rs 14,690 crore0.Overall refund outgo during the period increased by 26.19 per cent (Rs 11,375 crore as against Rs 9014 crore)while refunds to non corporate taxpayers grew by 61.7 per cent (Rs 2,149 crore against Rs 1,329 crore).

INDIRECT TAX

Indirect Tax or the tax that is levied on goods or services rather than on persons or organizations are of different types in India like Excise Duty, Customs Duty, Service Tax, and Securities Transaction Tax. In India, there are a series of Tax laws and regulations in order to control the indirect taxation, which can be either law, made by the central government or even can be state specific laws. As a result these taxes are an important part of the total cost. It is thus essential to make appropriate planning for such costs.

Nearly all of the activities that are subjected to indirect taxation range from manufacturing to those required for final consumption. Activities related to trading, imports, and services are also included in this list. As a result Indirect Tax has an impact on all business lines. At present the Indirect Taxes in India are under a transformation due to the changing fiscal reforms of the Indian government. Many new acts and laws are being introduced replacing the old laws and all related issues, which have become redundant. However, it should be remembered that such new laws while on one hand would create new opportunities, but also at the same time would lead to a certain extent of uncertainty and judicial proceedings.

In general, the Indirect Tax in India is a complex system of interconnecting laws and regulations, which includes specific laws of different states. For this there are many reliable organizations in India, which employs efficient Indirect Tax professionals to help their clients.

These tax professionals with their in-depth knowledge and wide-ranging experience offers effective planning methods to their clients in order to help in their cost minimization. The Indirect Taxation regime encompasses various types of taxes like Sales Tax, Service Tax, Custom and Excise Duties, VAT and Anti-Dumping Duties, and the organizations provide services in all these related fields.

In the recent year, the Indian government has undertaken significant reform of indirect taxation system. This includes the initiation of a region-based and state-level VAT on goods. However, it should be noted that as taxes still forms a barrier to inter-state trading in order to attain a secured market for the activities related to services and goods more reform is needed.

Some of the reforms that can be introduced for a better indirect taxation system in India are:

- The serialized set of Indirect Taxes so far activated at the central and state levels should be amalgamated and treated as a single tax.
- The integrated Indirect Tax should be neutral at all levels such that chances of fraudulence would be minimized
- The Central Sales Tax, which obstructs easy trading between different states, is being under the process of termination that would help to abolish the control measures on the inter-state trade

By the year 2010 the Indian government has planned to activate a goods and services tax neutral at all levels in order to fulfill these objectives. The government can undertake either an introduction of a national VAT or a system, which would permit both a state VAT, or a central VAT. Along with this if the government also can incorporate a central VAT that can be rebated, on the trade across the boundary lines, then there would be minimum chances of fraudulence.

INDIRECT TAX SYSTEM INDIA

Indirect Taxes Pre Reforms

The indirect tax structure was extremely irrational between the reforms. The Constitution gives the permission to levy a multitude of indirect taxes. But the most important ones are customs and excise duties charged by the Central government and sales tax excepting inter state sales tax to be charged by the state government. The indirect taxes levied by the centre like customs, excise and central sales tax and the major indirect taxes levied by the states and civic bodies like passenger and goods tax, electricity duty and octroi when taken together did not present a rational system.

Indirect Taxes Post Reforms

- Even post reforms, the indirect tax regime in India is still in the early stages of growth. Both the Central and State governments charge a multitude of indirect taxes. The central government charges tax on goods at the point of import, manufacture, inter state sales (Central sales tax or CST) and on provision of services.
- The state governments charge tax on goods sold within the state (Sales tax/Value Added Tax or VAT), and on the goods that enter the state.
- In the present scenario corporate would have to analyse the tax cost involved in a transaction, have enough backup documentation to support their tax positions and keep looking for ways for tax maximization.

Indirect Taxes

As per the Ministry Of Finance there has been significant development in planning for introducing the goods and services tax (GST) from April 1 2010.As a first step the rate of central sales tax (CST) is under proposal to be decreased to 2 per cent from April1 2008.The general rate of central value added tax has been decreased from 16 per cent to 14 per cent across all goods.

TAX BURDEN

Tax Burden is also known as Tax Incidence and means the research of the effect of a specific tax on the economic welfare of the people. The Burden of Tax falls on that group of people that has to pay the tax at the end of the day.

Taxes are charged by the state and it is an enforced contribution that the individual or the legal entity has to pay. The various kinds of taxes that have to be paid are income tax, sales tax, property tax, fuel tax, and luxury tax among others. The law of the land states from whom taxes are to be collected but the person who finally pays the Tax Burden is usually decided by the market. It is the market place that decides the person who is going to pay the Burden Tax for the taxes gets embedded with the costs of production.

The Burden of Tax depends on the quantity of product supplied and the demand for it and this is called the elasticities of demand and supply. Depending on it the Tax Burden can be absorbed either by the buyer which it does in the shape of higher prices post- tax or it may be absorbed by the seller in the shape of lower prices pre-tax. In case the supply elasticity is low then more of the Tax Burden is taken by the supplier. On the other hand if demand elasticity is low then more of the Burden Tax is taken by the customer.

Tax Burden in the case the seller is a firm that is competitive flows back to the production factors and this includes the capital investors who have to bear in the shape of loss of money to shareholders, entrepreneurs who have to bear in the shape of less salary of superintendence, landowners who have to bear in the shape of low rents, and workers who have to bear in the shape of lower salary.

The results of Tax Burden are:

- The employer passes on the Burden of Tax on the employee in the shape of lower salary If the employer has to provide his employee with health care facilities according to government regulations then too the Tax Burden will fall on the employee in the shape of lower salary
- Tax Burden puts on added pressure on the person that has to pay for it for it amounts in him paying more money as tax. And so the government must keep the rate of tax at such a level that everyone is able to bear the Burden of Tax.

TAX INCIDENCE

In economics, tax incidence is the analysis of the effect of a particular tax on the distribution of economic welfare. Tax incidence is said to "fall" upon the group that, at the end of the day, bears the burden of the tax. The key concept is that the tax incidence or tax burden does not depend on where the revenue is collected, but on the price elasticity of demand and price elasticity of supply. For example, a tax on apple farmers might actually be paid by owners of agricultural land or consumers of apples.

The theory of tax incidence has a number of practical results. For example, United States Social Security payroll taxes are paid half by the employee and half by the employer. However, economists think that the worker is bearing almost the entire burden of the tax because the employer passes the tax on in the form of lower wages. The tax incidence is thus said to fall on the employee.

GRAPHICAL ANALYSIS

Inelastic Supply, Elastic Demand

Because the producer is inelastic, he will produce the same quantity no matter what the price. Because the consumer is elastic, the consumer is very sensitive to price. A small increase in price leads to a large drop in the quantity demanded. The imposition of the tax causes the market price to increase from P without tax to P with tax and the quantity demanded to fall from Q without tax to Q with tax. Because the producer is inelastic, the quantity doesn't change much. Because the consumer is elastic and the producer is inelastic, the price doesn't change much. The producer is unable to pass the tax onto the consumer and the tax incidence falls on the producer. In this example, the tax is collected from the producer and the producer bears the tax burden. This is known as back shifting.

Similarly-elastic Supply and Demand

Most markets fall between these two extremes, and ultimately the incidence of tax is shared between producers and consumers in varying proportions. In this example, the consumers pay more than the producers, but not all of the tax. The area paid by consumers is obvious as the change in equilibrium price; the remainder, being the difference between the new price and the cost of production at that quantity, is paid by the producers.

Inelastic Demand, Elastic Supply

Because the consumer is inelastic, he will demand the same quantity no matter what the price. Because the producer is elastic, the producer is very sensitive to price. A small drop in price leads to a large drop in the quantity produced.

The imposition of the tax causes the market price to increase from P without tax to P with tax and the quantity demanded to fall from Q without tax to Q with tax. Because the consumer is inelastic, the quantity doesn't change much. Because the consumer is inelastic and the producer is elastic, the price changes dramatically.

The change in price is very large. The producer is able to pass almost the entire value of the tax onto the consumer. Even though the tax is being collected from the producer the consumer is bearing the tax burden. The tax incidence is falling on the consumer, known as forward shifting.

MACROECONOMIC PERSPECTIVE

The supply and demand for a good is deeply intertwined with the markets for the factors of production and for alternate goods and services that might be produced or consumed. Although legislators might be seeking to tax the apple industry, in reality it could turn out to be truck drivers who are hardest hit, if apple companies shift towards shipping by rail in response to their new cost. Or perhaps orange manufacturers will be the group most affected, if consumers decide to forgo oranges to maintain their previous level of apples at the now higher price. Ultimately, the burden of the tax falls on people—the owners, customers, or workers.

However, the true burden of the tax cannot be properly assessed without knowing the use of the tax revenues. If the tax proceeds are employed in a manner that benefits owners more than producers and consumers then the burden of the tax will fall on producers and consumers. If the proceeds of the tax are used in a way that benefits producers and consumers, then owners suffer the tax burden.

These are class distinctions concerning the distribution of costs and are not addressed in current tax incidence models. The US military offers major benefit to owners who produce offshore.

Yet the tax levy to support this effort falls primarily on American producers and consumers. Corporations simply move out of the tax jurisdiction but still receive the property rights enforcement that is the mainstay of their income.

Other Considerations of Tax Burden

Consider a 5% import tax applied equally to all imports and a direct refund of every penny of collected revenue in the form of a direct egalitarian "Citizen's Dividend" to every person who files Income Tax returns. At the macro level the people as a whole will break even. But the people who consume foreign produced goods will bear more of the burden than the people who consume a mix of goods.

The people who consume no foreign goods will bear none of the burden and actually receive an increase in utility. On the producer side, the tax burden distribution will depend on whether a firm produces its goods within the sovereignty or outside the sovereignty.

Firms that produce goods inside the sovereignty will increase their market share and their profits when compared to firms who offshore their production. And if the current mix of firms is tilted towards offshore production then the owners of firms will be burdened more than the consumers while the workers/employees will benefit from greater employment opportunity.

Clarification

The burden from taxation is not just the quantity of tax paid, but the magnitude of the lost consumer surplus or producer surplus. The concepts are related but different. For example, imposing a $1000 per gallon of milk tax will raise no revenue, but this tax will cause substantial economic harm. When examining tax incidence, it is the lost consumer and producer surplus that is important.

OTHER PRACTICAL RESULTS

The theory of tax incidence has a large number of practical results, although economists dispute the magnitude and significance of these results:

- Because businesses are more sensitive to wages than employees, payroll taxes, employer mandates, and other taxes collected from the employer end up being borne by the employee. The tax is passed onto the employee in the form of lower wages.
- If the government requires employers to provide employees with health care, some of the burden will fall on the employee as the employer will pass it on in the form of lower wages. Some of the burden will be borne by employer since both the supply of and demand for labour are highly inelastic and have few perfect substitutes. Employers need employees largely to the extent they can substitute employees for machines, and employees need employers largely to the extent they can become self-employed entrepreneurs. An uneducated population is therefore more susceptible to bearing the burden because they are more easily replaced by machines able to do unskilled work, and because they have less knowledge of how to make money on their own.
- Taxes on easily substitutable goods, such as oranges and tangerines, may be borne mostly by the producer because the demand curve for easily substitutable goods is quite elastic.
- Similarly, taxes on a business that can easily be relocated are likely be borne almost entirely by the residents of the taxing jurisdiction and not the owners of the business.
- The burden of tariffs on imported vehicles might fall largely on the producers of the cars because the demand curve for foreign cars might be elastic if car consumers may substitute a domestic car purchase for a foreign car purchase.
- If consumers drive the same number of miles regardless of gas prices, then a tax on gasoline will be paid for by consumers and not oil companies. Who actually bears the economic burden of the tax is not affected by whether government collects the tax at the pump or directly from oil companies.

APPRAISAL

Assessing tax incidence is a major economics subfield within the field of public finance. Most public finance economists acknowledge that nominal tax incidence is not necessarily identical to actual economic burden of the tax, but disagree greatly among themselves on the extent to which market forces disturb the nominal tax incidence of various types of taxes in various circumstances. The effects of certain kinds of taxes, for example, the property tax, including their economic incidence, efficiency properties and distributional implications, have been the subject of a long and contentious debate among economists.

The empirical evidence tends support different economic models under different circumstances. For example, empirical evidence on property tax incidents tends to support one economic model, known as the "benefit tax" view in suburban areas, while tending to support another economic model, known as the "capital tax" view in urban and rural areas. There is an inherent conflict in any model between considering many factors, which complicates the model and makes it hard to apply, and using a simple model, which may limit the circumstances in which its predictions are empirically useful.

TAX RATE

In a tax system and in economics, the tax rate describes the burden ratio at which a business or person is taxed. There are several methods used to present a tax rate: statutory, average, marginal, effective, effective average, and effective marginal. These rates can also be presented using different definitions applied to a tax base: inclusive and exclusive.

STATUTORY

A statutory tax rate is the legally imposed rate. An income tax could have multiple statutory rates for different income levels, where a sales tax may have a flat statutory rate.

AVERAGE

A marginal tax rate is the tax rate that applies to the last dollar of the tax base, and is often applied to the change in one's tax obligation as income rises:

To calculate the marginal tax rate on an income tax:

- Let m be the marginal tax rate.
- Let t be the tax liability.
- Let i be the taxable income.

$$m = \frac{\Delta t}{\Delta i}$$

For an individual, it can be determined by increasing or decreasing the income earned or spent and calculating the change in taxes payable. An individual's tax bracket is the range of income for which a given marginal tax rate applies. The marginal tax rate may increase or decrease as income or consumption increases, although in most countries the tax rate is progressive. In such cases, the average tax rate will be lower than the marginal tax rate: an individual may have a marginal tax rate of 45%, but pay average tax of half this amount. In a jurisdiction with a flat tax, everyone pays the same marginal tax rate. Some fixed amount of earnings is typically exempt from the flat tax, which means that not everyone pays the same average tax rate.

In economics, marginal tax rates are important because they are one of the factors that determine incentives to increase income; at higher marginal tax rates, some argue, the individual has less incentive to earn more. This is the foundation of the Laffer curve, which shows taxable income decreasing as a function of marginal tax rate, and therefore tax revenue begins to decrease after a certain point.

Public discussion of "high taxes" may refer to overall tax rates or marginal taxes. Marginal tax rates may be published explicitly, together with the corresponding tax brackets, but they can also be derived from published tax tables showing the tax for each income. It may be calculated noting how tax changes with changes in pre-tax income, rather than with taxable income. Marginal tax rates do not fully describe the impact of taxation. A flat rate poll tax has a marginal rate of zero, while a discontinuity in tax paid can lead to positively or negatively infinite marginal rates at particular points.

EFFECTIVE

An effective tax rate refers to the actual rate, i.e., the rate existing in fact. Both average and marginal tax rates can be expressed as effective tax rates. The effective tax rate is the amount of tax an individual or firm pays when all other government tax offsets or payments are applied, divided by the tax base.

If certain groups have high degrees of tax offsets compared to other groups, their effective tax rate will be different, even where their official tax rates and marginal tax rates will be equal. The effective rate of tax can often be discussed in terms of the effective marginal rate of tax - namely the amount of effective tax paid as a percentage of the last dollar earned or spent.

Effective Average

An effective average tax rate may differ from an average tax rate because some measure of income other than taxable income is used. For example, the Joint Committee on Taxation typically calculates the effective average tax rate as the ratio of taxes paid to a constructed measure of "economic income".

Effective Marginal

An effective marginal tax rate may differ from a marginal tax rate because the taxpayer may be in an income range in which she/he is subject to a phase-out of some exclusion or deduction. Where social security and other benefits are related to income, the combined tax and benefit effect can also be taken into account giving a result sometimes described as the marginal effective tax rate or the marginal deduction rate.

If the marginal deduction rate exceeds 100%, then an increase in gross income leads to a decrease in disposable income, discouraging attempts to increase income. When this occurs for low income individuals, it is known as the "poverty trap".

INCLUSIVE/EXCLUSIVE

Tax rates can be presented differently due to differing definitions of tax base, which can make comparisons between tax systems confusing. Some tax systems include the taxes owed in the tax base, while other tax systems do not include taxes owed as part of the base. In the United States, sales taxes are quoted exclusively and income taxes are quoted inclusively.

Value added tax countries often display this tax inclusively; however, Goods and Services Tax countries do not. For direct rate comparisons between exclusive and inclusive taxes, one rate must be manipulated to look like the other. When a tax system imposes taxes primarily on income, the tax base is a household's pre-tax income.

The appropriate income tax rate is applied to the tax base to calculate taxes owed. Under this formula, taxes to be paid are included in the base on which the tax rate is imposed.

If an individual's gross income is $100 and income tax rate is 20%, taxes owed equals $20. The income tax is taken "off the top", so the individual is left with $80 in after-tax money.

Some tax laws impose taxes on a tax base equal to the pre-tax portion of a good's price. These taxes do not include actual taxes owed as part of the base. A good priced at $80 with a 25% exclusive sales tax rate yields $20 in taxes owed. Since the sales tax is added "on the top", the individual pays $20 of tax on $80 of pre-tax goods for a total cost of $100.

In either case, the tax base of $100 can be treated as two parts—$80 of after-tax spending money and $20 of taxes owed. A 25% exclusive tax rate approximates a 20% inclusive tax rate after adjustment. By including taxes owed in the tax base, an exclusive tax rate can be directly compared to an inclusive tax rate.

Inclusive income tax rate comparison to an exclusive sales tax rate:

- Let t be the income tax rate. For a 20% rate, then t = 0.20

- Let a be the rate in terms of a sales tax.
- Let p be the price of the good.

The revenue that would go to the government:

$$t \times p$$

The revenue remaining for the seller of the good:

$$P - t \times p$$

To convert the tax, divide the money going to the government by the money the company nets:

$$a = \frac{t \times p}{p - t \times p} = \frac{t}{1 - t}$$

Therefore, to adjust any inclusive tax rate to that of an exclusive tax rate, divide the given rate by 1 minus that rate.

- 15% inclusive = 18% exclusive
- 20% inclusive = 25% exclusive
- 25% inclusive = 33% exclusive
- 33% inclusive = 50% exclusive
- 50% inclusive = 100% exclusive

TAX RATES IN INDIA

Foreign Investors | Previous Tax rates before 2008 Budget

Table. Individual Income Tax Rates

Taxable Income		**Tax Rate**
Over	Not Over	
0	Rs. 160,000[1]	0
Rs. 160,001	Rs. 300,000	10%
Rs. 300,001	Rs. 500,000	20%
Rs. 500,001	above	30%[2]

1. Rs. 190,000 for women and Rs. 240,000 for seniors.
2. An education cess of 3% is applicable.
3. (a) Tax exemption on interest in Non-Resident Account and on interest payable by a scheduled bank to Non-Resident Indians.

   (b) Tax exemption on the interest payable by a scheduled bank to a non-resident or a person who is not ordinarily resident on deposits in foreign currency where the acceptance of such deposits by the bank is approved by the RBI.

Table. Domestic Corporate and LLP Income Taxes Rates

	Tax Rate	Effective Tax Rate with surcharge and ed. cess
Domestic Corporations/Private Limited Companies	30%	33.99%[1]
Domestic Corporations/Public Limited Companies	30%	33.99%[1]
Limited Liability Partnership	30%	30.9%[2]

1. A surcharge of 10% of the income tax is levied, if the taxable income exceeds Rs. 1 million. Educational cess is also added.
2. An Educational Cess is added to the basic tax rates. Surcharge is not applicable to LLP. Unlike LLP's in the USA where they are pass-through entities for tax purposes, in case of LLP's in India, they are partially pass-through entities for tax paurposes. In India tax an LLP is required to pay income tax on 40% of its income; since an LLP is allowed to pay the balance of 60% as renumerations to it partners. Partners of an LLP are required to pay tax on the amount paid to them. Besides, LLP's are not required to pay dividend distribution tax or Minimum Alternate Tax (MAT).
3. All companies incorporated in India are deemed as domestic Indian companies for tax purposes, even if owned by foreign companies. Contact us for Incorporating in India

Table. Foreign Corporate Income Tax Rates

	Withholding Tax Rate for non-treaty froeign companies	Withholding Tax Rates for the USA companies Doing Business in India under the India USA Tax Treaty
Dividends	20%	15%[1]
Interest Income	20%	15%[1]
Royalties	30%	20%[2]
Technical Services	30%	20%[2]
Other income	55%	55%

1. Inter-corporate rates where there is minimum holding. There tax rates are applicable under the India USA Tax Treaty. For other countries the tax rates are different under the tax treaties between India and other countries, including Australia, Austria, Bangladesh, Belgium, Brazil, Belarus, Bulgaria, Canada, China, Cyprus, Czechoslovakia, Denmark, Finland, France, Germany, Greece, Hungary, Indonesia, Israel, Italy, Japan, Jordan, Kazakhstan, Kenya, Libya, Malta, Malaysia, Mauritius, Mongolia, Namibia, Nepal, Netherlands, New Zealand, Norway, Oman, Philippines, Poland, Qatar,

Romania, Singapore, South Africa, South Korea, Spain, Sri Lanka, Sweden, Switzerland, Syria, Tanzania, Thailand, Trinidad and Tobago, Turkmenistan, Turkey, U.A.E., U.A.R., U.K., U.S.A., Russian Federation, Uzbekistan, Vietnam and Zambia

2. 10% or 15% in some cases.
3. Withholding tax is charged on estimated income, as approved by the tax authorities.
4. There are other favourable tax rates under various tax treaties between India and other countries..

Wealth Tax

Net Taxable Wealth	Tax Rate	
Over	Not Over	
0	Rs.1,500,000	0
Rs.1,500,000	above	1%

Wealth tax is levied on non-productive assets whose value exceeds Rs.1.5 million. Productive assets like shares, debentures, bank deposits and investments in mutual funds are exempt from wealth tax. The non-productive assets include residential houses, jewelry, bullion, motor cars, aircraft, urban land, etc. Foreign nationals are exempt from wealth tax on non-Indian assets. In arriving at the net taxable wealth, any debt incurred in acquiring specified assets is deductible.

Gift Tax

Net Taxable Gift	Tax Rate	
Over	Not Over	
0	Rs.30,000	0
Rs.30,000	above	30%

Gifts to dependent relatives at the time of marriage are exempt upto Rs.100,000. Foreign nationals are exempt from gift tax on non-Indian assets.

Tax on cash withdrawal from banks: Withdrawn in the 2008 Budget. [0.1% tax used to be levied on cash withdrawals of over Rs 25,000 from banks on a day.]

ECONOMICS OF TAXATION

Taxation is any compulsory levy from individuals, households and firms to central or local government. The British economy imposes a wide range of taxes on people. The system is always evolving as the government seeks to develop and maintain a tax system that meets objectives and targets. In the financial year 2000-01, the British government received £377 billion in tax revenue.

The breakdown of this revenue is shown in the chart below:

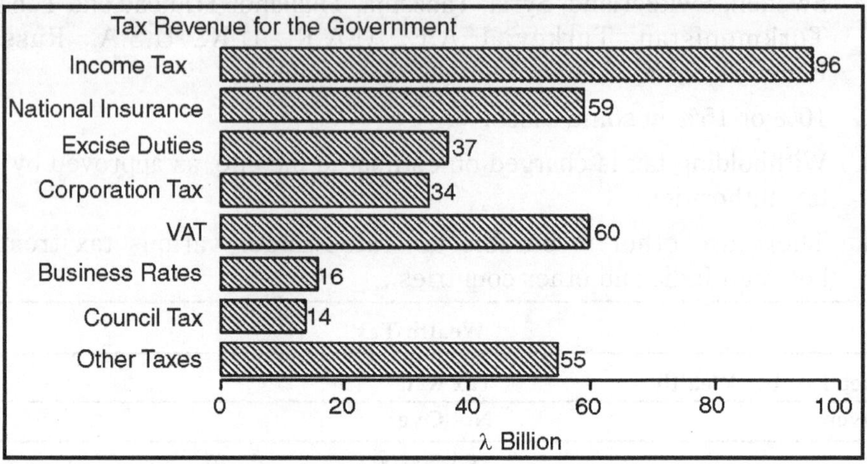

WHY DO WE NEED TO PAY TAXES

Taxation is levied for a number of reasons. To raise revenue to finance spending on goods and service by central and local government The government when managing the level of AD output and prices uses taxation. When demand is perceived as being too strong the government can increase direct taxation, to reduce the level of real disposable income and household spending. A progressive system of taxation can be utilised to achieve great equality in income and wealth between individuals and households Taxes can correct for externalities and other forms of market failure Import taxes may control imports and therefore help the country's international balance of payments and protect industries from overseas competition.

OBJECTIVES FOR THE TAX SYSTEM

- The Labour Government has identified six main objectives for its tax system - these are summarised below
- To keep the overall tax burden as low as possible
- To reduce tax rates on income to sharpen incentives to work and create wealth in the economy
- To maintain a broad tax base - having a range of taxes helps to keep each separate tax rate low
- To shift the balance of taxation away from taxes on income towards taxes on spending
- To ensure taxes are applied equally and fairly to everyone
- To use taxes to make markets work better

PROGRESSIVE REGRESSIVE AND PROPORTIONAL TAXES

Generally, indirect taxes are seen as regressive; the proportion of income paid in tax decreases as income rises. Direct taxes are progressive because the proportion of income paid in tax increases as income rises. With a progressive tax, the marginal rate of tax exceeds the average rate of tax.

As a result, progressive taxes act to reduce inequalities in the distribution of income. The post-tax distribution of income will be less dispersed than the pre-tax distribution.

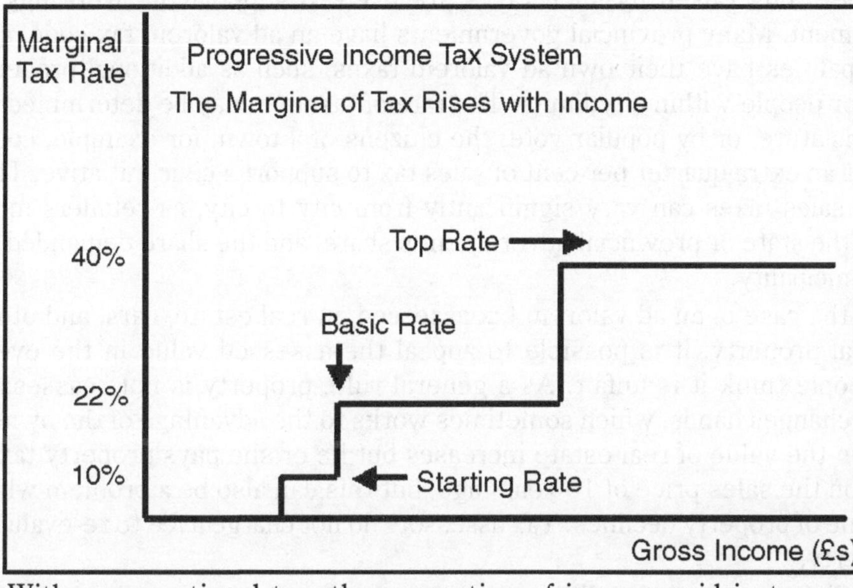

With a proportional tax, the proportion of income paid in tax remains constant as income changes. In this situation, the marginal rate of tax will be equal to the average rate of tax. Any tax that does not vary with income is called a lump sum tax.

TYPES OF TAXES

The Organisation for Economic Co-operation and Development (OECD) publishes perhaps the most comprehensive analysis of worldwide tax systems. In order to do this it has created a comprehensive categorisation of all taxes in all regimes which it covers:

AD VALOREM

An ad valorem tax is a type of tax which is levied on property according to its value. Under an ad valorem tax, people who own certain types of property are required to pay periodic taxes which represent a percentage of the assessed value of the property. One of the most widespread forms of this tax is the property tax which people are required to pay on real estate. The Latin phrase "ad valorem" means "according to value."

Depending on how regional laws concerning taxation are laid out, an ad valorem tax may be assessed when property is purchased, in the form of a sales tax or value added tax (VAT), or it may be levied later on a set basis, such as once a year or once a quarter. Ad valorem taxes can also be assessed on estates, imports, and in other circumstances where property of value changes hands.

The funds raised by such taxes are used to support the workings of government. Many provincial governments have an ad valorem tax code, and municipalities have their own ad valorem taxes, such as additional property taxes for people within city limits. The rate of taxation may be determined by the legislature, or by popular vote; the citizens of a town, for example, could vote for an extra quarter per cent of sales tax to support a civic initiative. This is why sales taxes can vary significantly from city to city, as retailers must collect the state or provincial government's share, and the share demanded by the municipality.

In the case of an ad valorem tax assessed on real estate, cars, and other personal property, it is possible to appeal the assessed value in the event that people think it is unfair. As a general rule, property is not reassessed until it changes hands, which sometimes works to the advantage of the owner, as when the value of real estate increases but he or she pays property taxes based on the sales price of 10 years ago, but this can also be a problem when the value of property declines. Tax assessors do not charge a fee to re-evaluate a property.

Legislatures occasionally battle over ad valorem taxation. Some people feel that such taxation is a very efficient and effective way to quickly raise money to fund various government enterprises, while others argue that these types of taxes penalize people for buying or maintaining property of value. Conservatives tend to favour a reduction in ad valorem taxes, while liberals often push for a maintenance or increase, under the argument that these funds are needed to support the smooth operation of the government.

BANK TAX

A bank tax is a proposed tax on banks. One of the earliest modern uses of the term "bank tax" occurred in the context of the Financial crisis of 2007–2010. On April 16, 2010, the International Monetary Fund (IMF) proposed the idea of a "financial stability contribution" (FSC), which many media have referred to as a "bank tax." It was proposed as one of three possible options to deal with the crisis.

These options were presented in response to an earlier request of the G-20 leaders, at the September 2009 Pittsburgh summit, for a investigative report on all possible options to deal with the crisis. Both before and after that IMF report, there was considerable debate amongst national leaders as to whether such a "bank tax" should be "global," "semi-global," or whether it should be applied only in certain nations.

CAPITAL GAIN TAX

As per Indian Income Tax laws, a capital gain tax is a voluntary tax payable on the sale of assets, investments, capital accumulation, and productivity.

A Capital Gain can be defined as an any income generated by selling a capital investment.

A capital investment can be anything from business stocks, paintings, and houses to family businesses and farmhouses. The 'gain' here, refers essentially to the difference between the price originally paid for the investment and money received upon selling it.

A capital gain can be categorized under the following heads, depending on how long the investment has been under your possession:

- *The Registrars of Companies in different states chiefly manage*:
  - *Short-term*: If you sell an investment within three years from the date of its purchase, it will be defined as a short-term capital gain. But if the investment is in the form of mutual funds/company shares, the allowed time duration is one year.
  - *Long-term*: If you sell an investment after three years from the date of its purchase, it will be defined as a long-term capital gain. However, selling mutual funds and company shares after one year will also constitute a long-term capital gain.
- In case of a short-term capital gain related to sale of property, the gained amount needs to be added to your total annual income. Then you'll be need to pay capital gain tax, depending on the total taxable amount.
- In case of a long-term capital gain related to sale of property, factors such as inflation are usually taken into consideration. The seller of the property needs to pay a tax not just on the real capital gain, but also on the projected gain as a result of inflation.
- You need to pay a capital gain tax on all your capital gains, though the government will allow you only a partial tax deduction in case you suffer a loss as a result of selling your investment.

Capital Gain Tax Rates

For short-term capital gains, you will be taxed depending on the tax slab relevant to you after you have added the capital gain to your annual income.

But if the transaction was levied with Securities Transaction Tax (STT), your gain will be taxed 10%.

For long term capital gains, you will be taxed 20%. But if the transaction was levied with STT, you need not pay any tax on your gain. In case of long term capital gains, you can either calculate your capital gain using an indexed acquisition cost, or you can choose not to opt for indexing.

CONSUMPTION TAX

Consumption Tax is applicable on the consumption of any type of good or service. This particular tax is based on consumption and not on income or labour. The Consumption Tax can be regarded as a sales tax, as this tax is also regressive in nature like the other pure sales taxes.

However, there are some remedies by which the Consumption Tax can be made progressive in nature. Some of the methods for reducing the regressive trait of this tax include use of exemptions, deductions, graduated rates, or rebates. This will in other terms allow accumulation of savings exempting the tax burdens.

History of the Consumption Tax

The Consumption Tax is more of a western concept than gaining grounds in the eastern countries. In the United States for consumption of goods and services, this tax was levied. The Consumption Tax was very popular out in the American countries as they are difficult to bring up at the levels of confiscation compared to that of the income tax.

Features of the Consumption Tax

The consumption Tax are a lot similar to those of the present income tax systems.

Some of the main characteristics of the tax on consumption are:

- All those who are paying this tax would be subjected to certain exemptions and a standard deduction such that those categorized, as the poor do not have to pay any tax
- All those who are liable to pay the Consumption Tax, will not enjoy any other deductions as this would not be allowed since their all savings are already subjected to deduction
- In order to estimate the total liability of the Consumption Tax there might be withholding of the system, however this poses problems for the taxpayers. This creates trouble, as they had to pay no tax throughout the year to receive a huge tax receipt at the termination of the assessed year

- All those paying the Consumption Tax enjoys the exemption of being taxed on all incomes placed in some investment projects, this is because this tax is only concerned with consumption
- In order to transform the regressive nature of the Consumption Tax and to make it a progressive tax, all the taxpayers should expend more on consumption such that they are liable to pay more taxes on consumption.

Generally, Consumption Taxes are more favoured than the income taxes, as these taxes do not depend on the investment rates. For the taxpayer, in order to buy one investment when he sells another investment, there is no extra tax imposed on the profit. This implies that the Consumption Tax in general favours investment policies and in turn this would increase the capital stock, productivity, and the size of the economy as a whole.

CORPORATE TAX

A company has been defined as a juristic person having an independent and separate legal entity from its shareholders. Income of the company is computed and assessed separately in the hands of the company. However the income of the company which is distributed to its shareholders as dividend is assessed in their individual hands. Such distribution of income is not treated as expenditure in the hands of company, the income so distributed is an appropriation of the profits of the company.

TAXABLE CORPORATE INCOME

The tax levied on a company's income is based on its legal residence. Companies of Indian origin are levied tax in India, while International companies are levied tax on earnings from their Indian operations. For International companies' royalty, interest, gains from sale of capital assets within India, dividends from Indian companies and fees for technical services are all treated as income arising in India.

TAX ON DISTRIBUTED PROFITS

Till 1997, a company was not required to pay any income tax on the amount of dividends declared, distributed or paid by such company. But such dividend was included in the income of the shareholders under the head "income from other sources". The finance act 1997 brought about changes to the rule.

- Tax On Distributed Profits Of The Domestic Company: The domestic company would be required to pay additional income tax on any amount declared, distributed or paid by such company by way of dividend on or after 1-06-1997,be it from current or accumulated profits. Such additional income tax shall be payable @ 10 per cent of the amount so distributed. Even if no income tax is payable by the company on it total income, the additional tax would have to be paid.

- Exemption Of Dividend In The Hands Of Shareholders: Such additional tax will have to be paid by the principal officer of the domestic company within 14 days from the date of:
  - Declaration of any dividend.
  - Distribution of any dividend.
  - Payment of any dividend, whichever is earlier.

CORPORATE TAX IN INDIA

Corporate tax rate in India is at par with the tax rates of other nations of the world. The corporate tax rate in India is based on the origin of the company.

If the company is domicile to India, then the tax rate is flat at 30%. But for a foreign company, then the tax rate depends on several other factors and considerations.

For companies that are domicile to India, tax is charged on the global income whereas for the foreign companies present in India, tax is charged on their income within Indian Territory. Incomes that are taxable for foreign companies include income from the capital assets in India, interest gained, income from sale of equity shares of the company, royalties, dividends earned, etc.

Domestic Corporate Income Taxes Rates

Incase of Domestic Corporations the effective tax rate as well the tax rate with surcharge as is 30%. It should be noted that if the taxable income is greater than Rs. 1 million then a surcharge of 10% of the tax on income is also levied. It is important to note the fact that all the companies formed in India are considered as Indian domestic companies, even for ancillary units with mother companies in foreign countries

Foreign Companies income tax rates:

- *For dividends*: 20% for non-treaty foreign companies and 15% incase of companies under the treaty based in the United States
- *For interest gains*: 20% for non-treaty foreign companies and 15% for companies under the treaty based in the United States
- *For royalties*: 30% for non-treaty foreign companies and 20% for companies under the treaty based in the United States
- For the technology based services in case of non-treaty foreign companies and 20% for companies under the treaty based in the United States

- *For all other kinds of income and gains*: 55% in case of non-treaty foreign companies and 55% for the companies under the treaty based in the United States
- Attention should be given on levying inter corporate rates in case holding is minimum
- Attention should be given on the fact that sanctions of the tax authorities on tax withholding
- Attention should be given on several of the tax treaties that India signed with other countries and also on the various encouraging tax rates

Some of the tax rebates under corporate tax rate in India:

- Gains pertaining to long term capital are subject to low tax incidence
- Venture capital funds and venture capital companies have special tax provisions
- Specula tax provisions are applicable for non resident Indians involved in activities in India
- Under the Finance Bill 1996, the minimum alternative tax (MAT) is levied on the corporate sector

ENVIRONMENTAL TAX

This includes natural resources consumption tax, Greenhouse gas tax, "sulfuric tax", and others. The stated purpose is to reduce the environmental impact by repricing.

EXCISES

Unlike an ad valorem, an excise is not a function of the value of the product being taxed. Excise taxes are based on the quantity, not the value, of product purchased. For example, in the United States, the Federal government imposes an excise tax of 18.4 cents per U.S. gallon of gasoline, while state governments levy an additional 8 to 28 cents per U.S. gallon. Excises on particular commodities are frequently hypothecated. For example, a fuel excise is often used to pay for public transportation, especially roads and bridges and for the protection of the environment.

A special form of hypothecation arises where an excise is used to compensate a party to a transaction for alleged uncontrollable abuse; for example, a blank media tax is a tax on recordable media such as CD-Rs, whose proceeds are typically allocated to copyright holders. Critics charge that such taxes blindly tax those who make legitimate and illegitimate usages of the products; for instance, a person or corporation using CD-R's for data archival should not have to subsidize the producers of popular music.

Excises are also used to modify consumption patterns. For example, a high excise is used to discourage alcohol consumption, relative to other goods. This may be combined with hypothecation if the proceeds are then used to pay for the costs of treating illness caused by alcohol abuse.

Similar taxes may exist on tobacco, pornography, etc., and they may be collectively referred to as "sin taxes". A carbon tax is a tax on the consumption of carbon-based non-renewable fuels, such as petrol, diesel-fuel, jet fuels, and natural gas. The object is to reduce the release of carbon into the atmosphere. In the United Kingdom, vehicle excise duty is an annual tax on vehicle ownership.

EXPATRIATION TAX

An Expatriation Tax is a tax on some who renounce their citizenship of some governments. The most significant Expatriation Tax is one found in the USA.

The American Jobs Creation Act of 2004, passed by the Republican-controlled government, amended section 877 of the Internal Revenue Code of the USA. Under the new law, any individual who has a net worth of $2 million or an average income-tax liability of $127,000 who renounces his or her citizenship and leaves the country is automatically assumed to have done so for tax avoidance reasons and is victim to severe tax laws.

FINANCIAL ACTIVITIES TAX

As a regulatory response and proposal to the financial crisis of 2007-2010, on April 16, 2010, the IMF proposed three types of global taxes on banks: First, the "Financial Stability Contribution" is a straight tax on a bank's gross profits—before deducting compensation. It would initially be at a flat rate, this would eventually be refined so that riskier businesses paid more. Second, the "Financial Activities Tax" aims directly at excess bank profit and pay. The third, which was not endorsed by the IMF, but not ruled out as administratively difficult, is a financial transaction tax.

FINANCIAL TRANSACTION TAX

A financial transaction tax is a tax placed on a specific type of financial transaction for a specific purpose. This term has been most commonly associated with the financial sector, as opposed to consumption taxes paid by consumers.

There are several types of financial transaction taxes. Each has its own purpose. Some have already been implemented, and some remain unimplemented concepts. Concepts are found in various organizations and regions around the world. Some are domestic and meant to be used within one nation; whereas some are multinational.

INCOME TAX

An income tax is a tax levied on the financial income of persons, corporations, or other legal entities. Various income tax systems exist, with varying degrees of tax incidence. Income taxation can be progressive, proportional, or regressive. When the tax is levied on the income of companies, it is often called a corporate tax, corporate income tax, or corporation tax. Individual income taxes often tax the total income of the individual, while corporate income taxes often tax net income.

The "tax net" refers to the types of payment that are taxed, which included personal earnings, capital gains, and business income. The rates for different types of income may vary and some may not be taxed at all.

Capital gains may be taxed when realised or when incurred. Business income may only be taxed if it is significant or based on the manner in which it is paid. Some types of income, such as interest on bank savings, may be considered as personal earnings or as a realised property gain. In some tax systems, personal earnings may be strictly defined where labour, skill, or investment is required; in others, they may be defined broadly to include windfalls.

Personal income tax is often collected on a pay-as-you-earn basis, with small corrections made soon after the end of the tax year. These corrections take one of two forms: payments to the government, for taxpayers who have not paid enough during the tax year; and tax refunds from the government for those who have overpaid. Income tax systems will often have deductions available that lessen the total tax liability by reducing total taxable income. They may allow losses from one type of income to be counted against another. For example, a loss on the stock market may be deducted against taxes paid on wages. Other tax systems may isolate the loss, such that business losses can only be deducted against business tax by carrying forward the loss to later tax years.

INFLATION TAX

An inflation tax is the economic disadvantage suffered by holders of cash and cash equivalents in one denomination of currency due to the effects of Expansionary monetary policy, which acts as a hidden tax that subtracts value from those assets. Many economists hold that the inflation tax affects the lower and middle classes more than the rich, as they hold a larger fraction of their income in cash, they are much less likely to receive the newly created monies before the market has adjusted with inflated prices, and more often have fixed incomes, wages or pensions. Some argue that inflation is a regressive consumption tax.

There are systemic effects of an expansionary monetary policy, which are also definitively taxing, imposing a financial charge on some as a result of the policy. Because the effects of monetary expansion or counterfeiting are never uniform over an entire economy, the policy influences capital transfers in the market, creating economic bubbles where the new monies are first introduced. Economic bubbles increase market instability, and therefore increase investment risk, creating the conditions common to a recession. This particular tax can be understood to be levied on future generations that would have benefited from economic growth, and it has a 100% transfer cost. One example of a strong supporter of this tax was the former Federal Reserve chair Beardsley Ruml.

INHERITANCE TAX

Inheritance tax, estate tax, and death tax or duty are the names given to various taxes which arise on the death of an individual. In United States tax law, there is a distinction between an estate tax and an inheritance tax: the former taxes the personal representatives of the deceased, while the latter taxes the beneficiaries of the estate. However, this distinction does not apply in other jurisdictions; for example, if using this terminology UK inheritance tax would be an estate tax.

POLL TAX

A poll tax, also called a per capita tax, or capitation tax, is a tax that levies a set amount per individual. It is an example of the concept of fixed tax. One of the earliest taxes mentioned in the Bible of a half-shekel per annum from each adult Jew was a form of poll tax. Poll taxes are administratively cheap because they are easy to compute and collect and difficult to cheat. Economists have considered poll taxes economically efficient because people are presumed to be in fixed supply.

However, poll taxes are very unpopular because poorer people pay a higher proportion of their income than richer people. In addition, the supply of people is in fact not fixed over time: on average, couples will choose to have fewer children if a poll tax is imposed. The introduction of a poll tax in medieval England was the primary cause of the 1381 Peasants' Revolt. Scotland was the first to be used to test the new poll tax in 1989 with England and Wales in 1990. The change from a progressive local taxation based on property values to a single-rate form of taxation regardless of ability to pay, led to widespread refusal to pay and to incidents of civil unrest, known colloquially as the 'Poll Tax riots'.

PROPERTY TAX

A property tax is a tax put on property by reason of its ownership. Property tax can be defined as "generally, tax imposed by municipalities upon owners of property within their jurisdiction based on the value of such property." There are three species of property: land, improvements to land and personal property. Real estate or realty is the combination of land and improvements to land.

Property taxes are usually charged on a recurrent basis. A common type of property tax is an annual charge on the ownership of real estate, where the tax base is the estimated value of the property. For a period of over 150 years from 1695 a window tax was levied in England, with the result that one can still see listed buildings with windows bricked up in order to save their owners money. A similar tax on hearths existed in France and elsewhere, with similar results. The two most common type of event driven property taxes are stamp duty, charged upon change of ownership, and inheritance tax, which is imposed in many countries on the estates of the deceased.

In contrast with a tax on real estate, a land value tax is levied only on the unimproved value of the land. Proponents of land value tax argue that it is economically justified, as it will not deter production, distort market mechanisms or otherwise create deadweight losses the way other taxes do. When real estate is held by a higher government unit or some other entity not subject to taxation by the local government, the taxing authority may receive a payment in lieu of taxes to compensate it for some or all of the foregone tax revenue.

In many jurisdictions, there is a general tax levied periodically on residents who own personal property within the jurisdiction. Vehicle and boat registration fees are subsets of this kind of tax. The tax is often designed with blanket coverage and large exceptions for things like food and clothing. Household goods are often exempt when kept or used within the household. Any otherwise non-exempt object can lose its exemption if regularly kept outside the household. Thus, tax collectors often monitor newspaper articles for stories about wealthy people who have lent art to museums for public display, because the artworks have then become subject to personal property tax. If an artwork had to be sent to another state for some touch-ups, it may have become subject to personal property tax in that state as well.

SOCIAL SECURITY TAX

Some countries with social security systems, which provide income to retired workers, fund those systems with specific dedicated taxes. These often differ from comprehensive income taxes in that they are levied only on specific sources of income, generally wages and salary. A further difference is that the total amount of the taxes paid by or on behalf of a worker is typically considered in the calculation of the retirement benefits to which that worker is entitled. Examples of retirement taxes include the FICA tax, a payroll tax that is collected from employers and employees in the United States to fund the country's Social Security system; and the National Insurance Contributions collected from employers and employees in the United Kingdom to fund the country's national insurance system.

These taxes are sometimes regressive in their immediate effect. For example, in the United States, each worker, whatever his or her income, pays at the same rate up to a specified cap, but income over the cap is not taxed. A further regressive feature is that such taxes often exclude investment earnings and other forms of income that are more likely to be received by the wealthy. The regressive effect is somewhat offset, however, by the eventual benefit payments, which typically replace a higher percentage of a lower-paid worker's pre-retirement income.

SALES TAX

Sales taxes are levied when a commodity is sold to its final consumer. Retail organizations contend that such taxes discourage retail sales. The question of whether they are generally progressive or regressive is a subject of much current debate. People with higher incomes spend a lower proportion of them, so a flat-rate sales tax will tend to be regressive. It is therefore common to exempt food, utilities and other necessities from sales taxes, since poor people spend a higher proportion of their incomes on these commodities, so such exemptions would make the tax more progressive. This is the classic "You pay for what you spend" tax, as only those who spend money on non-exempt items pay the tax.

A small number of U.S. states rely entirely on sales taxes for state revenue, as those states do not levy a state income tax. Such states tend to have a moderate to large amount of tourism or inter-state travel that occurs within their borders, allowing the state to benefit from taxes from people the state would otherwise not tax. In this way, the state is able to reduce the tax burden on its citizens.

The U.S. states that do not levy a state income tax are Alaska, Tennessee, Florida, Nevada, South Dakota, Texas, Washington state, and Wyoming. Additionally, New Hampshire and Tennessee levy state income taxes only on dividends and interest income. Only Alaska and New Hampshire do not levy a state sales tax. Additional information can be obtained at the Federation of Tax Administrators website.

In the United States, there is a growing movement for the replacement of all federal payroll and income taxes with a national retail sales tax and monthly tax rebate to households of citizens and legal resident aliens. The tax proposal is named FairTax. In Canada, the federal sales tax is called the Goods and Services tax and now stands at 5%.

The provinces of British Columbia, Saskatchewan, Manitoba, Ontario and Prince Edward Island also have a provincial sales tax [PST]. The provinces of Nova Scotia, New Brunswick, and Newfoundland and Labrador have harmonized their provincial sales taxes with the GST - Harmonized Sales Tax [HST], and thus is a full VAT. The province of Quebec collects the Quebec Sales Tax [QST] which is based on the GST with certain differences. Most businesses can claim back the GST, HST and QST they pay, and so effectively it is the final consumer who pays the tax.

TARIFFS

An import or export tariff is a charge for the movement of goods through a political border. Tariffs discourage trade, and they may be used by governments to protect domestic industries. A proportion of tariff revenues is often hypothecated to pay government to maintain a navy or border police. The classic ways of cheating a tariff are smuggling or declaring a false value of goods. Tax, tariff and trade rules in modern times are usually set together because of their common impact on industrial policy, investment policy, and agricultural policy. A trade bloc is a group of allied countries agreeing to minimize or eliminate tariffs against trade with each other, and possibly to impose protective tariffs on imports from outside the bloc. A customs union has a common external tariff, and, according to an agreed formula, the participating countries share the revenues from tariffs on goods entering the customs union.

TOLL

A toll is a taxor fee charged to travel via a road, bridge, tunnel, canal, waterway or other transportation facilities. Historically tolls have been used to pay for public bridge, road and tunnel projects. They have also been used in privately constructed transport links. The toll is likely to be a fixed charge, possibly graduated for vehicle type, or for distance on long routes. Shunpiking is the practice of finding another route to avoid payment of tolls. In some situations where tolls were increased or felt to be unreasonably high, informal shunpiking by individuals escalated into a form of boycott by regular users, with the goal of applying the financial stress of lost toll revenue to the authority determining the levy.

TRANSFER TAX

Historically, in many countries, a contract needed to have a stamp affixed to make it valid. The charge for the stamp was either a fixed amount or a percentage of the value of the transaction. In most countries the stamp has been abolished but stamp duty remains. Stamp duty is levied in the UK on the purchase of shares and securities, the issue of bearer instruments, and certain partnership transactions. Its modern derivatives, stamp duty reserve tax and stamp duty land tax, are respectively charged on transactions involving securities and land. Stamp duty has the effect of discouraging speculative purchases of assets by decreasing liquidity. In the United States transfer tax is often charged by the state or local government and can be tied to the recording of the deed or other transfer documents.

VALUE ADDED TAX/GOODS AND SERVICES TAX

A value added tax, also known as 'Goods and Services Tax', Single Business Tax, or Turnover Tax in some countries, applies the equivalent of a sales tax to every operation that creates value. To give an example, sheet steel is imported by a machine manufacturer. That manufacturer will pay the VAT on the purchase price, remitting that amount to the government. The manufacturer will then transform the steel into a machine, selling the machine for a higher price to a wholesale distributor.

The manufacturer will collect the VAT on the higher price, but will remit to the government only the excess related to the "value added". The wholesale distributor will then continue the process, charging the retail distributor the VAT on the entire price to the retailer, but remitting only the amount related to the distribution mark-up to the government. The last VAT amount is paid by the eventual retail customer who cannot recover any of the previously paid VAT. For a VAT and sales tax of identical rates, the total tax paid is the same, but it is paid at differing points in the process.

VAT is usually administrated by requiring the company to complete a VAT return, giving details of VAT it has been charged and VAT it has charged to others. The difference between output tax and input tax is payable to the Local Tax Authority. If input tax is greater than output tax the company can claim back money from the Local Tax Authority.

WEALTH TAX

Some countries' governments will require declaration of the tax payers' balance sheet, and from that exact a tax on net worth, as a percentage of the net worth, or a percentage of the net worth exceeding a certain level. The tax may be levied on "natural" or legal "persons".

ETHICS OF TAXATION

ETHICAL BASIS OF TAXATION

According to most political philosophies, taxes are justified as they fund activities that are necessary and beneficial to society. Additionally, progressive taxation can be used to reduce economic inequality in a society. According to this view, taxation in modern nation-states benefit the majority of the population and social development. A common presentation of this view, paraphrasing various statements by Oliver Wendell Holmes, Jr. is "Taxes are the price of civilization".

It can also be argued that in a democracy, because the government is the party performing the act of imposing taxes, society as a whole decides how the tax system should be organized. The American Revolution's "No taxation without representation" slogan implied this view. For traditional conservatives, the payment of taxation is justified as part of the general obligations of citizens to obey the law and support established institutions.

The conservative position is encapsulated in perhaps the most famous adage of public finance, "An old tax is a good tax". Conservatives advocate the "fundamental conservative premise that no one should be excused from paying for government, lest they come to believe that government is costless to them with the certain consequence that they will demand more government 'services'." Social democrats generally favour higher levels of taxation to fund public provision of a wide range of services such as universal health care and education, as well as the provision of a range of welfare benefits.

As argued by Tony Crosland and others, the capacity to tax income from capital is a central element of the social democratic case for a mixed economy as against Marxist arguments for comprehensive public ownership of capital. Many libertarians recommend a minimal level of taxation in order to maximize the protection of liberty.

Compulsory taxation of individuals, such as income tax, is often justified on grounds including territorial sovereignty, and the social contract. Defenders of business taxation argue that it is an efficient method of taxing income that ultimately flows to individuals, or that separate taxation of business is justified on the grounds that commercial activity necessarily involves use of publicly established and maintained economic infrastructure, and that businesses are in effect charged for this use. Georgist economists argue that all of the economic rent collected from natural resources is unearned income, and belongs to the community rather than any individual. They advocate a high tax on land and other natural resources to return this unearned income to the state, but no other taxes.

OPTIMAL TAXATION THEORY

Most governments need revenue which exceeds that which can be provided by non-distortionary taxes or through taxes which give a double dividend. Optimal taxation theory is the branch of economics that considers how taxes can be structured to give the least deadweight costs, or to give the best outcomes in terms of social welfare.

Ramsey problem deals with minimizing deadweight costs. Because deadweight costs are related to the elasticity of supply and demand for a good, it follows that putting the highest tax rates on the goods for which there is most inelastic supply and demand will result in the least overall deadweight costs.

Some economists sought to integrate optimal tax theory with the social welfare function, which is the economic expression of the idea that equality is valuable to a greater or lesser extent. If individuals experience diminishing returns from income, then the optimum distribution of income for society involves a progressive income tax. Mirrlees optimal income tax is a detailed theoretical model of the optimum progressive income tax along these lines.

Over the last years the validity of the theory of optimal taxation was discussed by many political economists. Canegrati demonstrated that if we move from the assumption that governments do not maximise the welfare of society but the probability of winning elections, the tax rates in equilibrium are lower for the most powerful groups of society, instead of being the lowest for the poorest as in the optimal theory of direct taxation developed by Atkinson and Joseph Stiglitz.

VIEWS OPPOSED TO TAXATION

Because payment of tax is compulsory and enforced by the legal system, some political philosophies view taxation as theft, or tyranny, accusing the government of levying taxes via force and coercive means. Voluntaryists, Individualist anarchists, objectivists, anarcho-capitalists, and libertarians see taxation as government aggression.

The view that democracy legitimizes taxation is rejected by those who argue that all forms of government, including laws chosen by democratic means, are fundamentally oppressive.

According to Ludwig von Mises, "society as a whole" should not make such decisions, due to methodological individualism. Libertarian opponents of taxation claim that governmental protection, such as police and defence forces might be replaced by market alternatives such as private defence agencies, arbitration agencies or voluntary contributions. Walter E. Williams, professor of economics at George Mason University, stated "Government income redistribution programmes produce the same result as theft. In fact, that's what a thief does; he redistributes income. The difference between government and thievery is mostly a matter of legality."

Discourse surrounding taxation generally places an emphasis on the intended benefits; healthcare, schools and so on, but rarely points to the harm caused by forced removal of possessions.

Taxation has also been opposed by communists and socialists. Karl Marx assumed that taxation would be unnecessary after the advent of communism and looked forward to the "withering away of the state". In socialist economies such as that of China, taxation played a minor role, since most government income was derived from the ownership of enterprises, and it was argued by some that taxation was not necessary. While the morality of taxation is sometimes questioned, most arguments about taxation revolve around the degree and method of taxation and associated government spending, not taxation itself.

EFFECTS OF INCOME TAXATION ON DIVISION OF LABOUR

If a tax is paid on outsourced services that is not also charged on services performed for oneself, then it may be cheaper to perform the services oneself than to pay someone else — even considering losses in economic efficiency.

For example, suppose jobs A and B are both valued at $1 on the market. And suppose that because of your unique abilities, you can do job A twice over in the same effort as it would take you to do job B. But job B is the one that you need done right now. Under perfect division of labour, you would do job A and somebody else would do job B. Your unique abilities would always be rewarded.

Income taxation has the worst effect on division of labour in the form of barter. Suppose that the person doing job B is actually interested in having job A done for him. Now suppose you could amazingly do job A four times over, selling half your work on the market for cash just to pay your tax bill. The other half of the work you do for somebody who does job B twice over but he has to sell off half to pay his tax bill. You're left with one unit of job B, but only if you were 400% as productive doing job A! In this case of 50% tax on barter income, anything less than 400% productivity will cause the division of labour to fail.

In summary, depending on the situation a 50% tax rate can cause the division of labour to fail even where productivity gains of up to 300% would have resulted. Even a mere 30% tax rate can negate the advantage of a 100% productivity gain.

NON-TAX REVENUE

Non-tax revenue or non-tax receipts are government revenue not generated from taxes.

Examples include:

- Aid from another level of government —for example, in the United States, federal grants may be considered non-tax revenue to the receiving states
- Aid from abroad
- Tribute or indemnities paid by a weaker state to a stronger one, often as a condition of peace after suffering military defeat. The war reparations paid by the defeated Central Powers after the First World War offer a well-known example.
- Revenue from state-owned enterprises
- Revenue from investment funds, sovereign wealth funds, or endowments

- Revenues from sales of state assets
- Rents, concessions, and royalties collected by the state when it contracts out the right to profit from some good or service to a private corporation. An example are contracts for resource extraction collected privately under license from state-owned lands
- Fines collected and assets forfeitured as a penalty. Examples include parking fines, court costs levied on criminal offenders
- Fees for the granting or issuance of permits or licenses. Examples include vehicle registration plate permits, vehicle registration fees, watercraft registration fees, building fees, driver's licenses, hunting and fishing licenses, fees for professional licensing, fees for visas or passports, fees for demolition, rezoning, and land grading, and sometimes for increasing stormwater run-off, destroying native vegetation, and cutting-down healthy trees.
- User fees collected in exchange for the use of many public services and facilities. Tolls charged for the use of toll roads are an example
- Donations and voluntary contributions to the state.

RECORDING OF TRANSFER PRICING AND TAXATION

A small operation managed by a few individuals was the typical beginning of a large corporation with a hundred operating affiliates dispersed around the world. Decision making was highly centralized and lines of communication were short. As the company grew, the founding management team found it more difficult to keep matters under control.

This problem was greatly exacerbated when operations within the company became physically separated. Centers of activity in different locations called for a different style of management. Funneling of all decisions from diverse locations through a small group of individuals, who no longer possess the necessary intimate awareness of the circumstances surrounding each decision, is a surefire prescription for stifling growth.

Growth is the name of the game for modern corporations. Growth entails individual operating affiliates taking appropriate action to enhance productivity, market share, and the scope of a company's product line. It has been found that operating affiliates physically separated from the parent organization can best achieve these objectives under a decentralized style of management. Responsibility now falls on the shoulders of the manager of an operating affiliate to make the necessary decisions that will lead to improved financial results, the universal measure of performance. The parent organization takes on a new role as coordinator and monitor of activities now that responsibility for operations has been transferred to the operating units.

Far from playing a passive role, the parent organization focuses its attention on optimizing the performance of its semiautonomous operating affiliates. To do this, the parent organization must establish, and articulate, a set of strategic goals and allocate limited corporate resources to the various operating affiliates to best achieve these goals. It must ensure that the short–term action plans of the operating affiliates are in accord with its long–term plans.

Top management positions in the operating affiliates must be filled with individuals capable of leading their affiliates in the right direction and an incentive system must be set up to induce managers to orient their thinking to the goals of the company.

Finally, the parent organization must set up a financial reporting and control system to monitor its global operations, to provide necessary information for the making of decisions and to evaluate the performance of the affiliate managers.

Although operating affiliates appear to be semiauton-omous units in that they are given a wide spectrum of decision–making responsibility in managing their local operations, they are not independent centers of corporate activity. They are often united in manufacturing and marketing a common product line, in the course of which they routinely buy and sell finished goods, components, or raw materials from one another.

These intra company exchanges of goods, components, and raw materials require a transfer price. The parent organization sets the transfer price after considering various factors with an eye on optimizing corporate performance as a whole. Transfer prices are often not negotiated and agreed on by the actual buyers and sellers of the goods and components being shipped between operating affiliates.

Yet transfer prices directly affect the revenue and cost of goods sold, and therefore, the profitability of the operating affiliates. Because the affiliate managers are monitored by a financial reporting and control system that scrutinizes their financial results, one can expect that affiliate managers have an entirely different perspective on transfer pricing than the executives of the parent organization.

Transfer pricing can easily embroil executives of the parent organization and the managers of operating affiliates in endless disputes. Some firms have even established an administrative panel for reviewing transfer prices to resolve sharp differences of opinion between those responsible for managing operating affiliates and those responsible for setting transfer prices.

TRANSFER PRICES AND TAXES

A global company with operations in many nations must deal with a new dimension of complexity in establishing transfer prices, which is not present when a company operates solely within the confines of a single nation. A company whose operations are within a single nation pays the same taxes on profits regardless of the transfer pricing policy.

The consolidation process, whether for financial or tax accounting purposes, eliminates intra company transactions to arrive at either a book profit or a before-tax profit. When a company transacts business through affiliate companies in different nations, however, transfer pricing provides a mechanism for shifting taxable profits between tax jurisdictions.

Tax authorities in various nations are concerned with the notion that transfer pricing, often set by parent organizations outside their jurisdiction, is based on minimizing taxes paid in their jurisdictions. There certainly is an element of truth in this contention, but there are other considerations in administering transfer prices than minimizing taxes. The setting of transfer prices provides a way of moving funds internationally for a variety of purposes, of circumventing currency exchange controls that threaten to choke the operations of a company, of minimizing the deleterious impact of other artificial barriers to trade such as duties and tariffs, and of reducing currency risk exposure.

A transfer pricing policy attempts to satisfy a multiple set of objectives. Some of these objectives call for high transfer prices, whereas others require low transfer prices. A company must select what it considers to be an optimal transfer price, which is a compromise price for best achieving divergent objectives.

This optimal transfer price may not be the one that minimizes taxes on profits. The selected transfer price may not be satisfactory both to the local tax authority and to the manager of an affiliate if it reduces the reported profitability of the affiliate. However, setting the transfer price is critical to optimizing the financial performance of the corporation as a whole, given the conditions that prevail at a point in time.

MINIMIZING TAXES

Tax authorities of most countries have guidelines or controls that are expected to be complied with in setting transfer prices. Management is not free to arbitrarily select transfer prices without having to substantiate their transfer price decisions. Nevertheless, there is still an element of choice where a selected transfer price may reduce the tax burden of a company. Suppose that a company consists of a parent organization and two operating affiliates—one in nation A, where the tax rate on profits is 30 per cent, and one in nation B, where the tax rate on profits is 40 per cent. The tax is applied to each affiliate's gross margin for illustrative purposes. The affiliate in nation A makes a product that is entirely sold through the affiliate in nation B. Two cases are considered—a low and a high transfer price.

Case I-Low Transfer Price

	Nation A Tax 30%	Nation B Tax 40%	Consolidated
Sales	$2000	$3200	$3200
Cost of Goods Sold	1500	2000	1500
Gross Margin	500	1200	1700
Tax	150	480	630
Net Income	$350	$720	$1070

Everything made in a factory in nation A is sold through a marketing organization in nation B. Therefore, total sales in nation A, calculated on the basis of an administered transfer price, is also the cost of goods sold in nation B. Sales in nation B of $3,200 is the net consolidated sales for the company, because all goods produced in nation A are sold in nation B.

The actual cost of manufacturing the goods in nation A is $1,500. Because nation B does not add value to the goods, the consolidated cost of goods sold for the company is also $1,500. The consolidated tax is the sum of the $150 and the $480 paid to the tax authorities of nations A and B, respectively.

The consolidated net income is $1,070, the sum of the net incomes of the two affiliates. Suppose that the transfer price is increased from $2,000 to $2,500 for goods shipped between the two affiliates. Consolidated sales, cost of goods sold, and gross margin are unaffected by the change in the transfer price, because it is netted out in the consolidation process. Taxes paid in each nation are no longer the same because of the change in the transfer price.

In case II, the increase in the transfer price shifts the profit to Nation A, which has the lower tax rate. The affiliate in nation A earns more taxable income and pays more in taxes than in case I. The affiliate in nation B earns less taxable income and pays less in taxes in case II than in case I. The net effect, as seen by comparing case II with case I, is that the company as a whole is paying less in taxes, which increases its consolidated net income.

It is true that had the two nations the same tax rate, the total taxes paid by the company, and the consolidated net income, would not be affected by changes in the transfer price. Even so, transfer prices determine what portion of total taxes are to be paid to the tax authority in nation A and to the tax authority in Nation B. Although the parent organization may be relatively insensitive concerning to whom it pays taxes, needless to say, the tax authorities are very much concerned as to which is collecting taxes.

The problem is compounded, from the point of view of a tax authority, because the transfer price is probably set by a parent organization not under its jurisdiction. The importance of transfer pricing to both managers and tax authorities can be appreciated when it is realized that between 40 per cent and 60 per cent of international trade involves goods moving between affiliates of the same company.

Corporate decisions on transfer prices do have a meaningful impact on what a tax jurisdiction collects. There are nations, islands, and localities where tax authorities exhibit little interest in transfer prices. Ireland, Puerto Rico, and other nations or areas designated as free trade zones or having special tax privileges may not tax corporate profits, or have a very low tax rate.

These nations or locales are interested in companies building plants on their soil for the social benefits that accrue from employment of individuals who might otherwise be unemployed. Companies operating in such nations or locales can substantially decrease their overall tax rate. The effective reduction in tax rates depends on the transfer prices of imported components and semi finished goods and the transfer prices of exported finished goods.

Granting tax concessions is one way for a nation to attract companies. At this time, eastern European nations offer tax incentives but do not have a prescribed accounting methodology to calculate profits, which makes it impossible to quantify the tax benefit. More than one company has set up an operation in eastern Europe to later discover that the government had a much different version in mind of the nature of the tax benefits than the investors anticipated.

Such shortsightedness by government officials has a deleterious impact on attracting other companies. Many nations are discovering that viewing business solely as a way to fill the public coffers may not be in their long-term best interests. Within the United States, states with high corporate tax rates have experienced companies moving to states with low corporate tax rates.

The higher they raise their corporate tax rates, the less they collect in taxes. As once companies moved from one state to another, now they move from one nation to another. In selecting a potential site, a businessman considers many factors, of which taxes are but one.

Some of these are social and political stability; a system of commercial law to resolve disputes; a set of acceptable accounting practices (both to assess tax liabilities and evaluate tax incentives); a labour force with the requisite skills and will to work; and an infrastructure of transportation, communication, and utility and social (education, medical care) services.

There are more locations that offer good potential sites for factories than before. Managers no longer feel that their factories must be anchored to one nation and have learned to manage far–flung operations. Nations must now compete for factories. Tax authorities in developed nations are beginning to realise that they may end up collecting less tax revenue in their eagerness to collect more tax revenue by raising tax rates.

The United States was forced to repeal a luxury tax on pleasure boats because pleasure boat construction virtually ceased with the passage of the new tax. New Jersey was forced to repeal a sales tax on trucks when truck selling companies moved their operations to nearby Pennsylvania. In both cases, tax revenues fell when tax rates were raised, and the tax authorities were forced to rescind tax increases. In a global economy, companies are mobile and will relocate to avoid especially burdensome taxes.

INTERNATIONAL FUNDING

Businesses operating in hard currency nations have the advantage of being able to transfer and convert currencies as necessary. Many nations, however, have currencies that lack convertibility, the so-called soft currencies. Transfer pricing provides a means of moving funds from one country to another, when direct currency convertibility is not possible.

If a nation has an affiliate that completes the manufacturing process and sells its output within that nation, funds can be moved out of that nation by increasing the transfer price for goods imported by the affiliate. The same objective can be accomplished by increasing the charges for services rendered by the parent organization to the affiliate, such as selling and administrative (S&A) fees, research and development (R&D) expenses, financial charges on transferred assets, and royalties for rights to patents and dividends.

Sometimes currency exchange controls focus on the amount of dividends that can be paid by an affiliate to its parent. A quasi–dividend can be paid by raising the transfer price of goods moving into the nation or by increasing corporate fees, financial charges, and royalty payments. Some nations with severe restrictions on dividend outflows will permit increases in transfer prices and service fees. These quasi–dividend payments are allowed because the local government recognizes that few companies can afford the luxury of investing in a nation that prohibits the company from earning a return on its investment.

However, actions such as these that drain funds out of a soft currency nation eventually result in some sort of currency exchange restriction. This often results in affiliate profits accumulating in a currency that may not be particularly desirable. Sometimes currency exchange restrictions can be bypassed by the affiliate making an investment, or lending funds, to an affiliate in another nation.

CONTROLLING REPORTED PROFITS

Shifts in transfer prices, corporate administrative fees, and other parent company charges to an affiliate are means of managing the affiliate's reported profitability. It may be in the interest of a parent organization to lower the reported profitability of an affiliate for reasons other than tax minimization. These include deflecting union demands for higher wages, reducing political pressure to nationalize or expropriate a profitable affiliate, and dissuading potential competitors from entering the market.

Lowering profitability is also a way to counter price controls that limit profitability. If a government has set price controls based on the cost of production plus a limited markup for profits, increases in the transfer price of goods sent to the affiliate lowers the profit margin of goods sold in that nation. This may permit goods to be sold at government decreed profit margins with the company as a whole still able to earn its normal profits.

A few nations have tax rates that are linked to profitability. The greater the profitability, the higher the tax rate. The logic behind this taxation policy is that there is a level of profits on investment that seems "excessive" to the government. Such excessive profitability should be punished by the government, and there is no greater punishment than taking away the excess profits through a higher tax rate.

By increasing the transfer price of goods being imported into the nation, the degree of profitability is decreased, lowering the tax rate and, presumably, restoring respectability in the eyes of the government. Alternatively, it may be in the interests of the parent organization to enhance the profitability of an affiliate. This may be done by lowering the transfer price of imported goods.

One reason for enhancing the profitability of an affiliate is to provide sufficient financial resources to the affiliate for it to withstand price cutting by competitive companies. Improving an affiliate's profitability, even at the cost of paying more in taxes, may allow the affiliate to borrow needed funds for operation from local banks and other financial institutions, to improve its credit rating to qualify for lower interest loans and to fund capital outlays from its own resources.

CIRCUMVENTING EXCHANGE CONTROLS

Governments with soft currencies often limit the amount of their currency that companies operating in their nations can exchange for other currencies. Their motivation is to discourage the selling of the domestic soft currency and the buying of a hard currency, which would exert downward pressure on the value of the local currency. In other words, exchange controls are set up to keep a soft currency from becoming softer.

From the point of view of a parent organization, restricting hard currency outflows inhibits an affiliate's ability to pay for imported components or other items necessary for its operations. Transfer prices for the needed components can be kept artificially low to expand the volume of goods that are being imported into a soft currency nation.

This sustains an affiliate's manufacturing operation without exceeding government decreed restrictions on converting soft currency to hard currency. But there is an adverse consequence because such a course of action results in a parent corporation accumulating even larger amounts of soft currency. These holdings of soft currency are constantly losing purchasing power through inflation.

The soft currency cannot be converted to a more desirable currency because of currency exchange restrictions and the soft currency, which has little value within the nation, has no value outside the nation. One of the knottiest problems associated with an operating affiliate in a soft currency nation is funding of hard currency imports necessary for its operation and obtaining a hard currency return on a hard currency investment.

Some companies will not set up an operation in a soft currency nation unless there is a prearranged means to earn hard currency to pay for hard currency imports and to provide a hard currency return on a hard currency investment. Pepsi Cola struck a barter deal for producing its soft drink in the former Soviet Union. Its soft ruble revenue, net of soft ruble expenses, is exchanged for Russian built tankers, which are then sold for hard currencies.

Oil companies will not set up operations in the Commonwealth of Independent States, and other soft currency nations, unless they receive a share of the output, which is shipped out of the nation and sold for hard currency. The easiest way for a company to earn hard currency in a soft currency nation would be to export a portion of its output to hard currency nations. However, most soft currency nations do not permit the hard currency revenue to remain with the company.

The hard currency revenue is exchanged for an equivalent amount of soft currency, which is then credited to the exporter's bank account. In essence, the national government receives the hard currency revenue from exports and pays soft currency to the exporter.

Sometimes international banks are at fault for imposing this condition on a nation as a means to guarantee repayment of international debt. Regardless of whether the nation or the international banks impose this condition, it is self-defeating because the economic development of a developing nation is held back by the inability of companies to earn sufficient hard currency to justify their investments.

MINIMIZING DUTIES AND TARIFFS

Duties and tariffs imposed on goods imported into a nation can be reduced by lowering the transfer price. This is the exact opposite of reducing taxes on profits by increasing the transfer price. Because the tariff rate is usually less than the tax rate on profits, lowering transfer prices to reduce import tariffs often results in a higher tax on profits. In some nations, however, tariffs on certain imported goods and commodities are not set by a corporate-determined transfer price but by an internationally posted price.

This can be done only for generic goods or commodities (oil), where there is an active market with published and verifiable prices. Sometimes tax authorities will reference costs not to a "transfer price" cost but to an internationally agreed standard. One example of this is tanker rates in the oil business. An oil company can manage the profitability, and therefore, the tax liability, of a refinery by the transfer price associated with international tanker transportation for moving oil to and from a refinery.

The tax authorities of many nations and the oil companies have agreed to a panel of experts determining a fair and representative tanker rate that is used for the computation of taxes independent of the transfer price, or internal cost, that oil companies charge for shipping oil among their affiliates. This eliminates arguments between tax authorities and oil companies concerning the appropriate shipping charge.

Determining the optimal transfer-pricing policy is further complicated when a nation in which an affiliate operates has an export subsidy programme or provides a tax credit on the value of exports. It may be advantageous to lower transfer prices to an affiliate whose output is exported to third parties or other affiliates in other nations to take advantage of these tax incentives.

The optimal transfer price depends on the nature of the export subsidy or tax credit, the volume of the affiliate's output that is exported from the nation, the relationship between taxes on profits and the generation of tax credits and on the capacity of the affiliate to utilize the tax credit or export subsidy. The nature of the taxes paid in a nation in the form of income taxes, duties and tariffs on imported goods, and export subsidies or tax credits on exported goods influence the setting of transfer prices.

There is no hard and fast rule on whether a high or a low transfer-pricing policy is best for a company. The particular circumstances of a company's operations in a nation and the nature of taxes and subsidies determine the best transfer-pricing policy. A transferpricing system integrated into a financial reporting and control system should be capable of analyzing "what" if scenarios to evaluate the effect of different transfer-pricing policies.

REDUCING CURRENCY EXCHANGE RISK

Changes in currency exchange rates result in transaction and translation gains and losses. More importantly, they affect the competitive position of an affiliate. If an affiliate manufactures and markets its goods in a nation, and imports components from another nation, a revaluation of the currency where the finished goods are being sold relative to the currency of its purchased components reduces manufacturing costs.

This makes the affiliate more competitive and profitable. A devaluation, on the other hand, increases the cost of imported components, making the affiliate less competitive and less profitable. Reality is much more complex than this simple example because affiliates may export and import components and finished goods to and from a variety of nations.

Changes in exchange rates benefit some affiliates and hurt others, and it may not be obvious because of the nature of buying and selling of goods and services. It is possible that a change in currency exchange rates that is adverse to a particular affiliate may be beneficial to the company as a whole because of the nature of the net exposure of the company to the affected currencies. Adjustments to transfer prices may affect currency holdings before an anticipated change in exchange rates takes place and may be able to restore a company's competitive position after the change has taken place.

Therefore, a financial reporting and control system should have the capacity to assess changes to both transfer prices and currency exchange rates to enable the parent organization to respond both to anticipated changes in currency exchange rates and to subsequent shifts in its competitive position.

TRANSFER PRICING AND JOINT VENTURES

A joint venture partner, a local partner owning a portion of an affiliate, and a minority shareholder are going to be as interested in transfer pricing as the local tax authority. Less often, a partnership is structured on the basis of a claim, or royalty, on revenue. More often, it is a claim on profits. If one party to a venture or partnership can influence revenue, costs, and profitability through transfer pricing, then the other party or partner, or a minority shareholder, will be deservedly concerned.

One way to manage transfer pricing with regard to having partners or minority shareholders is to formalize the setting of transfer prices in some verifiable manner such as a set markup above costs, another is to reference transfer prices to an observable market transaction. Either way minimizes the opportunity for one party to a partnership or joint venture to manipulate transfer prices to its advantage.

If the partners, participants, and minority shareholders feel that their interests are vulnerable by virtue of the other party to a business venture controlling transfer prices, then they may not contribute to the venture that which was expected of them. Avoiding these problems can be more easily said than done. Some years ago, Ford Motor Company purchased the minority shares of its partially owned subsidiaries because the company felt that it could not administer transfer pricing in a way that was fair to all concerned.

Some managements have made the strategic decision not to enter into joint ventures, or have local partners or minority shareholdings in corporate affiliates, where they can manage the profitability of the venture through transfer prices. Sometimes, the solution for a problem is to avoid the problem.

TRANSFER PRICING AND MANAGERIAL PERFORMANCE EVALUATION

It may be in the interest of the corporation as a whole to transfer in components that are more highly priced than those an affiliate can purchase from other sources. It may be in the interest of the corporation as a whole to transfer goods made in one affiliate to another affiliate for less than what the affiliate can sell them for to third parties. Although the corporation may gain by such a set of transfer prices for goods moving among affiliates, it does not serve the interests of the affiliate managers if they are subsequently judged on profitability.

This dichotomy of purpose in establishing a transfer-pricing policy for the good of the whole company, yet holding managers of affiliates accountable for profits that are contaminated, so to speak, by transfer prices has not been successfully addressed when transfer prices are different from market prices. In fact, this is one potent argument in favour of companies having transfer pricing policies based on the market price for comparable goods.

If transfer prices are set at the price for goods exchanged between unrelated parties, then there is no dichotomy of purpose in setting transfer prices and measuring performance. Managers of affiliates can be judged in an unbiased fashion on the profitability of their operations because they are buying and selling at market prices—the same prices that would prevail if they were independent companies.

The disadvantage of letting the market set transfer prices is that the parent corporation can no longer utilize transfer pricing as a means to pursue the overall optimization of the financial performance of the corporation. One possible approach to the dysfunctional aspects of setting transfer prices at other than market prices and measuring management performance of affiliates is to isolate and separately state the amount of inter company "profit" or "loss" that each affiliate is experiencing in its transactions with other affiliates.

This approach provides the parent organization with information on whether an affiliate is suffering from unwarranted decreased profitability or enjoying unwarranted increased profitability because of transfer pricing.

SETTING TRANSFER PRICES BY COST OF PRODUCTION

There are two general approaches for setting transfer prices: the cost of production and market prices associated with third party, or unrelated, transactions. The cost-of-production approach bases the price of goods to be transferred between affiliates on the variable cost of production, an allowance for fixed costs that are general in nature and are apportioned over the entire product line, and an allowance for fixed costs that can be apportioned among the individual products.

This latter category usually includes research and development costs and selling and administrative costs. The remaining components may include financial fees and royalties associated with tangible and intangible assets to be apportioned to individual products and the selection of an appropriate profit margin. The variable cost of production includes labour, material, and other direct costs that are consumed in the production of an item.

If the policy of the company is to hire and fire factory workers as production rises and falls, then labour is a variable cost. If a company is reluctant to let go of their workers when sales decline, then factory labour should be considered part of fixed costs. Factory labour costs are usually part variable and part fixed.

Other variable costs can be the unit financing and utility costs associated with machinery and processes used in the manufacture of a particular product and unit shipping costs.

These costs can also be treated as fixed costs depending on how the company's cost accounting system is set up. Fixed costs are all costs not included in variable costs. Fixed costs are the financing or depreciation costs of the factory; the overhead costs of marketing, accounting, and supervision; the cost of inventories, warehouses, insurance, utilities, communication, property taxes, and other non-variable cost items.

Fixed costs may not be entirely fixed in that there is some variation as production levels change. For instance, bonuses, which would be considered part of the fixed costs of having an executive suite, rise and fall with profits, which are related to production levels. The number of staff personnel in marketing, accounting, engineering, and other overhead functions can vary with the production level.

Some elements of fixed costs are allocated in the transfer price setting mechanism in a way that fairly apportions the fixed cost burden among the various products. Other elements of fixed costs can be apportioned more on the basis of the benefit derived by an individual product. One of these is research and development, where the allocation can be made over a product line in proportion to the degree of R&D expenditures associated with the development of an individual product.

Although there is general agreement that this is a fair way to apportion R&D expenses of successful undertakings, there is lack of agreement on how to apportion R&D expenses for failed projects. Some maintain that the allocation of expenses associated with failed R&D projects should be apportioned to all products on the basis that every product should bear the risk of failed R&D efforts.

Others object on the grounds that had the R&D effort succeeded, a particular product might not have benefited. Therefore, it makes no sense for the transfer price to contain the cost of a failed R&D effort, which, had it succeeded, would not be part of the transfer price of the product. The question as to the proper treatment of failed R&D projects is not an internal accounting matter.

Tax authorities are interested in who takes the write off of a failed R&D project. In the United States, the Internal Revenue Service (IRS) is concerned whether a transfer price contains a provision for failed R&D expenditures. If a transfer price contains only that portion of R&D expenditures that were successful with regard to a particular product, then failed R&D projects of a U.S.

corporation are being written off solely against U.S. income. A portion of the tax loss write-off is passed on to the tax authority of another nation by including an element of failed R&D expenditures in the transfer price. Another fixed cost element that can be separated and apportioned in a different manner than general fixed costs are services provided to an individual product.

These may be coordination and control expenses associated with a product; costs for enhancing the efficiency of operations for manufacturing the product or expanding the scope of its market; and the costs of recruiting and training of management and operations personnel associated with manufacturing, marketing, and repairing or servicing the product. The allocation of these service costs to individual products provides another element in deriving their transfer prices.

The derivation of the transfer price also includes elements for tangibles and intangibles associated with a product. Tangibles are the plant, equipment, and other physical assets dedicated to the manufacture of the product. Part of the transfer price provides a financial return for tangibles based on their value. Intangibles represent the technical knowledge and expertise and applicable patents that can be allocated to a particular product.

The transfer price also contains an element that provides a company with a return on intangibles. Intangible costs within a transfer price cannot be capriciously determined by management because intangible costs affect taxable profits. For this reason, the IRS has established guidelines for determining the intangible cost element in a transfer price.

An intangible cost element must be present if there are intangible costs associated with the manufacture or marketing of a product and must be so identified. Intangible costs can be proportioned in relation to the income attributable to the intangibles by units of production, sales, net or gross profits, or other reasonable methods. The fee for intangible property incorporated in a transfer price must be similar to what would have been arranged with an independent third party.

The last part of the cost approach in setting transfer prices is determining the proper profit margin on the goods made by one affiliate and shipped to another. This may be the average profit margin for the company as a whole or a profit margin associated with a specific product line. Regardless, the stipulated profit margin must be reconciled in some manner with the profitability of the company or a product line to satisfy the tax authorities.

The need for reconciliation of the profit and the various cost elements of the transfer price with the tax authorities sometimes results in the tax group within the finance department of a company being responsible for administering transfer prices. However, this choice may hinder general management from using transfer prices as a means to achieve corporate objectives.

The chief advantage of the cost of production approach for setting transfer prices is that the costs are available and are subject to quantification. For this reason, the production cost approach has been more common in the past than the market price approach. The chief disadvantage is that there is no real incentive for an affiliate to improve its manufacturing process, to enhance its efficiency, or to take steps to lower costs.

Mistakes, errors, inefficiencies in manning or machinery, management inattention to detail, worker carelessness, and excessive remuneration of white and blue collar workers alike may all be incorporated in the determination of costs and passed on to the affiliates in the transfer price. Another disadvantage is that both the tax authority and the affiliates may object to the nature of the apportionment of R&D, S&A, tangibles, and intangibles among the various products and the assigned profit margin.

SETTING TRANSFER PRICES BY MARKET PRICES

The disadvantages associated with the cost-of-production method of setting transfer prices can be mostly avoided by referencing transfer prices to third party transactions for identical, or nearly identical, products. If an affiliate can obtain the item being purchased from a third party for a certain price, then that price can be the basis for setting the transfer price.

The proponents of market-oriented transfer prices maintain that letting the market set the transfer price is inherently more fair than a production-cost-based system because one affiliate is not supporting the inefficiencies of another. If an affiliate receives only the global competitive price for its products, then there is an incentive for it to take whatever actions are needed to correct the inefficiencies in its operations that are resulting in higher costs.

In a truly decentralized operation, managers are expected to make their decisions on an independent basis, and unrelated companies are permitted to compete for the business of an affiliate, along with other affiliates. The parent organization does not set transfer prices and has little or no influence over the decisions made by the managers of the affiliates. No favour or special consideration is shown to fellow affiliates in the competitive process of selecting suppliers for components and goods. The hope, of course, is that everyone is kept on his or her competitive toes to produce salable goods at the lowest possible cost. This managerial philosophy, where each affiliate is treated as an independent company, is sometimes referred to as the small business unit (SBU) management philosophy.

The disadvantage is that, although each affiliate is focused on optimizing its operations, the end result may be suboptimal performance of the corporation as a whole. Suppose that affiliate X produces all of a component for a number of widget manufacturing affiliates.

Total demand for part X is 2 million per year. Affiliate X has $10 million in fixed annual costs, which include a profit margin on the investment in manufacturing facilities plus a return on the R&D investment for the development of part X. The variable costs for manufacturing part X is $5. The transfer price based on the fixed and variable costs of affiliate X supplying all other affiliates with part X is $10.

Volume of Sales: 2,000,000

Fixed Costs	$10,000,000
Variable Costs at $5 per Unit	10,000,000
Total Costs	$20,000,000
Transfer Price Based on Cost of Making 2,000,000	$10.00

Affiliate A is free to cut its best deal and obtains a quote of $9.50 from another company. Affiliate A does what is best for maximizing its profits and purchases 200,000 part X's from a third party for $9.50 rather than pay $10 to affiliate X. Affiliate X has lost a contract for 200,000 part X's and now operates on a basis of a sales volume of 1,800,000 per year.

Volume of Sales: 1,800,000

Fixed Costs	$10,000,000
Variable Costs at $5 per Unit	9,000,000
Total Costs	$19,000,000
Transfer Price Based on Cost of Making 1,800,000	$10.56

The remaining affiliates must pay a higher price because there is less sales volume to cover the fixed costs of affiliate X. The increase in transfer price to cover the fixed and variable costs is essentially equivalent to treating fixed costs as a component of variable costs, which it is not. Nevertheless, affiliate X must cover all its costs. When affiliate X announces the increase in price, affiliate B concludes a deal with a third party at $9.75 causing another loss of 200,000 for affiliate X.

Volume of Sales: 1,600.000

Fixed Costs	$10,000,000
Variable Costs at $5 per Unit	8,000,000
Total Costs	$18,000,000
Transfer Price Based on cost of Making 1,600,000	$11.25

Now it's time for affiliate C to say goodbye to affiliate X, as it maximizes its profit by reducing the cost of part X by paying $10.50 to another outside source. This is higher than the $10 price that applied when all the affiliates received part X from affiliate X. It is clear from the continuation of this exercise that, as each affiliate maximizes its profits by cutting costs, the corporation as a whole is being sub optimized.

Even if the various affiliates do not pay more than an average price of $10 per unit for part X in purchasing all part X's from outside sources, the global company is stuck with an affiliate with no sales and a fixed annual cost of $10 million that represents, in large measure, financing costs on plant and equipment. It is highly likely that the fixed costs in affiliate X contain an allowance for R&D expenses and product development that have to be recouped in the operation of a company, but do not have to be recouped by another company if it is essentially manufacturing a copy of part X.

Copying is fairly common in global commerce because patent protection is limited to the nation issuing the patent. Global companies often obtain patents in a number of nations, but this may not be possible for all nations. A company may manufacture a copy of a product in one of these nations. Although it is true that affiliate X is free to pursue patent infringement action against sales in a particular nation where it has patent protection, the time involved in enforcement proceedings and the legal expenses may make such protection prohibitively expensive.

Furthermore, there is no internationally recognized legal structure to handle patent infringements. In addition to R&D expenses, the fixed costs of affiliate X may also contain a service element for the benefit of the affiliates purchasing its output that may not be provided by third parties. By each affiliate "doing its own thing," the R&D and service costs cannot be covered.

One principal problem associated with using market reference points for transfer pricing is that the affiliates may be shipping components and parts that are not readily available from other firms. Most components and parts are specifically designed for a company's product line and are not available from third parties unless contracted for by an affiliate. Market prices for similarly designed components that cannot be actually used in the company's product line may not be relevant.

Moreover, the quality inherent in third-party quotes for similar parts may not be up to the standards imposed on products made within a global corporate family. There is no easy answer as to which approach for determining transfer prices should be followed. Both have their adherents and detractors. Either approach restricts transfer prices to something related to third-party, or market, transactions or to the cost of manufacture.

Surveys have shown that nations seem to exhibit cultural preferences as to which approach to follow and as to what motivates companies in setting transfer prices. Companies in some countries favour costbased transfer prices, whereas companies in other nations favour market-based transfer prices. U.S. based corporations have historically preferred setting transfer prices by the cost approach because the necessary data is available, whereas the necessary data for setting transfer prices on the basis of market transactions may not be available.

Oftentimes, market quotes for uniquely designed parts and components may have to be derived rather than observed because there are no market transactions for the precise item. Should General Motors set its transfer price on carburetors being shipped to Europe based on its cost of production or on what Toyota charges its U.S. transplants?

The two carburetors are not the same and do not have the same cost of production.

Furthermore, there may not be a data base available for prices for carburetors sold between related and unrelated parties from which to derive a market price. Preferences change with time.

Surveys done in the 1970s indicated that the preponderance of U.S. companies were motivated by tax minimization in setting transfer prices. More recent surveys indicate that companies are more interested in setting transfer prices on the basis of measuring the performance of affiliate managers and of providing reliable and unbiased information for the making of decisions. This change in attitude in U.S. companies may be the result of the United States becoming a relative tax haven compared to other nations.

Its corporate tax rate of 34 per cent, plus state taxes, is less than in many other industrialized nations, where tax rates range between 40 per cent and 55 per cent. A U.S. company's total tax bill may, in fact, be reduced by allocating more profits to the United States.

Regardless of changes in attitudes as to what is important in setting transfer prices, the essential point is that there is no unanimity on which approach to use and on what motivates companies in setting transfer prices.

Up to this point, an important assumption has been that the parent company has real control over transfer prices to manage corporate cash flows and the profits reported by affiliates and to overcome artificial barriers to trade in the form of custom duties, currency exchange, and price controls. Some recent surveys suggest that competitive forces and market conditions within a nation seem to be more important in setting transfer prices than decisions made by a parent organization.

If transfer prices are being set by exogenous commercial forces, then the presumption that a parent organization is able to achieve optimal financial performance of a global family of affiliates through the careful orchestration of transfer pricing is being challenged.

TAX CONSIDERATIONS

Taxation and transfer pricing are intimately entwined, because transfer pricing of goods, parts, and components moving in and out of a nation has a direct impact on taxes on profits and on the amount of duties and tariffs paid to the tax authority. The discussion on transfer pricing based on the cost-of-production approach shows an intimate involvement with the tax authority in the methodology for calculating various elements of the transfer price. There is little uniformity on taxation among nations. Taxes range from taxation of a corporation's activities to the "water's edge" or on its global earnings, the so-called "unitary tax." The state of California invented the unitary tax in the 1930s when movie companies in California began moving out of the state to avoid state taxes.

A unitary tax was applied against the global earnings of a company and the tax was determined by the proportion of a company's sales, property, and payroll within the state to its global sales, property, and payroll. The resulting tax had no relation to the degree of profitability of a company's operation in California. A company could operate at a loss in California and still pay a tax based on its global profits.

Needless to say, both foreign governments and multinational companies have vigorously fought the unitary tax. A number of court decisions confirmed or restricted unitary taxation over the years. Ultimately, opposition to the unitary tax succeeded. In November 1991, Alaska was the last state to abandon having a company's state tax liability based on the global earnings of the company.

The unitary tax still exists in a truncated form, where earnings are restricted to the "water's edge." The state tax is calculated on the portion of a company's activities within a state as compared to its activities within the United States. Although most other countries limit their assessment on what is to be taxed to the operations of a company within their jurisdiction, there is no universal agreement as to what constitutes revenue and expenses in the calculation of taxable income and no uniformity on tax rates.

Every nation decides what is subject to taxation and the applicable tax rates. The complexity of tax regulations, in general, and the diversity of tax laws among nations are such that it is necessary for an affiliate to retain the technical expertise necessary to understand and comply with local tax regulations.

The parent organization must retain the technical knowledge for its own tax jurisdiction and have sufficient knowledge of tax matters elsewhere to coordinate tax planning among the various affiliates. The vigour with which tax payments are enforced varies among nations.

Some countries with seemingly high tax rates permit an underground economy to flourish without much in the way of enforcing tax payments. The other side of the coin is the willingness of companies to adhere to tax laws. In some nations, a businessman who scrupulously follows the tax laws and pays what is owed to the tax authority will find himself at a competitive disadvantage.

NATURE OF TAXES

Taxes can be direct or indirect. The United States relies more on direct taxation, which is applied to each taxable entity. A U.S. corporation is taxed at 34 per cent on its profits. If a corporation pays a dividend to its shareholders, then the next taxable entity, the individual, pays a tax, which may be 28 per cent or more. This is double taxation.

Some nations, such as Germany, have two corporate tax rates on profits—one for retained profits and the other for distributed profits in the form of dividends. A lesser tax rate applies to profits that are distributed to shareholders to reduce the degree of double taxation.

Europe relies more on indirect taxes—particularly, the value added tax (VAT). The VAT is basically a tax applied to each stage of the production process and is not directly associated with the degree of profitability. Indeed, only a small portion of a VAT is associated with profits. Suppose that a company's manufacturing operations has the following financial results.

Wages, rents, interest, profit	$400,000
Outside purchases of goods and services for which VAT has already been paid	600,000
Total sales	$1,000,000

The additive method is to apply the VAT rate, say 10 per cent, to all costs associated with the production of goods, including profit and excluding purchases of goods and services from third parties for which the VAT has already been paid. In this case, $400,000 of a company's activities falls into this category resulting in a VAT of $40,000.

A simpler method of calculation is to take the gross sales of the company, subtract all purchases of goods and services for which VAT has already been paid, and apply the VAT rate to the balance.

Either method yields the same result. The VAT is essentially equivalent to a national sales tax, because every company associated with the production and marketing of goods and providing services pays a tax on whatever value it adds to the goods or services. The value added tax, like a sales tax, is a tax on consumption, whereas U.S. taxes are on income and profits.

Value added tax rates vary widely from country to country and according to the nature of the business. Certain European countries have low VAT rates for business transactions associated with food and high VAT rates for luxury products. Others attempt to have one rate that applies to most forms of commerce.

Because the VAT is not paid on items that have already been exposed to a value added tax, and with the European economy becoming more integrated, there is a powerful incentive for the European Community to harmonize VAT rates and coordinate the handling of VAT payments for products or components shipped between members of the European Community.

The amounts of value added by a company are frequently disclosed in European financial statements. In the excerpt from the British company, the company had gross revenues of 3,213 million pounds in 1987 of which 919.1 million pounds represents added value by the company. Of the total of 919.1 million pounds of added value, 496.8 million pounds was paid to the company's employees, 157.1 million pounds was paid in taxes to government tax authorities, and the remainder was paid to the internal and external providers of capital.

U.S. TAXATION OF GLOBAL COMPANIES

Nations have different ways of taxing global companies domiciled within their jurisdiction. If a parent corporation is domiciled in the United States, it does not pay taxes in the United States on profits earned by incorporated affiliates in other nations, unless the nation is considered a tax haven. This, in the United States, is known as Subpart F income, which will be discussed later under rein voicing centers.

Unlike an incorporated affiliate, a branch of a U.S. company located in a foreign nation is taxed directly on its earnings regardless of whether the earnings are remitted to the home office or not. The taxes paid on remitted and unremitted earnings are not the same, in that unremitted earnings have to be translated to U.S. dollars before a tax liability can be assessed, and therefore, are influenced by changes in currency exchange rates.

Taxes can also be calculated on the basis of the increase in the net worth of the branch, which can also be affected by changes in currency exchange rates. Sometimes a U.S. company will first open a branch operation in another country to permit startup losses to flow back to the parent organization.

When the branch becomes profitable, it may be reorganized as a wholly owned subsidiary, reducing the company's overall tax liability. U.S. based companies usually operate in the global market through operating affiliates whose stock is owned by the parent corporation. The parent corporation pays U.S. taxes only on the profits generated from dividends, royalties, and other service payments and fees paid by a non-U.S. domiciled affiliate to the parent organization.

Taxes paid on profits by affiliates in their nations of domicile can be treated either as a tax credit or a tax deduction by the parent organization in the calculation of its U.S. taxes. To the degree that a tax paid on profits to a foreign government is treated as a tax credit, the net effect of a company paying taxes on its profits in a foreign country is that these taxes are essentially paid for by the U.S. government foregoing an equivalent amount of U.S. source based tax revenue.

Obviously, taxes paid to foreign governments must pass certain criteria set forth by the Internal Revenue Service to be considered for a tax credit. Foreign tax credits apply to taxes paid on foreign source profits calculated in a conventional way as U.S. source profits. Tax credits are also available for foreign government withholding taxes on dividends, interest payments, and royalties paid by a foreign-based affiliate to a U.S. parent company.

There is a maximum permissible limit on tax credits linked to the ratio of foreign source income to total worldwide income multiplied by the tax liability of U.S. operations. This effectively limits the foreign tax credit to the U.S., not the foreign, tax rate. A company doing business in a nation with a higher tax rate on profits than in the United States does not receive a tax credit equal to the taxes paid to the foreign government.

The tax credit is based on the U.S. tax rate. With U.S. tax rates being lower than in most other industrialized nations, U.S. based global companies are not being fully compensated by tax credits on foreign income taxes. This may provide an incentive to shift taxable income back to the United States through changes in transfer prices. The U.S. tax authorities permit a credit for taxes paid on profits to other nations under the notion of tax equity and tax neutrality.

The principle of tax equity implies that a U.S. taxpaying entity with an operation in another nation should not pay more in taxes than having the operation domiciled in the United States. Were the equity principle absolutely true, a U.S. taxpaying entity would be indifferent, or neutral, to whether the operation was located in another nation or in the United States. Some maintain that the U.S. tax code does not adhere to the tax neutrality principle because a company doing business in New York City does not obtain a tax credit on its federal taxes for taxes paid to the state and city of New York on profits made in their jurisdiction.

A company with an affiliate in another nation not only receives a tax credit, which neutralizes its foreign and U.S. income taxes, but does not have to pay U.S. taxes on its foreign source earnings until those earnings are remitted to the parent in the form of a dividend, a royalty payment, or an equivalent thereof. As long as foreign source profits remain in the coffers of the affiliate, no taxes are due to the U.S. government, even though, under special circumstances, the affiliate may lend these funds to the parent company.

Deferral of dividend payments is essentially an interest-free loan made by the U.S. government to the foreign affiliate of a U.S. parent company on the amount of U.S. taxes due if, and when, these funds are repatriated to the U.S. parent. The principles of equity and neutrality built into the U.S. tax code were designed to provide an incentive for U.S. firms to invest overseas as part of the national policy of rebuilding war-torn nations. U.S. companies would be better off confining their activities within the United States, and would not invest in foreign affiliates, if the profits of these foreign affiliates were exposed to double taxation.

Qualified foreign taxes, which cannot be utilized as tax credits, may be used as a tax deduction. A tax deduction is not as valuable as a tax credit. Tax deductions apply when there are not sufficient U.S. taxes to be shielded by tax credits, or where the overall limitation on tax credits has been exceeded. Tax deductions can be carried back or carried forward, whichever is more useful.

REIN VOICING CENTERS

Some companies have set up rein voicing centers to manage all intra company trading of products. A rein voicing centre is at a single location, buying the output of the manufacturing affiliates and selling it to the marketing affiliates. Each affiliate receives or pays in its own currency, thus concentrating all intra company transaction currency exposure at the rein voicing centre.

The centre possesses the necessary data to assess the net currency exposure of intra company transactions and can enter into appropriate currency hedges. The centre may also receive better quotes from currency exchange dealers because all intra company currency exchange transactions are done at one location. The rein voicing centre can mark up the price of all products flowing through the centre to cover its administrative expenses. If there is little or no profitability associated with the operations of a rein voicing centre, it does not matter where the rein voicing centre is located from a tax viewpoint. However, it is possible to increase the markup to the point where corporate profit can be diverted from the nations where the goods are manufactured and marketed to the nation where the rein voicing centre is located. Now the location of the rein voicing centre is critical from a tax viewpoint.

In the 1960s, the U.S. government became concerned with the accumulation of profits in rein voicing centers located in tax havens. Tax havens were characterized as nations imposing no, or a very low, tax on profits, having a high degree of bank secrecy, and little or no currency controls. These nations consider financial activities of importance to their economy, provide modern communication facilities, and promote themselves as offshore financial centers.

Bahamas, Bermuda, Cayman Islands, Liberia, Panama, and Vanuatu have been identified as tax havens. It is possible to "run" a rein voicing centre through these nations without a physical presence of personnel or products. Profits can be easily diverted to tax havens by increasing the markup on selling prices, thus reducing tax liabilities to the nations where the products are manufactured and marketed.

If the criterion for determining a tax haven is satisfied, then the income earned by a rein voicing centre, or any corporate entity in the declared tax haven, is deemed Subpart F income. This income flows directly to the U.S. parent corporation and is taxed as though the income was earned in the United States.

TAXATION IMPACT ON TRANSFER PRICING

Companies operating in the United States are guided by Section 482 of the Internal Revenue Code when setting transfer prices. Specifically, the IRS, through the Secretary of the Treasury, has the right to "distribute, apportion, or allocate gross income, deductions, credits, or allowances... between or among... businesses, if he determines that such distribution, apportionment, or allocation is necessary in order to prevent evasion of taxes. The IRS has been granted wide latitude to do whatever it wants if the IRS deems that dealings between a U.S. parent and its affiliates do not meet its standards. For instance, the IRS can reallocate income and deductions if loans have been made between a parent corporation and an affiliate at an unrealistic interest rate. Unrealistic interest rates are those that would not occur for similar transactions between unrelated third parties.

This also applies to charging for services and use of property, and transfers of tangible and intangible property including lease payments and royalties. A reference to IRS guidelines has already been made in discussing R&D and intangible costs in setting transfer prices by the production cost approach. Basing transfer pricing on published data rather than corporate derived prices is another example of the close working relationship, voluntary or not, between tax authorities and managers responsible for transfer prices.

In general, the IRS standard for determining transfer pricing, and other dealings between a parent and its affiliates, is whether it is an "arm's-length" transaction—one that would occur between a company and a third party having no affiliation other than the commercial transaction under consideration. This is independent of whether the transfer price is based on the cost of production or on market prices.

If the transfer price between affiliates is seemingly out of line with a price that would have been charged to an unrelated party, then the IRS has the right to reallocate income or deductions according to what it feels to be the appropriate transfer price.

The IRS specifies various methods for establishing an appropriate transfer price. The preferred one is the comparable uncontrolled price method where prices are the same for goods sold to affiliate and to nonaffiliated companies.

The price for goods sold to an unrelated third party establishes the transfer price for goods transferred to an affiliate.

This method does not work when goods are not sold to third parties, but are totally transferred between affiliates. Under these circumstances, the second method for setting the transfer price is the resale price method. This is the price for which the company would sell the item to an unspecified third party. The third party would add the same comparable value as the affiliate and sell the completed product with an appropriate markup.

By netting the market price of the appropriate markup and the value added to the product by an affiliate, one can "back into" an appropriate transfer price from the point of view of the tax authority. The third method is the "cost plus" method, where the IRS permits three different ways of allocating costs (full absorption, direct cost, and incremental cost).

All these methods leave some margin of discretion as to what is the appropriate transfer price. If all these fail, as they frequently do for high-technology products, customised components, or subassemblies, then so-called fourth methods are permitted, such as determining transfer pricing on the basis of a predetermined profit for the foreign firm's operations and, through a netting process of accounting for applicable costs, establishing an appropriate transfer price.

Regardless of the methodology, the burden of proof in supporting a transfer price is with the taxpayer, not the IRS.

To confuse matters more, there have been occasions when the tax courts have rejected the notion of arm's-length transfer pricing in settling tax disputes between corporations and the IRS.

OTHER NATIONS' POLICIES CONCERNING TRANSFER PRICING

The tax authority in Canada views transfer pricing of goods similar to the way the United States does. Transfer pricing for services differs in that it is based on a pro rata sharing of actual incurred costs between the parent corporation and its affiliate, and not necessarily at an arm's-length price. Tax authorities in Japan follow a system comparable to that of the United States.

German tax code provisions permit the reallocation of domestic source income if revenue or income has been shifted to another nation through a transaction that is different from those that would have been entered into by unrelated parties. In other words, transfer pricing should be arm's-length, although the code is not specific in defining arm's-length pricing.

The United Kingdom is similar to Germany in not specifically defining arm's-length pricing. The Inland Revenue may adjust taxable income based on fairness and arm's-length criteria. Disputes between corporations and Inland

Revenue agents are frequently settled by negotiation, resulting in some sort of compromise between the two parties. This is unlike in Germany, where the adjustments made by the tax authorities are considered final, and unlike in the United States, where adjustments are litigated in tax courts.

Tax authorities in many nations are currently taking a much closer look at transfer pricing practices. Recently, the U.K. Inland Revenue recast the accounts of one non-British company operating in the United Kingdom and assessed back taxes of nearly 2 billion pounds. In the United States, there is growing political pressure for the IRS to take more vigorous action against foreign-owned companies operating through U.S. based affiliates.

This pressure stems from the realization that the aggregate expenses for foreign-owned businesses operating in the United States exceed aggregate revenues. This means that, in the aggregate, foreign-owned subsidiaries are claiming to operate at a loss, although individual foreign-owned subsidiaries may be paying taxes on profits.

Some foreign-owned affiliates operating in the United States have a twenty-year string of consecutive losses. This is not considered a realistic appraisal of performance because there are few profit-motivated foreign-based parent companies that would support twenty years of successive losses were they real. Poor or nonexistent profits for foreign-based affiliates operating in the United States are blamed on transfer pricing.

Transfer price manipulation is felt to have resulted in tax underpayments of between $12 and $50 billion. Legislation was passed in 1989 to require foreign-owned businesses in the United States to keep records, in English, of transactions with foreign related parties. Much of this legislation has to do with substantiating transfer pricing on either a cost or arm's length transaction with an unrelated third party.

A growing risk associated with manipulating transfer prices for the purpose of tax minimization. The risk is that the tax authorities will recast the company's statements with their own version of the proper transfer price, thus exposing a company to the risk of double taxation. Most nations have entered into tax treaties with various other nations with regard to taxing of affiliates of parent organizations domiciled in the treaty nations.

These treaties determine withholding taxes on dividends, interest, and royalties; relief from double taxation; and the types of taxes and organizations covered by the treaty. Overall exposure to taxation can be reduced by judicious structuring of the legal corporate entities of a parent company and its affiliates in accordance with the provisions of these treaties.

Some of these treaties contain formal agreements for the mutual examination of the tax returns of affiliates of a parent company. The tax returns of affiliates and parent organizations are exchanged and examined by the tax authorities to determine correct tax liabilities, detect tax avoidance maneuvers, scrutinize transfer pricing practices, and exchange information useful to the tax authorities.

These treaties also provide a forum for one tax authority to complain about the actions taken by another, when these actions are deemed detrimental to its interests. Recent developments in international cooperation of tax authorities include the establishment of a formal agreement on transfer prices.

The mutual agreement of various nations to reference a published source for tanker rates in determining oil company tax liabilities is an example of this. Australia and the United States are attempting to grant "advance determinations" of the proper transfer price for Australian companies' dealings with their U.S. affiliates. A recent survey has shown that about half of IRS tax examinations of multinational companies involve transfer prices. If a mutually agreeable methodology could be arranged between a company and the IRS, many of these tax examinations could be eliminated. The IRS is attempting to develop a procedure whereby a company and the IRS would mutually agree to a transfer-pricing agreement covering the distribution of finished goods, sales of raw materials and components, general and administrative expenses, and managerial and technical services.

If the taxpayer develops an acceptable transfer-pricing methodology, then the taxpayer and the IRS would enter into an advance-pricing agreement. The IRS would limit its examinations to an audit to ensure that the taxpayer has complied with the agreement. However, the taxpayer is obliged to submit pricing data of independent transactions, or an adequate substitute, to show that the transfer price possesses the necessary attributes of an arm's-length transaction.

The taxpayer is also responsible to show that the agreed transfer-pricing methodology is generating acceptable transfer prices from an arm's-length perspective. The preference of tax authorities in many nations for arm's-length transfer pricing may act as an inducement to switch from the cost-of-production to the market price approach in setting transfer prices because, presumably, they are one and the same.

The financial and taxation departments of multinational, or global, companies must deal daily with what are considered to be the most pressing issues in international accounting today. Those involved with transfer pricing must measure the consequences of their transfer-pricing decisions both on corporate profits and on current and potential tax liabilities.

Potential tax liabilities, stemming from tax authorities rejecting management's transfer price decisions, and substituting their own, are enormous. This must weigh heavily on the shoulders of those responsible for setting transfer prices.

TRANSFER PRICING AND TAXATION

A small operation managed by a few individuals was the typical beginning of a large corporation with a hundred operating affiliates dispersed around the world. Decision making was highly centralized and lines of communication were short.

As the company grew, the founding management team found it more difficult to keep matters under control. This problem was greatly exacerbated when operations within the company became physically separated. Centres of activity in different locations called for a different style of management. Funneling of all decisions from diverse locations through a small group of individuals, who no longer possess the necessary intimate awareness of the circumstances surrounding each decision, is a surefire prescription for stifling growth.

Growth is the name of the game for modern corporations. Growth entails individual operating affiliates taking appropriate action to enhance productivity, market share, and the scope of a company's product line. It has been found that operating affiliates physically separated from the parent organization can best achieve these objectives under a decentralized style of management.

Responsibility now falls on the shoulders of the manager of an operating affiliate to make the necessary decisions that will lead to improved financial results, the universal measure of performance. The parent organization takes on a new role as coordinator and monitor of activities now that responsibility for operations has been transferred to the operating units. Far from playing a passive role, the parent organization focuses its attention on optimizing the performance of its semiautonomous operating affiliates. To do this, the parent organization must establish, and articulate, a set of strategic goals and allocate limited corporate resources to the various operating affiliates to best achieve these goals. It must ensure that the short-term action plans of the operating affiliates are in accord with its long-term plans.

Top management positions in the operating affiliates must be filled with individuals capable of leading their affiliates in the right direction and an incentive system must be set up to induce managers to orient their thinking to the goals of the company. Finally, the parent organization must set up a financial reporting and control system to monitor its global operations, to provide necessary information for the making of decisions and to evaluate the performance of the affiliate managers.

Although operating affiliates appear to be semiautono-mous units in that they are given a wide spectrum of decision-making responsibility in managing their local operations, they are not independent centres of corporate activity. They are often united in manufacturing and marketing a common product line, in the course of which they routinely buy and sell finished goods, components, or raw materials from one another. These intra company exchanges of goods, components, and raw materials require a transfer price. The parent organization sets the transfer price after considering various factors with an eye on optimizing corporate perfor-mance as a whole.

Transfer prices are often not negotiated and agreed on by the actual buyers and sellers of the goods and components being shipped between operating affiliates. Yet transfer prices directly affect the revenue and cost of goods sold, and therefore, the profitability of the operating affiliates. Because the affiliate managers are monitored by a financial reporting and control system that scrutinizes their financial results, one can expect that affiliate managers have an entirely different perspective on transfer pricing than the executives of the parent organization. Transfer pricing can easily embroil executives of the parent organization and the managers of operating affiliates in endless disputes. Some firms have even established an administrative panel for reviewing transfer prices to resolve sharp differences of opinion between those responsible for managing operating affiliates and those responsible for setting transfer prices.

TRANSFER PRICES AND TAXES

A global company with operations in many nations must deal with a new dimension of complexity in establishing transfer prices, which is not present when a company operates solely within the confines of a single nation. A company whose operations are within a single nation pays the same taxes on profits regardless of the transfer pricing policy. The consolidation process, whether for financial or tax accounting purposes, eliminates intra company transactions to arrive at either a book profit or a before-tax profit. When a company transacts business through affiliate companies in different nations, however, transfer pricing provides a mechanism for shifting taxable profits between tax jurisdictions.

Tax authorities in various nations are concerned with the notion that transfer pricing, often set by parent organizations outside their jurisdiction, is based on minimizing taxes paid in their jurisdictions. There certainly is an element of truth in this contention, but there are other considerations in administering transfer prices than minimizing taxes. The setting of transfer prices provides a way of moving funds internationally for a variety of purposes, of circumventing currency exchange controls that threaten to choke the operations of a company, of minimizing the deleterious impact of other artificial barriers to trade such as duties and tariffs, and of reducing currency risk exposure.

A transfer pricing policy attempts to satisfy a multiple set of objectives. Some of these objectives call for high transfer prices, whereas others require low transfer prices. A company must select what it considers to be an optimal transfer price, which is a compromise price for best achieving divergent objectives. This optimal transfer price may not be the one that minimizes taxes on profits. The selected transfer price may not be satisfactory both to the local tax authority and to the manager of an affiliate if it reduces the reported profitability of the affiliate. However, setting the transfer price is critical to optimizing the financial performance of the corporation as a whole, given the conditions that prevail at a point in time.

MINIMIZING TAXES

Tax authorities of most countries have guidelines or controls that are expected to be complied with in setting transfer prices. Management is not free to arbitrarily select transfer prices without having to substantiate their transfer price decisions. Nevertheless, there is still an element of choice where a selected transfer price may reduce the tax burden of a company. Suppose that a company consists of a parent organization and two operating affiliates—one in nation A, where the tax rate on profits is 30 per cent, and one in nation B, where the tax rate on profits is 40 per cent. The tax is applied to each affiliate's gross margin for illustrative purposes. The affiliate in nation A makes a product that is entirely sold through the affiliate in nation B. Two cases are considered—a low and a high transfer price.

Table. Case I-Low Transfer Price

	Nation A	Nation B	Consolidated
	Tax 30%	Tax 40%	
Sales	$2000	$3200	$3200
Cost of Goods Sold	1500	2000	1500
Gross Margin	500	1200	1700
Tax	150	480	630
Net Income	$350	$720	$1070

Everything made in a factory in nation A is sold through a marketing organization in nation B. Therefore, total sales in nation A, calculated on the basis of an administered transfer price, is also the cost of goods sold in nation B. Sales in nation B of $3,200 is the net consolidated sales for the company, because all goods produced in nation A are sold in nation B. The actual cost of manufacturing the goods in nation A is $1,500. Because nation B does not add value to the goods, the consolidated cost of goods sold for the company is also $1,500. The consolidated tax is the sum of the $150 and the $480 paid to the tax authorities of nations A and B, respectively. The consolidated net income is $1,070, the sum of the net incomes of the two affiliates.

Suppose that the transfer price is increased from $2,000 to $2,500 for goods shipped between the two affiliates. Consolidated sales, cost of goods sold, and gross margin are unaffected by the change in the transfer price, because it is netted out in the consolidation process. Taxes paid in each nation are no longer the same because of the change in the transfer price. In case II, the increase in the transfer price shifts the profit to Nation A, which has the lower tax rate.

The affiliate in nation A earns more taxable income and pays more in taxes than in case I. The affiliate in nation B earns less taxable income and pays less in taxes in case II than in case I. The net effect, as seen by comparing case II with case I, is that the company as a whole is paying less in taxes, which increases its consolidated net income.

It is true that had the two nations the same tax rate, the total taxes paid by the company, and the consolidated net income, would not be affected by changes in the transfer price. Even so, transfer prices determine what portion of total taxes are to be paid to the tax authority in nation A and to the tax authority in Nation B. Although the parent organization may be relatively insensitive concerning to whom it pays taxes, needless to say, the tax authorities are very much concerned as to which is collecting taxes. The problem is compounded, from the point of view of a tax authority, because the transfer price is probably set by a parent organization not under its jurisdiction. The importance of transfer pricing to both managers and tax authorities can be appreciated when it is realised that between 40 per cent and 60 per cent of international trade involves goods moving between affiliates of the same company. Corporate decisions on transfer prices do have a meaningful impact on what a tax jurisdiction collects.

There are nations, islands, and localities where tax authorities exhibit little interest in transfer prices. Ireland, Puerto Rico, and other nations or areas designated as free trade zones or having special tax privileges may not tax corporate profits, or have a very low tax rate. These nations or locales are interested in companies building plants on their soil for the social benefits that accrue from employment of individuals who might otherwise be unemployed. Companies operating in such nations or locales can substantially decrease their overall tax rate. The effective reduction in tax rates depends on the transfer prices of imported components and semifinished goods and the transfer prices of exported finished goods. Granting tax concessions is one way for a nation to attract companies. At this time, eastern European nations offer tax incentives but do not have a prescribed accounting methodology to calculate profits, which makes it impossible to quantify the tax benefit. More than one company has set up an operation in eastern Europe to later discover that the government had a much different version in mind of the nature of the tax benefits than the investors anticipated. Such shortsightedness by government officials has a deleterious impact on attracting other companies.

Many nations are discovering that viewing business solely as a way to fill the public coffers may not be in their long-term best interests. Within the United States, states with high corporate tax rates have experienced companies moving to states with low corporate tax rates.

The higher they raise their corporate tax rates, the less they collect in taxes. As once companies moved from one state to another, now they move from one nation to another. In selecting a potential site, a businessman considers many factors, of which taxes are but one. Some of these are social and political stability; a system of commercial law to resolve disputes; a set of acceptable accounting practices (both to assess tax liabilities and evaluate tax incentives); a labour force with the requisite skills and will to work; and an infrastructure of transportation, communication, and utility and social (education, medical care) services.

There are more locations that offer good potential sites for factories than before. Managers no longer feel that their factories must be anchored to one nation and have learned to manage far-flung operations.

Nations must now compete for factories. Tax authorities in developed nations are beginning to realise that they may end up collecting less tax revenue in their eagerness to collect more tax revenue by raising tax rates. The United States was forced to repeal a luxury tax on pleasure boats because pleasure boat construction virtually ceased with the passage of the new tax. New Jersey was forced to repeal a sales tax on trucks when truck selling companies moved their operations to nearby Pennsylvania. In both cases, tax revenues fell when tax rates were raised, and the tax authorities were forced to rescind tax increases. In a global economy, companies are mobile and will relocate to avoid especially burdensome taxes.

INTERNATIONAL FUNDING

Businesses operating in hard currency nations have the advantage of being able to transfer and convert currencies as necessary. Many nations, however, have currencies that lack convertibility, the so-called soft currencies. Transfer pricing provides a means of moving funds from one country to another, when direct currency convertibility is not possible.

If a nation has an affiliate that completes the manufacturing process and sells its output within that nation, funds can be moved out of that nation by increasing the transfer price for goods imported by the affiliate. The same objective can be accomplished by increasing the charges for services rendered by the parent organization to the affiliate, such as selling and administrative fees, research and development expenses, financial charges on transferred assets, and royalties for rights to patents and dividends. Sometimes currency exchange controls focus on the amount of dividends that can be paid by an affiliate to its parent. A quasi-dividend can be paid by raising the transfer price of goods moving into the nation or by increasing corporate fees, financial charges, and royalty payments.

Some nations with severe restrictions on dividend outflows will permit increases in transfer prices and service fees. These quasi-dividend payments are allowed because the local government recognizes that few companies can afford the luxury of investing in a nation that prohibits the company from earning a return on its investment. However, actions such as these that drain funds out of a soft currency nation eventually result in some sort of currency exchange restriction. This often results in affiliate profits accumulating in a currency that may not be particularly desirable. Sometimes currency exchange restrictions can be bypassed by the affiliate making an investment, or lending funds, to an affiliate in another nation.

CONTROLLING REPORTED PROFITS

Shifts in transfer prices, corporate administrative fees, and other parent company charges to an affiliate are means of managing the affiliate's reported profitability. It may be in the interest of a parent organization to lower the reported profitability of an affiliate for reasons other than tax minimization.

These include deflecting union demands for higher wages, reducing political pressure to nationalize or expropriate a profitable affiliate, and dissuading potential competitors from entering the market. Lowering profitability is also a way to counter price controls that limit profitability. If a government has set price controls based on the cost of production plus a limited markup for profits, increases in the transfer price of goods sent to the affiliate lowers the profit margin of goods sold in that nation. This may permit goods to be sold at government decreed profit margins with the company as a whole still able to earn its normal profits.

A few nations have tax rates that are linked to profitability. The greater the profitability, the higher the tax rate. The logic behind this taxation policy is that there is a level of profits on investment that seems"excessive" to the government. Such excessive profitability should be punished by the government, and there is no greater punishment than taking away the excess profits through a higher tax rate. By increasing the transfer price of goods being imported into the nation, the degree of profitability is decreased, lowering the tax rate and, presumably, restoring respectability in the eyes of the government. Alternatively, it may be in the interests of the parent organization to enhance the profitability of an affiliate. This may be done by lowering the transfer price

of imported goods. One reason for enhancing the profitability of an affiliate is to provide sufficient financial resources to the affiliate for it to withstand price cutting by competitive companies. Improving an affiliate's profitability, even at the cost of paying more in taxes, may allow the affiliate to borrow needed funds for operation from local banks and other financial institutions, to improve its credit rating to qualify for lower interest loans and to fund capital outlays from its own resources.

CIRCUMVENTING EXCHANGE CONTROLS

Governments with soft currencies often limit the amount of their currency that companies operating in their nations can exchange for other currencies. Their motivation is to discourage the selling of the domestic soft currency and the buying of a hard currency, which would exert downward pressure on the value of the local currency. In other words, exchange controls are set up to keep a soft currency from becoming softer.

From the point of view of a parent organization, restricting hard currency outflows inhibits an affiliate's ability to pay for imported components or other items necessary for its operations. Transfer prices for the needed components can be kept artificially low to expand the volume of goods that are being imported into a soft currency nation. This sustains an affiliate's manufacturing operation without exceeding government decreed restrictions on converting soft currency to hard currency. But there is an adverse consequence because such a course of action results in a parent corporation accumulating even larger amounts of soft currency. These holdings of soft currency are constantly losing purchasing power through inflation.

The soft currency cannot be converted to a more desirable currency because of currency exchange restrictions and the soft currency, which has little value within the nation, has no value outside the nation. One of the knottiest problems associated with an operating affiliate in a soft currency nation is funding of hard currency imports necessary for its operation and obtaining a hard currency return on a hard currency investment.

Some companies will not set up an operation in a soft currency nation unless there is a prearranged means to earn hard currency to pay for hard currency imports and to provide a hard currency return on a hard currency investment.

Pepsi Cola struck a barter deal for producing its soft drink in the former Soviet Union. Its soft ruble revenue, net of soft ruble expenses, is exchanged for Russian built tankers, which are then sold for hard currencies. Oil companies will not set up operations in the Commonwealth of Independent States, and other soft currency nations, unless they receive a share of the output, which is shipped out of the nation and sold for hard currency.

The easiest way for a company to earn hard currency in a soft currency nation would be to export a portion of its output to hard currency nations. However, most soft currency nations do not permit the hard currency revenue to remain with the company. The hard currency revenue is exchanged for an equivalent amount of soft currency, which is then credited to the exporter's bank account.

In essence, the national government receives the hard currency revenue from exports and pays soft currency to the exporter. Sometimes international banks are at fault for imposing this condition on a nation as a means to guarantee repayment of international debt. Regardless of whether the nation or the international banks impose this condition, it is self-defeating because the economic development of a developing nation is held back by the inability of companies to earn sufficient hard currency to justify their investments.

MINIMIZING DUTIES AND TARIFFS

Duties and tariffs imposed on goods imported into a nation can be reduced by lowering the transfer price. This is the exact opposite of reducing taxes on profits by increasing the transfer price. Because the tariff rate is usually less than the tax rate on profits, lowering transfer prices to reduce import tariffs often results in a higher tax on profits.

In some nations, however, tariffs on certain imported goods and commodities are not set by a corporate-determined transfer price but by an internationally posted price. This can be done only for generic goods or commodities (oil), where there is an active market with published and verifiable prices. Sometimes tax authorities will reference costs not to a "transfer price" cost but to an internationally agreed standard. One example of this is tanker rates in the oil business. An oil company can manage the profitability, and therefore, the tax liability, of a refinery by the transfer price associated with international tanker transportation for moving oil to and from a refinery.

The tax authorities of many nations and the oil companies have agreed to a panel of experts determining a fair and representative tanker rate that is used for the computation of taxes independent of the transfer price, or internal cost, that oil companies charge for shipping oil among their affiliates. This eliminates arguments between tax authorities and oil companies concerning the appropriate shipping charge.

Determining the optimal transfer-pricing policy is further complicated when a nation in which an affiliate operates has an export subsidy programme or provides a tax credit on the value of exports. It may be advantageous to lower transfer prices to an affiliate whose output is exported to third parties or other affiliates in other nations to take advantage of these tax incentives.

The optimal transfer price depends on the nature of the export subsidy or tax credit, the volume of the affiliate's output that is exported from the nation, the relationship between taxes on profits and the generation of tax credits and on the capacity of the affiliate to utilize the tax credit or export subsidy.

The nature of the taxes paid in a nation in the form of income taxes, duties and tariffs on imported goods, and export subsidies or tax credits on exported goods influence the setting of transfer prices.

There is no hard and fast rule on whether a high or a low transfer-pricing policy is best for a company. The particular circumstances of a company's operations in a nation and the nature of taxes and subsidies determine the best transfer-pricing policy.

A transferpricing system integrated into a financial reporting and control system should be capable of analyzing "what" if scenarios to evaluate the effect of different transfer-pricing policies.

REDUCING CURRENCY EXCHANGE RISK

Changes in currency exchange rates result in transaction and translation gains and losses. More importantly, they affect the competitive position of an affiliate. If an affiliate manufactures and markets its goods in a nation, and imports components from another nation, a revaluation of the currency where the finished goods are being sold relative to the currency of its purchased components reduces manufacturing costs.

This makes the affiliate more competitive and profitable. A devaluation, on the other hand, increases the cost of imported components, making the affiliate less competitive and less profitable.

Reality is much more complex than this simple example because affiliates may export and import components and finished goods to and from a variety of nations. Changes in exchange rates benefit some affiliates and hurt others, and it may not be obvious because of the nature of buying and selling of goods and services.

It is possible that a change in currency exchange rates that is adverse to a particular affiliate may be beneficial to the company as a whole because of the nature of the net exposure of the company to the affected currencies. Adjustments to transfer prices may affect currency holdings before an anticipated change in exchange rates takes place and may be able to restore a company's competitive position after the change has taken place.

Therefore, a financial reporting and control system should have the capacity to assess changes to both transfer prices and currency exchange rates to enable the parent organization to respond both to anticipated changes in currency exchange rates and to subsequent shifts in its competitive position.

TRANSFER PRICING AND JOINT VENTURES

A joint venture partner, a local partner owning a portion of an affiliate, and a minority shareholder are going to be as interested in transfer pricing as the local tax authority. Less often, a partnership is structured on the basis of a claim, or royalty, on revenue. More often, it is a claim on profits.

If one party to a venture or partnership can influence revenue, costs, and profitability through transfer pricing, then the other party or partner, or a minority shareholder, will be deservedly concerned. One way to manage transfer pricing with regard to having partners or minority shareholders is to formalize the setting of transfer prices in some verifiable manner such as a set markup above costs, another is to reference transfer prices to an observable market transaction.

Either way minimizes the opportunity for one party to a partnership or joint venture to manipulate transfer prices to its advantage. If the partners, participants, and minority shareholders feel that their interests are vulnerable by virtue of the other party to a business venture controlling transfer prices, then they may not contribute to the venture that which was expected of them.

Avoiding these problems can be more easily said than done. Some years ago, Ford Motor Company purchased the minority shares of its partially owned subsidiaries because the company felt that it could not administer transfer pricing in a way that was fair to all concerned.

Some managements have made the strategic decision not to enter into joint ventures, or have local partners or minority shareholdings in corporate affiliates, where they can manage the profitability of the venture through transfer prices. Sometimes, the solution for a problem is to avoid the problem.

TRANSFER PRICING AND MANAGERIAL PERFORMANCE EVALUATION

It may be in the interest of the corporation as a whole to transfer in components that are more highly priced than those an affiliate can purchase from other sources. It may be in the interest of the corporation as a whole to transfer goods made in one affiliate to another affiliate for less than what the affiliate can sell them for to third parties. Although the corporation may gain by such a set of transfer prices for goods moving among affiliates, it does not serve the interests of the affiliate managers if they are subsequently judged on profitability. This dichotomy of purpose in establishing a transfer-pricing policy for the good of the whole company, yet holding managers of affiliates accountable for profits that are contaminated, so to speak, by transfer prices has not been successfully addressed when transfer prices are different from market prices.

In fact, this is one potent argument in favour of companies having transfer pricing policies based on the market price for comparable goods. If transfer prices are set at the price for goods exchanged between unrelated parties, then there is no dichotomy of purpose in setting transfer prices and measuring performance. Managers of affiliates can be judged in an unbiased fashion on the profitability of their operations because they are buying and selling at market prices—the same prices that would prevail if they were independent companies.

The disadvantage of letting the market set transfer prices is that the parent corporation can no longer utilize transfer pricing as a means to pursue the overall optimization of the financial performance of the corporation. One possible approach to the dysfunctional aspects of setting transfer prices at other than market prices and measuring management performance of affiliates is to isolate and separately state the amount of inter company "profit" or "loss" that each affiliate is experiencing in its transactions with other affiliates. This approach provides the parent organization with information on whether an affiliate is suffering from unwarranted decreased profitability or enjoying unwarranted increased profitability because of transfer pricing.

SETTING TRANSFER PRICES BY COST OF PRODUCTION

There are two general approaches for setting transfer prices: the cost of production and market prices associated with third party, or unrelated, transactions. The cost-of-production approach bases the price of goods to be transferred between affiliates on the variable cost of production, an allowance for fixed costs that are general in nature and are apportioned over the entire product line, and an allowance for fixed costs that can be apportioned among the individual products.

This latter category usually includes research and development costs and selling and administrative costs. The remaining components may include financial fees and royalties associated with tangible and intangible assets to be apportioned to individual products and the selection of an appropriate profit margin.

The variable cost of production includes labour, material, and other direct costs that are consumed in the production of an item. If the policy of the company is to hire and fire factory workers as production rises and falls, then labour is a variable cost. If a company is reluctant to let go of their workers when sales decline, then factory labour should be considered part of fixed costs. Factory labour costs are usually part variable and part fixed. Other variable costs can be the unit financing and utility costs associated with machinery and processes used in the manufacture of a particular product and unit shipping costs. These costs can also be treated as fixed costs depending on how the company's cost accounting system is set up.

Fixed costs are all costs not included in variable costs. Fixed costs are the financing or depreciation costs of the factory; the overhead costs of marketing, accounting, and supervision; the cost of inventories, warehouses, insurance, utilities, communication, property taxes, and other non-variable cost items.

Fixed costs may not be entirely fixed in that there is some variation as production levels change. For instance, bonuses, which would be considered part of the fixed costs of having an executive suite, rise and fall with profits, which are related to production levels. The number of staff personnel in marketing, accounting, engineering, and other overhead functions can vary with the production level.

Some elements of fixed costs are allocated in the transfer price setting mechanism in a way that fairly apportions the fixed cost burden among the various products. Other elements of fixed costs can be apportioned more on the basis of the benefit derived by an individual product. One of these is research and development, where the allocation can be made over a product line in proportion to the degree of RandD expenditures associated with the development of an individual product.

Although there is general agreement that this is a fair way to apportion RandD expenses of successful undertakings, there is lack of agreement on how to apportion RandD expenses for failed projects.

Some maintain that the allocation of expenses associated with failed RandD projects should be apportioned to all products on the basis that every product should bear the risk of failed RandD efforts. Others object on the grounds that had the RandD effort succeeded, a particular product might not have benefited. Therefore, it makes no sense for the transfer price to contain the cost of a failed RandD effort, which, had it succeeded, would not be part of the transfer price of the product.

The question as to the proper treatment of failed RandD projects is not an internal accounting matter. Tax authorities are interested in who takes the write off of a failed RandD project. In the United States, the Internal Revenue Service (IRS) is concerned whether a transfer price contains a provision for failed RandD expenditures.

If a transfer price contains only that portion of RandD expenditures that were successful with regard to a particular product, then failed RandD projects of a U.S. corporation are being written off solely against U.S. income. A portion of the tax loss write-off is passed on to the tax authority of another nation by including an element of failed RandD expenditures in the transfer price.

Another fixed cost element that can be separated and apportioned in a different manner than general fixed costs are services provided to an individual product.

These may be coordination and control expenses associated with a product; costs for enhancing the efficiency of operations for manufacturing the product or expanding the scope of its market; and the costs of recruiting and training of management and operations personnel associated with manufacturing, marketing, and repairing or servicing the product. The allocation of these service costs to individual products provides another element in deriving their transfer prices.

The derivation of the transfer price also includes elements for tangibles and intangibles associated with a product. Tangibles are the plant, equipment, and other physical assets dedicated to the manufacture of the product. Part of the transfer price provides a financial return for tangibles based on their value. Intangibles represent the technical knowledge and expertise and applicable patents that can be allocated to a particular product. The transfer price also contains an element that provides a company with a return on intangibles.

Intangible costs within a transfer price cannot be capriciously determined by management because intangible costs affect taxable profits. For this reason, the IRS has established guidelines for determining the intangible cost element in a transfer price. An intangible cost element must be present if there are intangible costs associated with the manufacture or marketing of a product and must be so identified. Intangible costs can be proportioned in relation to the income attributable to the intangibles by units of production, sales, net or gross profits, or other reasonable methods. The fee for intangible property incorporated in a transfer price must be similar to what would have been arranged with an independent third party.

The last part of the cost approach in setting transfer prices is determining the proper profit margin on the goods made by one affiliate and shipped to another. This may be the average profit margin for the company as a whole or a profit margin associated with a specific product line. Regardless, the stipulated profit margin must be reconciled in some manner with the profitability of the company or a product line to satisfy the tax authorities.

The need for reconciliation of the profit and the various cost elements of the transfer price with the tax authorities sometimes results in the tax group within the finance department of a company being responsible for administering transfer prices.

However, this choice may hinder general management from using transfer prices as a means to achieve corporate objectives. The chief advantage of the cost of production approach for setting transfer prices is that the costs are available and are subject to quantification. For this reason, the production cost approach has been more common in the past than the market price approach.

The chief disadvantage is that there is no real incentive for an affiliate to improve its manufacturing process, to enhance its efficiency, or to take steps to lower costs. Mistakes, errors, inefficiencies in manning or machinery, management inattention to detail, worker carelessness, and excessive remuneration of white and blue collar workers alike may all be incorporated in the determination of costs and passed on to the affiliates in the transfer price. Another disadvantage is that both the tax authority and the affiliates may object to the nature of the apportionment of RandD, SandA, tangibles, and intangibles among the various products and the assigned profit margin.

SETTING TRANSFER PRICES BY MARKET PRICES

The disadvantages associated with the cost-of-production method of setting transfer prices can be mostly avoided by referencing transfer prices to third party transactions for identical, or nearly identical, products.

If an affiliate can obtain the item being purchased from a third party for a certain price, then that price can be the basis for setting the transfer price. The proponents of market-oriented transfer prices maintain that letting the market set the transfer price is inherently more fair than a production-cost-based system because one affiliate is not supporting the inefficiencies of another.

If an affiliate receives only the global competitive price for its products, then there is an incentive for it to take whatever actions are needed to correct the inefficiencies in its operations that are resulting in higher costs.

In a truly decentralized operation, managers are expected to make their decisions on an independent basis, and unrelated companies are permitted to compete for the business of an affiliate, along with other affiliates. The parent organization does not set transfer prices and has little or no influence over the decisions made by the managers of the affiliates. No favour or special consideration is shown to fellow affiliates in the competitive process of selecting suppliers for components and goods. The hope, of course, is that everyone is kept on his or her competitive toes to produce salable goods at the lowest possible cost.

This managerial philosophy, where each affiliate is treated as an independent company, is sometimes referred to as the small business unit (SBU) management philosophy. The disadvantage is that, although each affiliate is focused on optimizing its operations, the end result may be suboptimal performance of the corporation as a whole.

Suppose that affiliate X produces all of a component for a number of widget manufacturing affiliates. Total demand for part X is 2 million per year.

Affiliate X has $10 million in fixed annual costs, which include a profit margin on the investment in manufacturing facilities plus a return on the RandD investment for the development of part X. The variable costs for manufacturing part X is $5. The transfer price based on the fixed and variable costs of affiliate X supplying all other affiliates with part X is $10.

Table. Volume Of Sales: 2,000,000

Fixed Costs	$10,000,000
Variable Costs at $5 per Unit	10,000,000
Total Costs	$20,000,000
Transfer Price Based on Cost of Making 2,000,000	$10.00

Affiliate A is free to cut its best deal and obtains a quote of $9.50 from another company. Affiliate A does what is best for maximizing its profits and purchases 200,000 part X's from a third party for $9.50 rather than pay $10 to affiliate X. Affiliate X has lost a contract for 200,000 part X's and now operates on a basis of a sales volume of 1,800,000 per year.

Table. Volume Of Sales: 1,800,000

Fixed Costs	$10,000,000
Variable Costs at $5 per Unit	9,000,000
Total Costs	$19,000,000
Transfer Price Based on Cost of Making 1,800,000	$10.56

The remaining affiliates must pay a higher price because there is less sales volume to cover the fixed costs of affiliate X. The increase in transfer price to cover the fixed and variable costs is essentially equivalent to treating fixed costs as a component of variable costs, which it is not. Nevertheless, affiliate X must cover all its costs. When affiliate X announces the increase in price, affiliate B concludes a deal with a third party at $9.75 causing another loss of 200,000 for affiliate X.

Table. Volume Of Sales: 1,600.000

Fixed Costs	$10,000,000
Variable Costs at $5 per Unit	8,000,000
Total Costs	$18,000,000
Transfer Price Based on cost of Making 1,600,000	$11.25

Now it's time for affiliate C to say goodbye to affiliate X, as it maximizes its profit by reducing the cost of part X by paying $10.50 to another outside source. This is higher than the $10 price that applied when all the affiliates received part X from affiliate X. It is clear from the continuation of this exercise that, as each affiliate maximizes its profits by cutting costs, the corporation as a whole is being sub optimized. Even if the various affiliates do not pay more than an average price of $10 per unit for part X in purchasing all part X's from outside sources, the global company is stuck with an affiliate with no sales and a fixed annual cost of $10 million that represents, in large measure, financing costs on plant and equipment.

It is highly likely that the fixed costs in affiliate X contain an allowance for RandD expenses and product development that have to be recouped in the operation of a company, but do not have to be recouped by another company if it is essentially manufacturing a copy of part X. Copying is fairly common in global commerce because patent protection is limited to the nation issuing the patent. Global companies often obtain patents in a number of nations, but this may not be possible for all nations.

A company may manufacture a copy of a product in one of these nations. Although it is true that affiliate X is free to pursue patent infringement action against sales in a particular nation where it has patent protection, the time involved in enforcement proceedings and the legal expenses may make such protection prohibitively expensive. Furthermore, there is no internationally recognized legal structure to handle patent infringements.

In addition to RandD expenses, the fixed costs of affiliate X may also contain a service element for the benefit of the affiliates purchasing its output that may not be provided by third parties. By each affiliate "doing its own thing," the RandD and service costs cannot be covered. One principal problem associated with using market reference points for transfer pricing is that the affiliates may be shipping components and parts that are not readily available from other firms. Most components and parts are specifically designed for a company's product line and are not available from third parties unless contracted for by an affiliate. Market prices for similarly designed components that cannot be actually used in the company's product line may not be relevant. Moreover, the quality inherent in third-party quotes for similar parts may not be up to the standards imposed on products made within a global corporate family.

There is no easy answer as to which approach for determining transfer prices should be followed. Both have their adherents and detractors. Either approach restricts transfer prices to something related to third-party, or market, transactions or to the cost of manufacture. Surveys have shown that nations seem to exhibit cultural preferences as to which approach to follow and as to what motivates companies in setting transfer prices.

Companies in some countries favour costbased transfer prices, whereas companies in other nations favour market-based transfer prices. U.S. based corporations have historically preferred setting transfer prices by the cost approach because the necessary data is available, whereas the necessary data for setting transfer prices on the basis of market transactions may not be available. Oftentimes, market quotes for uniquely designed parts and components may have to be derived rather than observed because there are no market transactions for the precise item.

Should General Motors set its transfer price on carburetors being shipped to Europe based on its cost of production or on what Toyota charges its U.S. transplants? The two carburetors are not the same and do not have the same cost of production. Furthermore, there may not be a data base available for prices for carburetors sold between related and unrelated parties from which to derive a market price.

Preferences change with time. Surveys done in the 1970s indicated that the preponderance of U.S. companies were motivated by tax minimization in setting transfer prices. More recent surveys indicate that companies are more interested in setting transfer prices on the basis of measuring the performance of affiliate managers and of providing reliable and unbiased information for the making of decisions.

This change in attitude in U.S. companies may be the result of the United States becoming a relative tax haven compared to other nations. Its corporate tax rate of 34 per cent, plus state taxes, is less than in many other industrialized nations, where tax rates range between 40 per cent and 55 per cent. A U.S. company's total tax bill may, in fact, be reduced by allocating more profits to the United States. Regardless of changes in attitudes as to what is important in setting transfer prices, the essential point is that there is no unanimity on which approach to use and on what motivates companies in setting transfer prices.

Up to this point, an important assumption has been that the parent company has real control over transfer prices to manage corporate cash flows and the profits reported by affiliates and to overcome artificial barriers to trade in the form of custom duties, currency exchange, and price controls. Some recent surveys suggest that competitive forces and market conditions within a nation seem to be more important in setting transfer prices than decisions made by a parent organization. If transfer prices are being set by exogenous commercial forces, then the presumption that a parent organization is able to achieve optimal financial performance of a global family of affiliates through the careful orchestration of transfer pricing is being challenged.

TAX CONSIDERATIONS

Taxation and transfer pricing are intimately entwined, because transfer pricing of goods, parts, and components moving in and out of a nation has a direct impact on taxes on profits and on the amount of duties and tariffs paid to the tax authority. The discussion on transfer pricing based on the cost-of-production approach shows an intimate involvement with the tax authority in the methodology for calculating various elements of the transfer price. There is little uniformity on taxation among nations. Taxes range from taxation of a corporation's activities to the "water's edge" or on its global earnings, the so-called "unitary tax." The state of California invented the unitary tax in the 1930s when movie companies in California began moving out of the state to avoid state taxes. A unitary tax was applied against the global earnings of a company and the tax was determined by the proportion of a company's sales, property, and payroll within the state to its global sales, property, and payroll. The resulting tax had no relation to the degree of profitability of a company's operation in California. A company could operate at a loss in California and still pay a tax based on its global profits.

Needless to say, both foreign governments and multinational companies have vigourously fought the unitary tax. A number of court decisions confirmed or restricted unitary taxation over the years. Ultimately, opposition to the unitary tax succeeded. In November 1991, Alaska was the last state to abandon having a company's state tax liability based on the global earnings of the company. The unitary tax still exists in a truncated form, where earnings are restricted to the "water's edge." The state tax is calculated on the portion of a company's activities within a state as compared to its activities within the United States.

Although most other countries limit their assessment on what is to be taxed to the operations of a company within their jurisdiction, there is no universal agreement as to what constitutes revenue and expenses in the calculation of taxable income and no uniformity on tax rates. Every nation decides what is subject to taxation and the applicable tax rates. The complexity of tax regulations, in general, and the diversity of tax laws among nations are such that it is necessary for an affiliate to retain the technical expertise necessary to understand and comply with local tax regulations. The parent organization must retain the technical knowledge for its own tax jurisdiction and have sufficient knowledge of tax matters elsewhere to coordinate tax planning among the various affiliates.

The vigour with which tax payments are enforced varies among nations. Some countries with seemingly high tax rates permit an underground economy to flourish without much in the way of enforcing tax payments. The other side of the coin is the willingness of companies to adhere to tax laws. In some nations, a businessman who scrupulously follows the tax laws and pays what is owed to the tax authority will find himself at a competitive disadvantage.

NATURE OF TAXES

Taxes can be direct or indirect. The United States relies more on direct taxation, which is applied to each taxable entity. A U.S. corporation is taxed at 34 per cent on its profits. If a corporation pays a dividend to its shareholders, then the next taxable entity, the individual, pays a tax, which may be 28 per cent or more. This is double taxation. Some nations, such as Germany, have two corporate tax rates on profits—one for retained profits and the other for distributed profits in the form of dividends. A lesser tax rate applies to profits that are distributed to shareholders to reduce the degree of double taxation.

Europe relies more on indirect taxes—particularly, the value added tax (VAT). The VAT is basically a tax applied to each stage of the production process and is not directly associated with the degree of profitability. Indeed, only a small portion of a VAT is associated with profits. Suppose that a company's manufacturing operations has the following financial results.

Wages, rents, interest, profit	$400,000
Outside purchases of goods and services for which VAT has already been paid	600,000
Total sales	$1,000,000

The additive method is to apply the VAT rate, say 10 per cent, to all costs associated with the production of goods, including profit and excluding purchases of goods and services from third parties for which the VAT has already been paid. In this case, $400,000 of a company's activities falls into this category resulting in a VAT of $40,000. A simpler method of calculation is to take the gross sales of the company, subtract all purchases of goods and services for which VAT has already been paid, and apply the VAT rate to the balance. Either method yields the same result. The VAT is essentially equivalent to a national sales tax, because every company associated with the production and marketing of goods and providing services pays a tax on whatever value it adds to the goods or services. The value added tax, like a sales tax, is a tax on consumption, whereas U.S. taxes are on income and profits. Value added tax rates vary widely from country to country and according to the nature of the business. Certain European countries have low VAT rates for business transactions associated with food and high VAT rates for luxury products. Others attempt to have one rate that applies to most forms of commerce. Because the VAT is not paid on items that have already been exposed to a value added tax, and with the European economy becoming more integrated, there is a powerful incentive for the European Community to harmonize VAT rates and coordinate the handling of VAT payments for products or components shipped between members of the European Community.

The amounts of value added by a company are frequently disclosed in European financial statements. In the excerpt from the British company, the company had gross revenues of 3,213 million pounds in 1987 of which 919.1 million pounds represents added value by the company. Of the total of 919.1 million pounds of added value, 496.8 million pounds was paid to the company's employees, 157.1 million pounds was paid in taxes to government tax authorities, and the remainder was paid to the internal and external providers of capital.

U.S. TAXATION OF GLOBAL COMPANIES

Nations have different ways of taxing global companies domiciled within their jurisdiction. If a parent corporation is domiciled in the United States, it does not pay taxes in the United States on profits earned by incorporated affiliates in other nations, unless the nation is considered a tax haven. This, in the United States, is known as Subpart F income, which will be discussed later under rein voicing centres.

Unlike an incorporated affiliate, a branch of a U.S. company located in a foreign nation is taxed directly on its earnings regardless of whether the earnings are remitted to the home office or not. The taxes paid on remitted and unremitted earnings are not the same, in that unremitted earnings have to be translated to U.S. dollars before a tax liability can be assessed, and therefore, are influenced by changes in currency exchange rates. Taxes can also be calculated on the basis of the increase in the net worth of the branch, which can also be affected by changes in currency exchange rates. Sometimes a U.S. company will first open a branch operation in another country to permit startup losses to flow back to the parent organization. When the branch becomes profitable, it may be reorganized as a wholly owned subsidiary, reducing the company's overall tax liability.

U.S. based companies usually operate in the global market through operating affiliates whose stock is owned by the parent corporation. The parent corporation pays U.S. taxes only on the profits generated from dividends, royalties, and other service payments and fees paid by a non-U.S. domiciled affiliate to the parent organization. Taxes paid on profits by affiliates in their nations of domicile can be treated either as a tax credit or a tax deduction by the parent organization in the calculation of its U.S. taxes. To the degree that a tax paid on profits to a foreign government is treated as a tax credit, the net effect of a company paying taxes on its profits in a foreign country is that these taxes are essentially paid for by the U.S. government foregoing an equivalent amount of U.S. source based tax revenue.

Obviously, taxes paid to foreign governments must pass certain criteria set forth by the Internal Revenue Service to be considered for a tax credit. Foreign tax credits apply to taxes paid on foreign source profits calculated in a conventional way as U.S. source profits. Tax credits are also available for foreign government withholding taxes on dividends, interest payments, and royalties paid by a foreign-based affiliate to a U.S. parent company. There is a maximum permissible limit on tax credits linked to the ratio of foreign source income to total worldwide income multiplied by the tax liability of U.S. operations. This effectively limits the foreign tax credit to the U.S., not the foreign, tax rate. A company doing business in a nation with a higher tax rate on profits than in the United States does not receive a tax credit equal to the taxes paid to the foreign government.

The tax credit is based on the U.S. tax rate. With U.S. tax rates being lower than in most other industrialized nations, U.S. based global companies are not being fully compensated by tax credits on foreign income taxes. This may provide an incentive to shift taxable income back to the United States through changes in transfer prices.

The U.S. tax authorities permit a credit for taxes paid on profits to other nations under the notion of tax equity and tax neutrality. The principle of tax equity implies that a U.S. taxpaying entity with an operation in another nation should not pay more in taxes than having the operation domiciled in the United States.

Were the equity principle absolutely true, a U.S. taxpaying entity would be indifferent, or neutral, to whether the operation was located in another nation or in the United States. Some maintain that the U.S. tax code does not adhere to the tax neutrality principle because a company doing business in New York City does not obtain a tax credit on its federal taxes for taxes paid to the state and city of New York on profits made in their jurisdiction.

A company with an affiliate in another nation not only receives a tax credit, which neutralizes its foreign and U.S. income taxes, but does not have to pay U.S. taxes on its foreign source earnings until those earnings are remitted to the parent in the form of a dividend, a royalty payment, or an equivalent thereof.

As long as foreign source profits remain in the coffers of the affiliate, no taxes are due to the U.S. government, even though, under special circumstances, the affiliate may lend these funds to the parent company. Deferral of dividend payments is essentially an interest-free loan made by the U.S. government to the foreign affiliate of a U.S. parent company on the amount of U.S. taxes due if, and when, these funds are repatriated to the U.S. parent. The principles of equity and neutrality built into the U.S. tax code were designed to provide an incentive for U.S. firms to invest overseas as part of the national policy of rebuilding war-torn nations. U.S. companies would be better off confining their activities within the United States, and would not invest in foreign affiliates, if the profits of these foreign affiliates were exposed to double taxation.

Qualified foreign taxes, which cannot be utilized as tax credits, may be used as a tax deduction. A tax deduction is not as valuable as a tax credit. Tax deductions apply when there is not sufficient U.S. taxes to be shielded by tax credits, or where the overall limitation on tax credits has been exceeded. Tax deductions can be carried back or carried forward, whichever is more useful.

REIN VOICING CENTRES

Some companies have set up rein voicing centres to manage all intra company trading of products. A rein voicing centre is at a single location, buying the output of the manufacturing affiliates and selling it to the marketing affiliates. Each affiliate receives or pays in its own currency, thus concentrating all intra company transaction currency exposure at the rein voicing centre. The centre possesses the necessary data to assess the net currency exposure of intra company transactions and can enter into appropriate currency hedges. The centre may also receive better quotes from currency exchange dealers because all intra company currency exchange transactions are done at one location.

The rein voicing centre can mark up the price of all products flowing through the centre to cover its administrative expenses. If there is little or no profitability associated with the operations of a rein voicing centre, it does not matter where the rein voicing centre is located from a tax viewpoint. However, it is possible to increase the markup to the point where corporate profit can be diverted from the nations where the goods are manufactured and marketed to the nation where the rein voicing centre is located. Now the location of the rein voicing centre is critical from a tax viewpoint.

In the 1960s, the U.S. government became concerned with the accumulation of profits in rein voicing centres located in tax havens. Tax havens were characterized as nations imposing no, or a very low, tax on profits, having a high degree of bank secrecy, and little or no currency controls. These nations consider financial activities of importance to their economy, provide modern communication facilities, and promote themselves as offshore financial centres. Bahamas, Bermuda, Cayman Islands, Liberia, Panama, and Vanuatu have been identified as tax havens.

It is possible to "run" a rein voicing centre through these nations without a physical presence of personnel or products. Profits can be easily diverted to tax havens by increasing the markup on selling prices, thus reducing tax liabilities to the nations where the products are manufactured and marketed. If the criteria for determining a tax haven is satisfied, then the income earned by a rein voicing centre, or any corporate entity in the declared tax haven, is deemed Subpart F income. This income flows directly to the U.S. parent corporation and is taxed as though the income was earned in the United States.

TAXATION IMPACT ON TRANSFER PRICING

Companies operating in the United States are guided by Section 482 of the Internal Revenue Code when setting transfer prices. Specifically, the IRS, through the Secretary of the Treasury, has the right to "distribute, apportion, or allocate gross income, deductions, credits, or allowances... between or among... businesses, if he determines that such distribution, apportionment, or allocation is necessary in order to prevent evasion of taxes. The IRS has been granted wide latitude to do whatever it wants if the IRS deems that dealings between a U.S. parent and its affiliates do not meet its standards. For instance, the IRS can reallocate income and deductions if loans have been made between a parent corporation and an affiliate at an unrealistic interest rate.

Unrealistic interest rates are those that would not occur for similar transactions between unrelated third parties. This also applies to charging for services and use of property, and transfers of tangible and intangible property including lease payments and royalties. A reference to IRS guidelines has already been made in discussing RandD and intangible costs in setting transfer prices by the production cost approach. Basing transfer pricing on published data rather than corporate derived prices is another example of the close working relationship, voluntary or not, between tax authorities and managers responsible for transfer prices.

In general, the IRS standard for determining transfer pricing, and other dealings between a parent and its affiliates, is whether it is an "arm's-length" transaction—one that would occur between a company and a third party having no affiliation other than the commercial transaction under consideration. This is independent of whether the transfer price is based on the cost of production or on market prices. If the transfer price between affiliates is seemingly out of line with a price that would have been charged to an unrelated party, then the IRS has the right to reallocate income or deductions according to what it feels to be the appropriate transfer price.

The IRS specifies various methods for establishing an appropriate transfer price. The preferred one is the comparable uncontrolled price method where prices are the same for goods sold to affiliated and to nonaffiliated companies. The price for goods sold to an unrelated third party establishes the transfer price for goods transferred to an affiliate.

This method does not work when goods are not sold to third parties, but are totally transferred between affiliates. Under these circumstances, the second method for setting the transfer price is the resale price method. This is the price for which the company would sell the item to an unspecified third party. The third party would add the same comparable value as the affiliate and sell the completed product with an appropriate markup. By netting the market price of the appropriate markup and the value added to the product by an affiliate, one can "back into" an appropriate transfer price from the point of view of the tax authority. The third method is the "cost plus" method, where the IRS permits three different ways of allocating costs (full absorption, direct cost, and incremental cost). All these methods leave some margin of discretion as to what is the appropriate transfer price.

If all these fail, as they frequently do for high-technology products, customised components, or subassemblies, then so-called fourth methods are permitted, such as determining transfer pricing on the basis of a predetermined profit for the foreign firm's operations and, through a netting process of accounting for applicable costs, establishing an appropriate transfer price.

Regardless of the methodology, the burden of proof in supporting a transfer price is with the taxpayer, not the IRS. To confuse matters more, there have been occasions when the tax courts have rejected the notion of arm's-length transfer pricing in settling tax disputes between corporations and the IRS.

OTHER NATIONS' POLICIES CONCERNING TRANSFER PRICING

The tax authority in Canada views transfer pricing of goods similar to the way the United States does. Transfer pricing for services differs in that it is based on a pro rata sharing of actual incurred costs between the parent corporation and its affiliate, and not necessarily at an arm's-length price.

Tax authorities in Japan follow a system comparable to that of the United States. German tax code provisions permit the reallocation of domestic source income if revenue or income has been shifted to another nation through a transaction that is different from those that would have been entered into by unrelated parties. In other words,

transfer pricing should be arm's-length, although the code is not specific in defining arm's-length pricing. The United Kingdom is similar to Germany in not specifically defining arm's-length pricing. The Inland Revenue may adjust taxable income based on fairness and arm's-length criteria. Disputes between corporations and Inland Revenue agents are frequently settled by negotiation, resulting in some sort of compromise between the two parties. This is unlike in Germany, where the adjustments made by the tax authorities are considered final, and unlike in the United States, where adjustments are litigated in tax courts.

Tax authorities in many nations are currently taking a much closer look at transfer pricing practices. Recently, the U.K. Inland Revenue recast the accounts of one non-British company operating in the United Kingdom and assessed back taxes of nearly 2 billion pounds. In the United States, there is growing political pressure for the IRS to take more vigourous action against foreign-owned companies operating through U.S. based affiliates.

This pressure stems from the realization that the aggregate expenses for foreign-owned businesses operating in the United States exceed aggregate revenues. This means that, in the aggregate, foreign-owned subsidiaries are claiming to operate at a loss, although individual foreign-owned subsidiaries may be paying taxes on profits. Some foreign-owned affiliates operating in the United States have a twenty-year string of consecutive losses. This is not considered a realistic appraisal of performance because there are few profit-motivated foreign-based parent companies that would support twenty years of successive losses were they real.

Poor or nonexistent profits for foreign-based affiliates operating in the United States are blamed on transfer pricing. Transfer price manipulation is felt to have resulted in tax underpayments of between $12 and $50 billion. Legislation was passed in 1989 to require foreign-owned businesses in the United States to keep records, in English, of transactions with foreign related parties. Much of this legislation has to do with substantiating transfer pricing on either a cost or arm'slength transaction with an unrelated third party. A growing risk associated with manipulating transfer prices for the purpose of tax minimization.

The risk is that the tax authorities will recast the company's statements with their own version of the proper transfer price, thus exposing a company to the risk of double taxation. Most nations have entered into tax treaties with various other nations with regard to taxing of affiliates of parent organizations domiciled in the treaty nations. These treaties determine withholding taxes on dividends, interest, and royalties; relief from double taxation; and the types of taxes and organizations covered by the treaty. Overall exposure to taxation can be reduced by judicious structuring of the legal corporate entities of a parent company and its affiliates in accordance with the provisions of these treaties.

Some of these treaties contain formal agreements for the mutual examination of the tax returns of affiliates of a parent company. The tax returns of affiliates and parent organizations are exchanged and examined by the tax authorities to determine correct tax liabilities, detect tax avoidance maneuvers, scrutinize trans- fer pricing practices, and exchange information useful to the tax authorities. These treaties also provide a forum for one tax authority to complain about the actions taken by another, when these actions are deemed detrimental to its interests.

Recent developments in international cooperation of tax authorities include the establishment of a formal agreement on transfer prices. The mutual agreement of various nations to reference a published source for tanker rates in determining oil company tax liabilities is an example of this. Australia and the United States are attempting to grant "advance determinations" of the proper transfer price for Australian companies dealings with their U.S. affiliates. A recent survey has shown that about half of IRS tax examinations of multinational companies involve transfer prices. If a mutually agreeable methodology could be arranged between a company and the IRS, many of these tax examinations could be eliminated.

The IRS is attempting to develop a procedure whereby a company and the IRS would mutually agree to a transfer-pricing agreement covering the distribution of finished goods, sales of raw materials and components, general and administrative expenses, and managerial and technical services. If the taxpayer develops an acceptable transfer-pricing methodology, then the taxpayer and the IRS would enter into an advance-pricing agreement. The IRS would limit its examinations to an audit to ensure that the taxpayer has complied with the agreement.

However, the taxpayer is obliged to submit pricing data of independent transactions, or an adequate substitute, to show that the transfer price possesses the necessary attributes of an arm's-length transaction. The taxpayer is also responsible to show that the agreed transfer-pricing methodology is generating acceptable transfer prices from an arm's-length perspective.

The preference of tax authorities in many nations for arm's-length transfer pricing may act as an inducement to switch from the cost-of-production to the market price approach in setting transfer prices because, presumably, they are one and the same. The financial and taxation departments of multinational, or global, companies must deal daily with what are considered to be the most pressing issues in international accounting today. Those involved with transfer pricing must measure the consequences of their transfer-pricing decisions both on corporate profits and on current and potential tax liabilities. Potential tax liabilities, stemming from tax authorities rejecting management's transfer price decisions, and substituting their own, are enormous. This must weigh heavily on the shoulders of those responsible for setting transfer prices.

LEGAL AND TAX CONSIDERATIONS

Over the last few years, India has emerged as a leading destination for companies wishing to outsource their software development, and business process requirements. International companies have either entered into contracts with Indian service companies or set up their own facilities through Joint Ventures and Indian subsidiaries.

Indian Government has been a catalyst in the growth of the Indian software and BPO industry through the tax incentives provided to exporters. These incentives are aimed largely at maximizing exports, thereby resulting in an inflow of foreign exchange into India. Industrial policy reforms have eliminated the licensing requirements except for certain select sectors, removed restrictions on investment and expansion and facilitated easy access to foreign technology and direct investment. This has contributed to increased inflow of foreign exchange into India.

FOREIGN INVESTMENT POLICY

Foreign investment is permitted in virtually every sector, except those of strategic concern such as defence (opened up recently to a limited extent) and rail transport. Foreign companies are permitted to set up Wholly Owned Subsidiaries in India. No prior approval from the exchange control authorities (RBI) is required, except for certain specified activities. The investment should be in accordance with the prescribed guidelines and the details of the investment should be filed with the authorities within the prescribed time limit. This investment procedure is commonly known as the "automatic approval route". Foreign Investment Promotion Board (FIPB) of the Government of India is constituted mainly to promote inflow of FDI into the country, as also to provide appropriate institutional arrangements, transparent procedures and guidelines for investment promotion and to consider and approve proposals for foreign investment.

AUTOMATIC APPROVAL ROUTE AND FIPB ROUTE

Foreign investment into India is governed by the Foreign Direct Investment (FDI) policy of the Government and the Foreign Exchange Management Act, 1999 (FEMA). With increasing liberalisation of the Indian economy, generally, there is no need to obtain prior approval of the Government of India for a fresh investment to be made into an Indian company (only procedural filings have to be made with the Reserve Bank of India (RBI), the Indian central bank). In certain cases, however, and also for investment in certain specified sectors, prior approval is required. Further, investment in certain specified sectors is subject to foreign equity caps.

Outsourcing vs. Software Development Centre

The determination of whether to outsource to an Indian software services company or set up one's own facility is largely a business decision. A long term requirement could make investment in a subsidiary worthwhile. Recent transfer pricing regulations may however have an impact on the pricing of the services provided by the subsidiary. A requirement for highly specialized work may also point to setting up one's own facility. The need to exercise control over valuable intellectual property and maintenance of confidentiality is also a key factor. The slowdown since 2001 has also seen some hybrid structures, for e.g. where the Indian company sets up a separate entity, is assured a steady stream of business and grants the customer an option to purchase the business later. This would have the effect of leveraging on the benefits of outsourcing while sheltering the associated risks.

SOFTWARE OUTSOURCING ARRANGEMENTS

Contractual Protection

Where at least one party is a foreign entity, the parties can choose the law governing the contract. The negotiating power of international customers would typically weigh in favour of choosing a governing law of the customer. The parties may also choose a foreign venue for arbitration. A Foreign arbitral award would be recognized in India if the country of venue has signed either the New York or Geneva conventions and has been notified as having reciprocal relations with India in the matter of enforcement of foreign awards. A foreign arbitral award would generally be more easily enforced in India than a foreign court judgment.

If dispute resolution is to be held in India, it is generally recommended that the parties opt for arbitration because litigation in India can be long drawn and subject to delays. However, it is possible to obtain quick injunctive relief in case of intellectual property violations.

Contract Liability Concerns

Indian law does not contain statutory provisions or case law dealing specifically with liability issues arising from development of software. However, customers should keep in mind that under Indian law, compensation can be awarded for breach of contract only in relation to damages that naturally arise in the usual course of things and which the parties knew would result from such breach. It cannot extend to any remote or indirect losses. Further, Indian courts rarely award large damages for breach of contract. Delays in the justice system also make speedy recovery of money difficult. This may impact the ability of customers to recover fees paid or obtain damages in Indian courts.

Copyright and Protection of Intellectual Property

It is generally difficult to patent software programmes in India. Under copyright law, the software developer, being an independent contractor, would be the author of the works and therefore, the owner. However, Indian law permits the parties to agree that the customer would be the owner of the copyright.

Under Indian law, in the absence of anything to the contrary, it is presumed that an assignment or license of a copyright work would be limited to 5 years and to the territory of India.

Further, the assignment may lapse if the work product is not made use of within one year. Accordingly, the contract would need to mention specific language to overcome these presumptions.

An assignment agreement must also specifically describe the work to be assigned. It is important to note that the knowing violation of copyright in India is a criminal offence. It is possible to obtain reasonably quick injunctive relief from Indian courts for intellectual property violation. However, it is important that the customer chooses an IP friendly jurisdiction.

The Business Software Alliance has had some success in obtaining Anton Pillar orders from Indian courts and conducting raids on distributors of pirated software. Another remedy that could be used is criminal breach of trust, if the developer has misused proprietary software or know-how provided by the customer.

India does not have a statute governing the protection of confidential information and trade secrets. Further, there is no statute dealing with data protection or privacy matters. One would typically obtain protection through a civil action under common law.

Recently, the central government and some state governments have expressed an interest in bringing forth a separate legislation for data protection in an effort to attract more investment in BPO activities. Another option would be to file an action for criminal breach of trust.

This is based on the principle that confidential information is provided "in trust" and any misuse would amount to a breach of trust. Criminal action has its advantages in that the individuals involved will be put to inconvenience in terms of personal appearance before the court, the perceived stigma and the restrictions on traveling out of India.

TAX ISSUES

Under Indian law, software and BPO companies would typically be exempt from tax in relation to income earned from export of software out of India if the fees are received in convertible foreign currency.

This may affect certain types of outsourcing arrangements, for example, where the customer wishes to outsource the work from its existing Indian subsidiary. Payment of fees in Indian Rupees could significantly increase the cost, because the developer would seek to recover the tax payable on its margins.

Another important issue is the possibility that the customer may be held to have a permanent establishment in India if it transfers testing equipment to the developer for use while developing the software.

Another relevant issue is the taxation on Information Technology related services. In an attempt to boost the growth of software exporting, Government of India has exempted export of services and also secondary services consumed in exported services from service tax.

As mentioned earlier, India's software companies are largely exempt from tax. However, it is possible that the exemption may be removed or substantially reduced in the future. In such event, the Vendor would seek to increase its fees. The customer must recognize this as a reasonable possibility and perhaps, obtain fixed, tax inclusive costs, at least in the short term.

OUTSOURCING THROUGH OWNERSHIP MODEL

Foreign Investment Regulations

Software development and BPO services is now under the automatic route and no foreign investment approvals are required to set up a wholly owned subsidiary; only certain filings need to be made after receipt and issue of share capital. However, acquisition of shares in an existing Indian company may still require a prior foreign investment approval.

Choice of Vehicle - Private Company

Most foreign corporations set up their subsidiaries as private limited companies with liability limited by share capital. This entity is similar but not identical to an unlisted C Corporation in the USA and has no flow-through taxation. A private company can have a maximum of 50 shareholders, must restrict the transferability of its shares and is prohibited from making invitations to the public for subscription to shares, debentures or deposits.

A private company is generally less regulated than a public company. It must have at least 2 shareholders. Regulations relating to personal presence of shareholders at shareholder meetings, and limitations on transfer of shares under exchange control laws would require a careful structuring of share capital investment into the subsidiary.

Funding the Venture

Restrictions imposed by Indian exchange control laws on the ability of an Indian company to obtain short term debt from abroad make it difficult to fund the subsidiary through loan funds. Inflexible buy back regulations make a buyback of share capital difficult. Hence, the parent would typically seek to fund only the capital costs through share capital. One could possibly consider funding the operating expenses by the holding company making trade advances to the subsidiary for services to be performed.

Software Technology Park Units

Most foreign corporations interested in engaging in development of software and BPO services in India set up their Indian subsidiaries as Software

Technology Park Units. This is not a separate legal entity but merely a status obtained from the government. The STP status entitles the company to substantial tax benefits, subject to it meeting certain export commitments. An STP unit would need to be a customs bonded area. This means that it can be at a location of the Company's choosing but must be in an area demarcated specifically for STP operations. Some formalities on entry and removal of goods would apply. In practice, most companies handle these requirements with ease.

Activities of an STP

The permitted activities of an STP do not cover just software development activities. An STP's activities could include:

- Software development
- Hardware design, digital signal processing;
- Business process outsourcing, including medical transcription services, customer relations, document processing and call centres.

On site services through deputed personnel would also be covered. Because an STP is supposed to be engaged primarily in export activities, its ability to make sales within the Indian market is limited to the equivalent of 50% of its total exports. Further, restrictions under both STP regulations and tax laws would limit the ability of the Indian subsidiary to outsource work to another Indian STP.

Export Requirements for STP Units

The export related commitments that need to be satisfied by an STP Unit are driven largely by the Government's objective of maximizing the country's foreign exchange reserves. These commitments are as follows:

- Exports of US$ 0.25 million or 5 times the CIF value of imported capital goods, whichever is higher (if no capital goods are imported, the US$ 0.25 million requirement would apply).
- An annual Net Foreign Exchange Earnings as a Percentage of Exports (NFEP) of 10%. This means that the inflow of foreign exchange earned by the company should be at least 10% more than the outflow of foreign exchange out of India.
- Both the requirements need to be satisfied over a period of 5 years. The value of capital goods would cover the entire CIF value - cost, insurance and freight. However, the value of exports would cover only the landed cost. Further, it may be noted that in considering the outflow of foreign exchange, the dividend distributed to the holding company would also need to be considered.

INCOME TAX BENEFITS

An STP Unit in India would be entitled to enjoy the remainder of a 10 year tax holiday commencing from April 1, 2000 to March 31, 2009. (The Indian tax year runs from April 1 to March 31).

The tax benefit would apply only if the software/service is exported out of India and payment is received in convertible foreign exchange. It would also not cover profits earned from domestic business or income other than from STPI services. The tax holiday will not cover dividend distribution.

The STP Unit cannot be set up as a result of the re-organization or break up of an existing business and not more than 20% of its hardware should constitute hardware previously used by another business. Hence, in an acquisition, a careful structuring may be required in order to preserve the tax holiday.

Transfer Pricing Regulations

Indian tax laws have recently included provisions relating to transfer pricing, requiring pricing of transactions between associated enterprises to be at arms length. Even in the case of a tax exempt software company, this assumes significance because if the tax authorities conclude that the consideration payable to the Indian subsidiary is not at arms length, the enhanced income determined by the authorities would be subject to tax and would be the basis of possible penalties. Typically, companies opt for a cost plus method or standard per diem rates. Since these developments are relatively recent, there is no consensus yet on what would be an acceptable pricing formula.

Indirect Tax

An STP company can import capital goods and consumables without payment of any customs duty. However, the higher the value of imported goods, the higher will be the export commitment, as above.

The company would also be exempt from payment of excise duty on manufacture of goods, when purchased from the manufacturer and can claim a refund on sales tax paid by the supplier on sale of the product to the STP.

Tax Benefits for Non-STP Companies

Even if a software exporting company does not have an STP unit, it can avail of the general exemption for profits derived from export of computer software under Indian tax laws. At present, 30% of such export income is tax exempt.

Procedure for Setting up the STP

Setting up the STP Unit involves compliance with numerous regulatory procedures that would typically take about 3 months. After company incorporation, a detailed STP application has to be prepared, that would include the prescribed application form, a project report, projected 5 year accounts and details of expenses and foreign exchange remittances.

This would involve substantial work from the company officials. After obtaining the STP registration, certain other formalities need to be completed relating to customs bonding and obtaining tax registrations.

OPERATING A BUSINESS IN INDIA

Company Law - Indian company law is based on the English Companies Act of 1948. Key requirements include mandatory board and shareholder meetings, shareholder approval in respect of certain matters, appointment of officers, restrictions on loans and investments, etc.

Exchange Control

The Indian Rupee is fully convertible on the current account though control remains on the capital account. Doing business in India involves wading through India's complex exchange control regulations that restrict the remittance of foreign exchange out of India.

Employment Laws

Indian employee laws are considered to be somewhat restrictive in terms of requirements relating to lay offs, closure of business, etc. BPO companies need to be particularly concerned about rules relating to flexible working hours, holidays and employment of women at night as well as regulation of leave policies

Stock Options: Exchange control restrictions that limited the amount that an employee could remit out of India for purchase of foreign stock have been lifted in the case of listed stock of holding companies. Subject to the employer fulfilling certain requirements, employees receiving foreign stock can also claim a tax status similar to the ISO status in the USA.

India many believe has just the right "climate" for entrepreneurial development and in 2007 India is the place to be in. It provides a great combination of skill and competency. Combine that with the right investment climate and the ever improving technological efficiency, you find that the great Indian time has arrived. The India boom is here to stay. The heat is on and it's only getting hotter.

BUSINESS OPPORTUNITIES IN INDIA

While looking at the prospect of doing business in India it would be prudent to see what options are available to a Non Indian company to invest in India. Since 1991 India has undergone a sea of change in its outlook toward foreign investment and global collaboration.

Add to that the phenomenon called Internet and you really have an explosive combination. It's no wonder that software and Internet services have really led India's outward push. Outsource2india has been providing high-quality and technology-driven services to a wide range of global customers since the year 1999.

Outsource to O2I and get access to proficient, professional and cost-effective services. Outsource 2india provides a range of competent services which include call centre services, data entry services, engineering services, financial services, creative services, web analytics services, healthcare services, digital image editing services, software services, Research and Analysis services and a host of other additional services. While most of the policies are not specific to any industry, there are special provisions that relate only to the IT industry. Once you have decided to invest in India, the next question is naturally, how do I set up operations? There are primarily 2 ways to get your work done.

- Having your own setup
- Outsource the work to a local company

HAVING YOUR OWN SETUP

Many foreign investors prefer to have their own setup in India. This gives them better control over management of the organization.

It is also the best guarantee that the company's processes are being followed. Furthermore this may in some cases tend to be preferable, especially if the volume of work is large or the work is sensitive in nature.

However there are also disadvantages in this approach. One is regarding flexibility. Often these branches or subsidiaries are bound by the policies of the parent company and this may make it unwieldy when it comes to Indian legal and cultural framework.

Secondly, management of a remote setup is always more difficult, especially if the work involved is intermittent and small in volume.

Basically there are four types of direct foreign investment businesses in India:

- Branch Office
- 100% Subsidiary
- Joint Venture Companies
- Acquiring Existing Indian companies

Branch office:

It's really simple to set up a branch office in India. You are allowed to open a branch office if you are engaged in manufacturing or trading for the following activities:

- To represent your company in various matters in India e.g. acting as buying/selling agents in India, etc.
- To conduct research work in which the parent company is engaged provided the results of the research work are made available to the Indian companies
- To undertake export and import trading activities
- To promote the possible technical and financial collaborations between the Indian companies and overseas companies

Under this setup, you will not be allowed to do any sales in India for any of your products or services. However if you are only looking at doing your software development or IT enabled services, then this is the easiest option.

Wholly Owned Companies :

If you would like to hand over control to the local management or would like to sell your products in India then look at this option. For the software industry, the Government of India allows up to 100% ownership by the Foreign Investor. Also, if you were to set up your office in an Export Processing Zone (EPZ), Software Technology Park (STP) or Electronic Hardware Technology Park (EHTP), then you will automatically be given permission for 100% ownership. The catch though is that you will have to export at least 75% of the final output out of India.

Many of India's States have at least one of these Parks. Automatic approvals are given by the Secretariat for Industrial Approval for setting up 100% Export Oriented Units. These zones are designed to provide internationally competitive infrastructure facilities and duty-free and low cost environment. Various monetary and non-monetary incentives are granted which include import duty exemption, complete tax holiday, decentralized "single window clearance," etc.

Establishing units in EPZ or STPs have the following advantages:

- Duty Free imports
- Tax free income
- Readymade infrastructure
- Housing and living facilities

Joint Venture Companies:

This is a common form of investment, because it allows the Foreign Investor and the Indian partner to do what each does best - the foreign partner brings in technology, systems and products and the Indian partner takes care of Human resources, marketing and legal and tax issues.

This is a special favourite for foreign companies just moving into India, since it gives you the distribution channel to get sales moving quickly. However over the long term you may prefer to move to a 100% subsidiary, to establish greater control. This is commonly done by means of stock buyouts or fresh investments. Both Wholly owned Companies and Joint ventures may be registered as Private Limited Liability or Public Limited Liability. Currently the government allows 51% shareholding by foreign companies in all but a small list of companies (these companies are essential to India's national security).

Acquisition of existing Indian Companies:

You have also the option of acquiring a company already existing in India. Such acquisition could take place through the issue of fresh capital and/or transfer of shares of an existing Indian company to the foreign investor with the effect of transferring control. Shares of an Indian company could be acquired from another foreign investor, subject to RBI approval. This will give you the advantage of a readymade setup. The Foreign Exchange Regulations Act (FERA) makes it necessary that Reserve Bank of India (India's Federal Reserve Bank) permission be taken prior to acquisition of shares in an Indian company by a foreign investor.

Similar permission is required in case of transfer of shares from you to a person resident in India. Either the transferor or the transferee can apply for permission. However be careful with this one. If the company is listed on the stock exchange, then you cannot hold more that 5% of the total paid up capital and all Foreign investors and Non Resident Indians (in case there's more than one) cannot own in total more than 24% of the capital.

CORPORATE TAX AND OTHER INCENTIVES

The corporate income tax effective rate for domestic companies is 35% while the profits of branches in India of foreign companies are taxed at 45%. Companies incorporated in India (any setup other than a branch) even with 100% foreign ownership, are considered domestic companies under the Indian laws. However, the New Export-Import Policy of 1992 provides substantial tax incentives for investments in Export. Major exporters are allowed to operate bank accounts abroad to facilitate trade.

Companies that sell in the Indian market as well as international markets may deduct export earnings from their tax liabilities. Exporters and other foreign exchange earners have been permitted to retain 25% of their foreign exchange earnings in foreign currency. For 100% Export Oriented Units and units in Export Processing Zones, Electronic Hardware Technology Parks, retention up to 50% is allowed.

Other incentives include:

- Tax holiday for a period of 5 continuous years in the first 8 years from the year of commencement of production
- Exemption from taxes on exports earnings even after the period of tax holiday

- Exemption from central and state taxes on production and sale
- Permission to install machinery on lease
- Freedom to borrow self-liquidating foreign currency loans at the prime rate of interest
- Inter-unit transfers of finished goods among exporting units

OUTSOURCING YOUR WORK TO INDIA

The other option is to completely outsource your work to Indian companies. This has it's own advantages. For example

- For intermittent jobs, it may make better sense to pay only when you have work
- Also if the volume of work were small, it would always be difficult to achieve economy of scale
- Outsourcing ensures that while you may not be the best in a certain area, you are giving the work to someone who's really good at it. That leaves you to focus on what you do best
- Many Indian companies do a lot of business with International customers, so they would often be able to bring in expertise and advice from their earlier work
- Lastly but definitely not least, you have no legal hurdles to overcome when you outsource

When companies go through M&A deals what are the key tax issues that arise? How far do tax laws and other laws encourage or constrict M&A, inbound and outbound? For starters, inbound deals have a foreign buyer and an Indian target, while outbound deals are the opposite.

"Inbound acquisitions have recently become the flavour of the season with a good number of deals ringing the bells of some of the finest Indian fast-growing corporates," says Mr Girish Vanvari, Executive Director - M&A Tax, KPMG, India.

He cites as examples: Heidelberg's purchase of 51 per cent stake in Mysore Cements, EDS Corp's acquisition of 52 per cent stake of MphasiS BFL, Kohlberg Kravis Roberts (KKR) buying up Indian software unit Flextronics, and Holcim taking up stake in Gujarat Ambuja Cement.

"These transactions require a lot of structuring such that they are tax-efficient, compliant with SEBI (Securities and Exchange Board of India), FDI (Foreign Direct Investment) regulations and so forth," points out Mr Vanvari. "The Heidelberg's acquisition in the BIFR-reported (Board of Industrial and Financial Reconstruction) Mysore Cements triggered off the SEBI takeover code.

Heidelberg compulsorily made an open offer for 22.15 per cent stake at a price higher than their acquisition price," he recounts.

"The acquisition of 51 per cent stake was made on a preferential basis subject to the approval of the shareholders in their extraordinary general meeting." Thus, corporate law provisions come in to full play in deals involving companies.

What about the EDS Corp deal? "This merger is subject to the approval of the Bombay and Karnataka High Courts. Also required are sanctions of the stock exchanges, shareholders, creditors, and regulatory authorities," explains Mr Vanvari.

"Tax neutrality of this merger will be on the compliance with the `amalgamation' conditions laid down under Section 2(1B) of the Income-Tax Act, 1961." In contrast, KKR's acquisition of 85 per cent of Flextronics did not trigger the takeover code, distinguishes Mr Vanvari. Because "the Indian entity had applied for voluntary delisting and been delisted from BSE and NSE in 2005."

Not all proposals sail through, as for example the US glassmaker Guardian Industries' idea to set up a separate wholly owned glass venture in the country. "It ran into rough weather with the FIPB (Foreign Investment Promotion Board) since the company already had a joint venture partner in India, and its partner would not grant a no-objection certificate to Guardian," narrates Mr Vanvari. "Any M&A in India has to be carefully planned and executed, cutting through a wide spectrum of tax and regulatory issues such as exchange control, income-tax, capital market regulations and so forth," he opines. "From tax perspective it would be important to structure these transactions into the country in a tax efficient manner, taking into account manner of funding, and choice of the holding company jurisdiction."

OUTBOUND ACQUISITIONS

Recently we have had many outbound acquisitions. Such as: Patni's acquisition of the US-based Cymbal Corporation for about $68 million; Dr Reddy's acquisition of Betapharm in Germany for $570 million, and Terapia in Romania for $324 million; Suzlon's acquisition of Eve Holding in Belgium for $526 million; Aban Loyd's acquisition of Sinvest ASA in Norway for $445 million; and Matrix Labs acquiring Docpharma in Belgium for $320 million. And the deal meter keeps ticking! "Outbound acquisitions are guided not only by the tax laws of the foreign companies but also the political relationships, free trade agreements (FTAs) and double taxation avoidance agreements between these countries," says Mr Vanvari. "Deal structuring from tax perspective has become one of the most important factors for structuring transactions in the recent times such that the transaction is tax neutral or has minimum tax outflow."

It should enthuse professionals that a lot of tax planning is possible because good tax treaties are in place with many countries. Yet, areas that need appropriate attention, according to Mr Vanvari, are: 'substance' test, tax outflow, capital gains, dividend, interest and royalty, withholding taxes and elimination of double taxation.

"Tax, legal and financial due diligence of the target company is of utmost importance," he alerts. For, such an exercise can result in `a good understanding of the laws governing the target company,' so that you can structure the transactions appropriately.

EVALUATING YOUR BUSINESS'S LEGAL STRUCTURE

One of the many roles you will have to play in your business is that of security guard. You have to make sure that the company remains safe—nothing enters that could harm your business and nothing leaves that could reduce its value. The more you can use legal protections to safeguard your business, the easier this task becomes.

There are many ways to protect the business, its assets, and employees—one critical way is to conduct business within the most appropriate legal framework. The legal framework you use to support your business can affect your tax payments, legal liability, and potential for future investment.

As an entrepreneur, you must make decisions and take legal actions to structure your business. Otherwise, the law will make those decisions for you, and that can be detrimental. Even if you've never officially selected a legal form for your business, you are operating within the parameters of a legal form. States typically hold undeclared businesses to be sole proprietorships or partnerships, leaving you personally responsible for debts and injuries. Instead of ignoring this issue, take the time to select an appropriate legal structure after consulting an attorney and accountant. If you are in business, you're currently operating under one of the following legal structures:

- Sole proprietorship
- Partnership
- Corporation
- S corporation
- Limited liability company (LLC)
- Nonprofit corporation

The important question now is whether your legal form is appropriate for your business and its plan for growth. The factors that affect this important decision are listed below. Read these carefully and then complete My Business's Legal Form to see if you should talk with a lawyer and accountant about changing your current legal structure.

FACTORS AFFECTING THE CHOICE OF LEGAL STRUCTURE

While you should consider many factors in choosing the legal structure of your business, not all factors will apply to every business. Several key issues, however, will apply to most:

Control

Who is the decision maker? The decision maker will control management, determine who receives profits, decide whether to get loans or solicit investors, and be solely responsible for the company's financial losses.

Taxes

Tax liability is a major concern for business owners. The amount of taxes paid yearly can make or break a business.

Liability

Some legal structures do not protect personal assets from business debts. If you do not want to personally pay the debts of your business, consider a legal structure that will protect your personal assets.

Transferability of Ownership

Depending upon the legal structure, one person's ownership in a business may be transferred to another owner in whole or in part simply by the exchange of a piece of paper.

Longevity of the Business

Not all business forms are perpetual. Some forms of business cease when the entrepreneur exits the business.

Raising Capital

Simple entities such as sole proprietorships and general partnerships are restricted in their ability to raise capital.

Most often, entrepreneurs are concerned with all of these important issues. The key is to identify the legal structure that best meets your needs and the needs of your business as it grows.

This tough decision should not be made without adequate counsel from an attorney, an accountant, and other advisers. In an ideal world, you would select a legal form of business understanding every legal and tax implication.

The reality is that you must rely on the advice of your attorneys and accountants to make this decision.

Attorneys and accountants can anticipate many situations based on their experience and on the information you provide. Still, the legal structure of the business is your decision to make and live with. Use My Business's Legal Form to check that the structure you operate under best covers the factors you are concerned about from the list above and best align with your business's strategy and goals. The legal form of your business can't be an afterthought. Your profits, your peace of mind, and even your business may depend upon using the right structure. Schedule appointments with your lawyer and accountant now to review your company's legal form.

5

Two Systems of Public Finance: Entrepreneurial and Taxation

Why study public financial administration separately from business finance? Modern public financial administration liberally borrows the tools and concepts of business management. Financial management in business seeks to increase the value of the firm to its owners by judicious allocation and control of its resources. Public financial management uses similar analytic, technical, and managerial tools to allocate and control, but governments differ from private businesses in terms of resource constraints, ownership, and objectives. In particular, governments may tax to enlarge their resources, "ownership" is not clear because many stakeholders share a legitimate interest in government decisions, and the value of government services is neither easy to quantify nor reflected in a single measure. And behind all these differences lies the unique power of government to tax, prohibit, and punish.

This capacity to coerce, even in democracies, makes governments different from proprietary businesses and voluntary organizations; the reflection of those differences makes public financial administration distinct from many fundamental practices of business finance. Both sorts of entities are interested in fiscal sustainability, that is, the ability to operate over the long term without reducing the standards of life below those currently enjoyed and even to improve that standard.

Many different organizations—private businesses, nonprofit organizations, and governmental agencies—provide the goods and services that we use every day, including both those necessary for life itself and those that make life more enjoyable. Private businesses sell us food and clothing, cars and television sets, and so on: a vast range of commodities that we purchase for survival and enjoyment. The same applies to services: We go to movies run by private companies, travel across the country on privately operated airlines, and hire the neighbour to feed our cats when we go on vacation.

All these and many more goods and services are provided under market principles of voluntary exchange: Businesses provide those services to us in exchange for the payment we make to them. No payment, no service. Much the same applies for many nonprofit organizations, like hospitals and social service organizations, that operate on the basis of charges and government contracts. Other services come from voluntary associations or clubs—the services of the county historical museum, the local neighbourhood association, or a local youth organization.

Their operations are financed by a variety of contributions and fees. Although most voluntary organizations do not require payment before service is rendered, they still need to be paid by someone, voluntarily, in order to survive, because those who provide the resources that are used in providing services need to be paid for those resources.

Finally, we receive services of police departments, school systems, the judicial and regulatory systems, the social safety net, and so on, from governments. But these services are financed differently. Rather than operating from finance by voluntary exchange or by voluntary contribution, governments provide goods and services paid by taxes or other revenues raised by law. This revenue comes not from voluntary purchase or contribution, but, even in a democracy, from the operation of a revenue system based on legal requirement for payment, backed, if necessary, by force or threat of force.

That is coercion, something we dislike and distrust. In our open and free society, why have a public sector? The reason is that government services are uniquely essential to life: Most countries leave the provision of life's necessities—food, clothing, and usually shelter—to the private sector. But when government fails, the private sector cannot function and citizens are "bereft of even the most basic conditions of a stable existence: law and security, trust in contracts, and a sound medium of exchange." Without a government that does its job in at least some basic areas, the private sector itself cannot properly function.

MARKET FAILURE AND THE FUNCTIONS OF GOVERNMENT

Why can't private businesses selling their products in free markets be relied upon to provide all goods and services that ought to be available? The argument for the efficiency of markets is powerful. The President's Council of Economic Advisors explains: "If markets are competitive and function smoothly, they will lead to prices at which the amount sellers want to supply equals the amount buyers demand. Moreover, the price in any market will simultaneously equal the benefit that buyers get from the last unit consumed and the cost of producing the last unit supplied.

These two conditions ensure efficiency: when they hold in all markets, the Nation's labour and other resources are allocated to producing a particular good or service if and only if consumers would not be willing to pay more to have those resources employed elsewhere." Markets cause the productive capacity of the economy to be used to produce what people want most and cause the least possible amount of resources to be used in that production. In a world of limited resources, it is a valuable result.

But there remains an important role for government, even if private markets can deliver most goods and services, and deliver them at low cost. Indeed, there is an important cooperative relationship between healthy government and healthy markets. Markets need government to function efficiently: "Deals must be enforced and fraud discouraged.

Without a governmental legal system to guarantee property rights and enforce contracts, corporate organizations and market exchange would be virtually impossible. Anarchy and the free market are not synonymous." Government— at least its protective elements—is necessary if markets are to exist. And governments can obtain important information from market data, use markets as efficient mechanisms for implementing public policy, and acquire goods and services in market transactions to provide government services.

The market economy needs government to function properly, and governments need the market economy if they are to serve the public interest. The role of government, however, extends beyond simply allowing markets to operate, because a system of markets is not always able "to sustain 'desirable' activities or to stop 'undesirable' activities." What makes some services a governmental responsibility? Why can't private action be relied upon to provide police and urban fire protection, primary education, environmental protection, public health, national defence, and so on? Individuals demand these services, and we expect businesses to respond to customer demand in their quest for profit. Why do markets fail, and thereby create an economic need for government?

PUBLIC GOODS

Some goods will not be supplied in the market or, if supplied, will be supplied in insufficient amounts because of their very nature.

The problem comes from two properties:

- Nonexhaustion, or nonrivalry, occurs when benefits of the service can only be shared, meaning that a given quantity of the service can be enjoyed by additional people with no reduction in benefit to the existing population.
- Inability to exclude nonpayers occurs when benefits cannot be easily limited to those who have paid for the services.

The properties reflected in Figure distinguish private goods, public goods, and two intermediate kinds of goods—toll goods and common-pool goods.

Table. The Elements of Nonappropriability

	Exhaustion or Rivalry	
	Alternate Use	**Joint Use**
	Private Goods	**Toll Goods**
Feasible Exclusion	*Examples*: Food clothing, television sets	*Example*: Turnpikes, toll bridges, motion pictures
	Common-Pool Resources	**Public Goods**
Not Feasible	*Examples*: Aquifers, fishing grounds, petroleum reserves	*Examples*: National defence, system of justice, vector control

What do these public-good properties mean? When services are nonrival, use of the service by one person does not preclude concurrent full use by others at no additional cost of providing that service. The cost of providing service to additional users, once the service has been provided for someone, equals zero (its marginal cost is zero). Economic efficiency requires that the price paid by the buyer (the value of resources given up by the buyer to make the purchase) not exceed the additional cost of producing the purchased good or service. A private business will charge a price higher than zero, the efficient price, because it cannot afford to do otherwise.

Therefore, too little of the good or service will be purchased and consumed, and its price will be too high, compared with quantities and prices in a fully functioning market. When exclusion of those who have not paid for the service is not feasible, a seller could not successfully charge a price; people not paying would receive the service as completely as those who paid. Private goods do not have appropriability problems: One person's use of the good eliminates the possibility of anyone else using it (additional service means extra cost, and sellers charge to cover that cost), and exclusion is feasible. Obviously, the full range of ordinary commodities and services are private goods. The only way an individual can receive the benefits from a private good is by paying for it; there are no effects on others, and it is possible to separate payers from nonpayers.

Public goods include national defence, mosquito abatement, pollution control, and disease control.

The common characteristics of these services are:

- Once they are made available, denial to those who have not paid is impossible, and
- Any number of people can consume the same good at the same time without diminishing the amount of that good available for anyone else to consume (nonexhaustion, or nonrivalry).

Consider mosquito abatement. When a given level of control is provided, all people in the area of control receive the same service. Other people could enter the control district and receive that same service without any additional abatement cost. Many people can simultaneously consume that service, once it has been provided, without diminishing the amount of service available to others (the marginal cost of service is zero), and there is no mechanism to deny service to those not paying for it.

Individuals in the service area may value the abatement service differently (reaction to mosquito bites varies among individuals), but all receive the same level of service. This is completely different from the situation with a private good, like a hamburger: When you eat that burger, it is gone and not available for consumption by anyone else—no nonrivalry.

The failure of exclusion is the other public-good characteristic. Within the range of exclusion failure, if someone provides the services, all receive that service. When one structure in an urban area receives fire protection, given the propensity of fires to spread, nearby structures receive protection as well. (The public good is fire protection, not fire fighting; when the equipment is putting out the fire at Smith's house, it is not available to put out the fire anywhere else.

Extinguishing Smith's fire, however, provides fire protection equally to many neighbours.) Obviously, there are geographic limits to that range of nonappropriability: Fire protection provided in Bloomington, Indiana, will not extend to the people in Jackson, Mississippi. Within a specific geographic area, however, all receive the service regardless of payment, whether they want it or not. Such is the special monopoly position of governments: Not only are alternative providers unavailable, but residents also do not have the option of not paying for the service because public revenue systems operate independently from service delivery. A governor of Kentucky recognized the difference between operating the state and operating his successful business: "Hell, governing Kentucky is easier than running Kentucky Fried Chicken. There's no competition." Payment regardless of preference or consumption is, of course, a unique feature of government provision.

Toll goods and common-pool goods have one public-good characteristic but not both. Toll goods are nonrival: One person can consume the service to its fullest while not reducing the amount of service someone else may consume. For these goods, however, exclusion is feasible; boundaries can separate payers and nonpayers. Examples include drive-in movies and toll roads: Up to a congestion point, a larger number of people can consume these services without exhausting the service concurrently available to others. Common-pool goods are goods or services for which exclusion is not feasible, but there are competing and exhaustive uses. Examples include aquifers, oil and gas deposits, and fisheries.

There are no normal means of exercising exclusive property rights on the resource, but when used, the resource becomes unavailable for others. Left to private processes, the resource may be rapidly exhausted because it is valuable and is not, in its natural state, subject to normal ownership controls. (Firstcome-first-served is a normal allocation principle, so getting those resources out of the ground as quickly as possible is advantageous to any private user —and is why governments frequently intervene in markets for natural resources. That is another element of market failure.) Sidebar 1–1 describes one common-pool resource problem and how government action sought to remedy it.

EXTERNALITIES

Market transactions between buyer and seller may affect third parties. The consequences may be negative—as with the exhaust fumes from automobiles—or positive— as with the protection provided pregnant women when a boy receives a rubella vaccination—but, either way, that value is unlikely to be fully recognized in the market transaction. For these goods and services, the private return from their consumption is substantial, so the market will not fail to provide. It will not, however, provide at a socially reasonable level.

An attractive externality causes the good in question to be underproduced. In the case of the rubella vaccination, those people who are vaccinated receive the benefit of reduced probability that they will contract the disease, a direct benefit to them for which they could be expected to pay. But they also provide protection against the disease to others in that they will not infect others if they themselves do not have the disease. That is a third-party, or external, effect of the vaccination.

It is unlikely that everyone considering the vaccination will take full account of these benefits when weighing the advantages of vaccination against the disadvantages (minimal discomfort and some small risk of adverse reaction, time spent and inconvenience met in receiving the injection, and the out-of-pocket price of the service), and some will decide not to be vaccinated. Fewer people would be vaccinated than would be in the best economic interests of society, because of the external benefits from the personal choice about vaccination. Governments require young boys to get rubella vaccinations not simply to protect them—rubella itself is not much worse than a common cold—but because we do not want them to give the disease to a pregnant woman and cause birth defects in her child.

An undesirable externality has the opposite effect, an overproduction of the good. Automobile operators choose to pay the operating costs of their cars to enjoy the great personal value of mobility that cars provide, without full attention to the undesirable health and esthetic effects of the exhaust fumes produced by their vehicles or of the congestion delays caused by having many vehicles competing for highway space. Again, this leads to a misallocation of resources: more car miles traveled than would be the case if their operators based their choices on the full social cost of using the car. Governments regularly subsidize or tax to try to correct these market failures caused by externalities.

For instance, governments may pay producers or consumers of goods with positive externalities to encourage more consumption of the good in recognition of benefits to third parties. They may also levy corrective taxes to make purchasers and sellers respond to the external damage done by other products. The idea is to make buyers and sellers respond to the external effects of the product, to bring the third-party effect into their decision-making in an economically tangible way.

FAILURE OF COMPETITION

The efficiencies of markets arise from competition among firms. When only a few firms serve a market, those firms may exercise monopoly power to charge prices higher than justified by economic conditions and, thereby, to collect excess profits. Governments watch markets to ensure that barriers do not prevent new firms from entering such markets, because entry of new firms in the industry is the best deterrent to monopoly pricing. And governments strictly police practices that unfairly restrain trade.

Sometimes governments choose to regulate industries that, because of cost advantage to larger firms (or increasing returns to scale), seem destined to be dominated by a few large firms (the natural monopoly case). This may be the situation for electrical, telephone, water, and some other utilities, although new technologies (e.g., lower production cost for alternative electricity generators with small production capacity, and diverse telecommunication systems) have opened new competitive options in many such industries. As this occurs, governments have rightly moved from strategies of legalistic regulation of firm operations and the prices they charge to removing barriers to the entry of new firms, thereby allowing competition to allocate resources and establish reasonable prices for products. Nevertheless, expecting private businesses to regulate failures of competition—without the government's prompting—is not reasonable.

INCOMPLETE MARKETS AND IMPERFECT INFORMATION

Governments often intervene in markets when customers have incomplete information about products and there is fear that unfettered market forces will not provide necessary information in a timely fashion. Governments test (or supervise the testing of) new drugs, guard against the sale of hazardous products, establish certain disclosure standards, and so forth. The market may ultimately provide information—but not until after much grief and suffering by the unwary. Insurance markets can present special problems of adverse selection and moral hazard. Adverse selection occurs when insurance purchasers impose higher-than- average costs on sellers (in health insurance, for instance, those more likely to purchase insurance are those more likely to need care) or when sellers exclude such potential purchasers (health insurance companies seek to exclude those more likely to require care).

It is a particular problem for provision of private prescription drug insurance (or the voluntary Medicare prescription drug benefit programme): people vary widely in the extent to which they have high drug expenses, and both high- and low-expense people generally know into which group they fall. The only takers of a plan with premiums that reflect average prescription expenses would be those with high expenses, and, hence, the finances of the plan would be doomed. Insurance sellers rely on having both sets of people in the premium pool. Moral hazard is a problem when those with insurance have an incentive to cause the insured event to happen or to be less than diligent in averting the insured event. For example, with health insurance, there is a tendency for people to seek more treatment when the third party, the insurance company, is paying for it.

In a case of government failure, federally subsidized flood insurance (premiums for the federal National Flood Insurance Programme represent only about 38% of what a full premium would be) makes people more willing to build in floodplains and in coastal areas, thus increasing the loss when the inevitable flood occurs, as with Hurricane Katrina in 2005; and federal bank deposit insurance with coverage to high deposit levels makes people less interested in considering the financial strength of the institutions holding their deposits. Reasoned government intervention involves securing widespread coverage (to prevent adverse selection) and regulating markets to ensure that decision-makers see the accurate cost implications of those choices. Social insurance systems (public pension, health and disability, unemployment, etc.) throughout the world stem from these market problems.

ECONOMIC STABILIZATION

Governments seek to stabilize the macroeconomy, in other words, preventing high unemployment, controlling inflation that could erode purchasing power and distort financial markets, and improving the prospects for economic growth and a higher quality of life. Governments use monetary policy (manipulation of the money supply) and fiscal policies (changes in expenditure and taxation) to correct for these aggregate failures of the market, although there is continuing controversy about the extent to which those policies can make an active improvement in performance. Nevertheless, evidence does indicate that poor government decisions in use of national resources and financing of government programmes in a misguided fashion can cause severe economic problems. Central governments worry about the condition of the national economy, whereas subnational units (states, regions, cities, etc.) seek to improve their own particular share of that national economy.

And some governments attempt industrial policy, targeted subsidies and tax advantages designed to stimulate particular industries, in the belief that they can increase economic growth and reduce unemployment by giving an extra boost to activities destined to be national or even global leaders. Again, the capacity of politicians and government bureaucrats to pick winners better than can markets is decidedly mixed, but that does not stop them from trying as they arrange the public finances. There is also not much evidence to support the idea that subnational government use of targeted tax and expenditure programmes can have much of an effect on economic development, but that does not stop the political leaders from trying.

The Economist succinctly explains why industrial and economic development policy, whether national, state, or local, has such a low success rate: "Neither economists nor emperors can be relied upon to pick winners. The best bet is entrepreneurial trial and error." Government money spent to assist particular industries is, sadly, often badly spent, because even the well-advised government usually guesses wrong. If lawmakers really knew how to do this, would there be poverty anywhere?

REDISTRIBUTION

Markets distribute products of the economy to those people having resources (talents, properties, etc.), not distinguishing whether those resources were earned, inherited, stolen, or whatever. Those who own the resources get the goods. People with few resources—property or skills—may fall below acceptable living standards and may be destined to a life of poverty in a pure market economy. Governments may correct injustices in the distribution of affluence in society, seeking to improve the conditions faced by the less well-to-do that the market alone would leave them with.

Some argue for a degree of redistribution out of a social conscience and a desire for a safety net for all humanity; others argue for a degree of redistribution out of a fear that the poor will revolt, taking property from the affluent. Regardless of motives, most politicians believe that the public wants some protection for the very poor and at least some mild redistribution by the government of the result produced by pure operation of the market.

Those concerns are reflected both in government spending programmes and in systems for finance of those programmes. Governments employ a variety of different approaches towards redistribution. These include tax structures that levy relatively higher tax burdens on highaffluence households than on low-affluence ones (income taxes that levy higher effective rates on high-income households), direct income payments to low-affluence families (the earned income tax credit), programmes that provide assistance services for which only low-affluence families qualify, or programmes available to all that low-income families use more heavily (unemployment benefit programmes). However, the United States makes less aggressive use of active tax and transfer programmes to handle problems of poverty than do other wealthy nations, preferring programmes of economic expansion that benefit everyone, trusting that economic expansion will take care of the economic bottom as it benefits the economic top. As a result, the gap between highest and lowest incomes and the level of poverty in the United States is considerably wider than in other wealthy nations.

Modern societies argue about where to draw the line between government provision and market provision of goods and services. Many governments have downsized the public sector to achieve efficiency, in the belief that market provision may offer more service options to the public, more flexibility in service response, and lower operating costs. With those possible advantages, it is no surprise that privatization of government operations is an attractive option. After considering the appropriate functions of government, as we did in the last part, it is also reasonable to explore the range for which various forms of privatization may be reasonable.

Privatization encompasses:

- Transfer to the private sector of governmentowned businesses that operate in goods and services markets that do not have significant market failures,
- Transfer to the private sector of government-owned businesses with natural monopoly power, especially telecommunications and electricity, and
- Contracting out of publicly financed services to private businesses, using service contracts or franchise agreements. This latter variety of privatization is possibly amenable to pure public goods; the former two may be accompanied by government regulation of prices, returns, or other conditions of operation.

ARGUMENTS SUPPORTING PRIVATIZATION

Several logical arguments have been offered in support of privatization. *These are three of the most frequently used*:

- *Smaller government*: Some argue for a smaller public sector and fewer public bureaucrats, resulting in a shrunken scope of government, largely as a matter of philosophy. Because governments may spend without producing services (e.g., the check writing of the American Social Security system) and may be deeply involved in the private economy without even spending (e.g., the safety regulations applied to private industry), privatization, while reducing government production, may or may not reduce the size of government or state involvement in the economy. This therefore provides a weak basis for privatization.

- *Operating efficiency and response to clients*: Governments produce under the political-bureaucratic system of central command and control, often driven from a desire to employ people with minimal attention to the need to at least cover costs of operation. State enterprises frequently lack a hard budget constraint and, when they operate at a loss, receive a government subsidy to cover it. This situation blunts any incentive for efficient operations. To survive, private businesses must respond to direct customer demand and must constrain prices out of concern for competition from other businesses. That environment drives private business towards operating efficiency and improved responsiveness to customers, but only if the new private businesses face a competitive business environment. There is no reason to believe that a private monopolist city water company would be more efficient and responsive than a government monopolist city water company serving the same territory under the same regulatory conditions. The cost reduction associated with improved operating efficiency is a frequent objective of government privatizations in the United States. However, a number of studies have found the Veterans Health Administration hospital system to be a better performer than the systems available to other Americans. It is not always the case that a private system will outperform a government one—provided the incentives, direction, and will are strong.
- *Cash*: Sale of government-operated enterprises may bring revenue to the government. The inflow, assuming a buyer can be found, would occur at sale. Operating profits in the future would disappear, although the enterprise would then be subject to the tax system. Unfortunately, many government assets produce no revenue or produce revenue that is less than operating cost. That makes their value extremely low. This is a problem that countries of the former Soviet Union have had to face as they try to move into a market economy. Many state enterprises have high production costs and, even with private ownership, the product will not sell on national or international markets at a price sufficient to cover those costs. Although the old central plans invested heavily in these plants, their privatized value has proved to be low— except in natural resource sectors. In other environments, the revenues have proved substantial. The cumulative total has been estimated at over $1 trillion through the second part

of 1999; the annual flow of privatization proceeds has exceeded $100 billion in the last part of the 1990s.

Other motives behind privatization include lack of appropriate personnel or expertise to perform the service, provide greater operating flexibility, quicken implementation of the programme, increase the pace of innovation, and improve quality of service.

However, it is important to understand that all government services are not equally susceptible to outsourcing and not all motives will be satisfied in any particular privatization programme.

The largest transactions involve formerly nationalized industries under old concepts of the economic role of government or of the need to keep "socially or eco nomically significant" industries under state control: telecommunications, petroleum and petrochemicals, gas distribution, automobile manufacturing, electricity generation and distribution, airlines, steel making, and so on. Between 1990 and 2000, 36 per cent of privatization proceeds came from telecommunications, 16 per cent from power, 15 per cent from financial institutions, 10 per cent from oil and gas, and 17 per cent from other industries.

Government operation of these industries has been notoriously bad because of political influences on service decisions (e.g., a city gets served by the national airline because an important politician lives there) and on operations (e.g., the industry is seen as employer of last resort and the resulting bloated payrolls prevent it from ever producing its product at a competitive cost). Governments in the United States have been less active in recent privatization than those in Western Europe, Latin America, Asia, New Zealand, and Australia. Many of the big international privatizations, however, have been in industries never publicly owned in the United States. Privatization of roads, airports, the postal system, schools, and the like raise much more interesting social, political, and economic issues than the state sale of telephone or petrochemical companies.

PRODUCTION/PROVISION

The American privatization issue frequently concerns the provision-production dichotomy. Goods and services provided by a government because of market failure need not be produced by that government. Provision means government intervention to ensure availability or, generally, to finance the service; it does not require production by the government.

The production choice should be made according to which entity—a government department, a private entity, or another government—would supply the desired quantity and quality of service at least cost to the citizens of the providing government.

The distinction between government and private production and provision can be clarified by example:

- Government provision/government production. The city street department plows the streets after a heavy snowfall. The job uses department managers, department employees, department equipment, and department supplies.
- Government provision/private production. The county hires a private appraisal firm to estimate values of real estate in the county for use in computing property tax bills. The firm does the work with its managers, employers, equipment, and supplies. Another example: The U. S. Department of Defence hires private firms to provide food and other support services to military units in the field. Outsourcing is almost certainly the most common privatization practiced in the United States. It is a major element in President Bush's management agenda for the federal government, which intends competitive sourcing for federal tasks that are readily available in the commercial marketplace.
- Private provision/government production. A racetrack pays a city for extraordinary traffic control services on race days.
- Private provision/private production. A private manufacturer patrols its factory site with its own security employees. Neighbouring properties may receive some protection spillover from this security activity.

Some cities, especially in California, have provided a full range of services entirely by contract. Such an arrangement is called the Lakewood Plan after an early contract city. Production by contract is probably limited more than anything else by the ability to design a contract specifying the service qualities to be delivered.

Even parts of the judicial system may be privately produced: California permits litigants to hire private jurists when court congestion or special expertise makes such a procedure attractive to both parties, and private firms have undertaken contractual operation of correction facilities. School districts have similarly chosen private production through vouchers or charter schools.

In these systems, the school district provides financing but the educational service is actually produced by another entity. The production choice should be kept open for possible privatization; the idea of government action is to provide services of desired quantity and quality at the least cost to the economy. When might contracting not be an efficient option?

One study suggests that in-house production may be warranted when:

- "There are very few potential suppliers,
- Costs of switching from one producer to another are high,

- Information about the production process and supplier performance is expensive to obtain, and
- The good or service being provided cannot be clearly defined."

In other words, the option would be difficult if contracts would be especially difficult to write and the public would end up being confronted with a monopoly supplier. Otherwise, out-of-government production can be an efficient option. Privatization of provision is a more difficult problem. For public goods, the market will not function because the private supplier will not charge an efficient price for the service because of nonrivalry and inability to exclude. Business firms provide goods and services because they intend to make money, not for the sheer enjoyment of providing the goods or services.

If it is not possible to charge people for the good or service, a business firm will seldom provide it. Furthermore, the price will exceed the cost of providing service to an additional consumer. The expectation of government provision of public goods is strong, but occasionally governments will provide private goods as well and often do a very bad job of it. Organizational problems, particularly lack of appropriate production incentives, cause high costs, undesirable production strategies, and a bland product designed by an uneasy consensus. Governments provide toll goods (highways, bridges, etc.), and sometimes they do about as well as the private producer would do. But even some toll goods are provided by private businesses.

For instance, in France eight public/private joint ventures and one private company operate the toll highway/tunnel system, the most extensive auto toll system in Europe. Evidence indicates that fewer resources will be wasted if government avoids provision of private goods. Some observers of public fiscal problems have suggested that privatization would relieve pressures on government finances. That is a realistic response if the service being privatized in fact lacks substantial public-good features; one wonders why, in such a case, the government got involved in its provision. On the other hand, to expect private firms to provide public goods at desirable levels is folly.

At best, the private firm may be contracted to produce the public good provided by the government. Privatization cannot be a general and complete cure for fiscal problems, no matter how inefficient a troubled government might be. For public goods, efficient private provision cannot substitute for inefficient government provision of public goods. That does not mean that market incentives cannot help, however, in guiding provision by government.

BUILDING SOCIAL DECISIONS FROM PRIVATE PREFERENCES

The logic of moving from individual choice to choices made by society is built on three fairly simple tenets. First, individuals are the best judges of their own well-being and generally act to improve that well-being as they see it. There is no scientific principle that leads us to reject or accept the judgments made by individuals about their own lives. Dictators or philosopher-kings may accurately make those determinations, but others should not assume that responsibility. Second, the welfare of the community depends on the welfare of the individuals in that community.

In other words, communities are made up of people, and community welfare increases only if the welfare of those in the community is improved. From that comes the third tenet, judging the impact of a social action on the welfare of the community. The Pareto criterion, named after a nineteenth-century economist, holds that if at least one person is better off from a policy action and no person is worse off, then the community as a whole is unambiguously better off for the policy. Does a social action harming anyone, despite improving the condition of many individuals, improve the welfare of society as a whole? It cannot be indisputably argued that such an action improves the well-being of society, regardless of the numbers made better off, because the relative worth of those harmed cannot scientifically be compared with those helped.

Such a proposed policy would fail the Pareto criterion for judging social action. With those standards, we can analyse the implications of nonappropriability on public provision. Suppose that only five people would be influenced by construction of a levee to protect a small area from periodic flooding of a river.

The cost of that levee is $20,000. Each individual in this community knows the maximum sacrifice that he or she would be willing to make to have that levee as compared to having no levee at all. Presumably it would not be larger than the individual damage avoided by having levee protection. These are the individual benefit numbers in Table. The levee, we assume, would be a public good: Each individual could use it without diminishing its availability to anyone else in the community, and exclusion of nonpayers is not feasible. First, would the levee be built without public action, that is, by individual action only?

The cost of the levee is $20,000; the most that any single individual will pay to get the levee built is $9,000. Thus, the levee would not be produced by any single individual. If the levee only cost $8,500 to construct, however, we suspect individual D would build the levee for his or her benefit, and four other people in the community would receive benefits from the levee without payment. (The four would be free riders.) Once the levee is there, it serves all because of its public-good features.

The initially presumed construction cost, however, is such that the maximum individual benefit is less than the cost of the project, so the levee will not be built by private action. Is the levee economically desirable for the community, in the sense that the value of the levee is greater than the resources going into the construction of the levee?

Table. Individual Benefits from the Project

Individual	Individual Benefit	
A	8,000	
B	7,000	
C	6,000	Total cost = $20,000
D	9,000	
E	6,000	
Total benefit	$36,000	

The social cost, the value of the resources being used in the construction of the levee, equals $20,000. The social benefit of the levee, the sum of the improved welfare of the individuals with the levee, equals $36,000. Because social benefits are greater than social costs, it is a desirable project for the community.

A responsive government would act to provide the levee and would raise sufficient funds through the revenue structure to finance the project. If the government levied an equal per-capita tax—a payment based on the coercive power of government rather than the voluntary payment of market exchange—on the community to finance the levee, all individuals would still be better off with the levee and the tax than without the combination. Government can thus provide a desired service that public-good features prevent private action from providing.

A second example yields additional insights. Assume that the community receives benefits from a project as shown in Table. The project, possibly a levee in another location, is a public good. The cost of the project is $20,000. Because the sum of individual benefits is less than the cost of the project, the project resources would be worth more in other uses than in the particular use being considered.

Suppose, however, that the project decision will be made at a referendum among the people in the community, with a simple majority required for passage. The referendum also includes the method to be used to finance the project: an equal per-capita tax (project cost divided by number of people in the community, or $4,000 per person).

If the people in the community vote according to their individual net gain or loss from the project, it will be approved. Does voter approval make the project desirable for the community? Not at all, because the project misallocates resources: It consumes resources that would have a greater value in other use.

The majority vote may misallocate resources when used for public decisions, as may any technique that does not involve comparisons of social cost and social return.

Table. Individual Benefits from the Project

Individual	Individual Benefit	Cost Share	Individual Gain
A	$5,000	$4,000	$1,000
B	5,000	4,000	1,000
C	2,000	4,000	–2,000
D	1,000	4,000	–3,000
E	6,000	4,000	2,000
Total	$19,000	$20,000	

A third example further emphasizes the limits of scientific principles in public decision making. Table resents individual benefits from a project with a total cost of $12,500 and an equal per-capita tax method of distributing project costs. Total benefits do exceed total cost, so the project apparently represents an appropriate way to use scarce resources, and the project would be approved by majority vote if the people voted according to their individual gains or losses. The project, however, does leave one individual worse off. Is the loss to E less important to the community than the gains of A, B, C, and D? That answer requires a value judgment about the worth of the individuals to society, a judgment with which science and Pareto cannot help.

One option would be to distribute costs in exactly the same proportion as individual benefits. That is the approach shown in the last column of Table. Any project for which total benefits exceed total cost has possible cost distributions from which all will be made better off. There is no redistribution of individual cost from which all will be made better off for projects like that demonstrated in Table, but choices about situations like that shown in Table are difficult. Politicians make such decisions regularly, but not with scientific justification. One voting rule would ensure that only projects that pass the Pareto criterion could be approved. That rule is unanimity, if we assume that people will not vote for policies contrary to their own best interest.

This rule is seldom used, because reaching decisions often requires substantial costs. James Buchanan and Gordon Tullock identify two elements constituting the full cost of making a community decision. The first element, the cost of reaching the decision, the "time and effort... which is required to secure agreement," rises as the agreement percentage required for the decision rises. As more of the group must agree on any issue, the effort invested in bargaining, arguing, and discussion normally rises. That investment is a real cost because the effort could have been directed to other uses.

The second element, the external costs, or the cost from group "choices contrary to the individual's own interest," falls as the agreement percentage rises. (These are the costs imposed by a simple majority choice on individuals C and D in Table. Those costs could have been prevented by requiring a higher vote for approval.) The optimal choice percentage—the lowest combination of the two cost elements—usually would require neither unanimity nor one-person rule because the former has excessive decision costs and the latter has excessive external costs. Certain decisions are more dangerous to minorities (the losers in decisions) than others. For instance, many juries must reach a unanimous verdict because of the very high external costs that juries can place on people. For similar reasons, constitutional revision has high-percentage vote requirements.

Table. Individual Benefits from the Project

Individual	Individual Benefit	Cost Share	Individual Gain	Individual Share of Total Benefits	Benefit-Based Cost Share
A	$3,000	$2,500	$ 500	15%	$1,875
B	5,000	2,500	2,500	25%	3,125
C	8,000	2,500	5,500	40%	5,000
D	3,000	2,500	500	15%	1,875
E	1,000	2,500	–1,500	5%	625
Total	$20,000	$12,500		100%	$12,500

POLITICS, REPRESENTATION, AND GOVERNMENT FINANCE

Decisions about public spending, raising revenue, borrowing, and so on are not the product of mechanical rationality. They are intensely political and involve personal interests, interest groups, political parties, and the process of representation. Even the clearest preferences of any particular individual are usually filtered through representation, and that one preference becomes part of a vote that may or may not be in the majority whose choice prevails. The many elements that produce a fiscal choice are diverse, but a framework devised by Anthony Downs for exploring the process of representation can help with an understanding of what influences these decisions.

He hypothesizes that political parties in a democracy operate to obtain votes to retain the income, power, and prestige that come with being in office. Parties are not units of principle or of ideals but are primarily seekers of votes. A lack of perfect knowledge, however, permeates the system: Parties do not always know what citizens want; citizens do not always know what the government in power or its opposition has done, is doing, or should be doing to try to serve citizen interests. Information that would reduce this ignorance is expensive to acquire.

The scarcity of knowledge obscures the path that would lead from citizen preferences to their votes. Neither political parties nor elected representatives know exactly what the voters want, and the voters do not know exactly what the government is up to. Several consequences for the representative process result. First, some people are politically more important than others because they can influence government action. Democratic government will not treat everyone with equal deference in a world of imperfect knowledge. One person, one vote is the ideal slogan, but it doesn't represent political influence particularly well. Second, specialists in influencing people will appear, and some will emerge as representatives of the people.

These individuals will try to convince the government that the policies they support, and that directly benefit them, are good for and desired by the electorate. Information provided by these individuals will be filtered to provide only data consistent with the supported cause. A rational government will discount these claims, but it cannot ignore them. Third, imperfect information makes a government party susceptible to bribery simply because the party in power needs resources to persuade voters to keep it in power. Parties out of power are susceptible as well, but they have less to sell. It is no accident that corruption scandals involve more Republicans when the Republicans are in power and more Democrats when the Democrats are in power. Political influence is a necessary result of imperfect information combined with the unequal distribution of income and wealth in society. Parties have to use economic resources to provide and obtain information. Lobbying is a rational response to the lack of perfect information, but an important imbalance of interests influences the lobbying process. Suppose a direct subsidy to industry is being considered.

This subsidy is of great total value to that industry. The total subsidy paid by taxpayers, of course, exactly equals the subsidy received by the industry. However, each taxpayer bears only a small individual share of that total subsidy. Who will undertake the expense of lobbying on the measure? The industry will, not the taxpayer, because the net benefit of lobbying is positive for the industry (comparing the substantial cost of lobbying with the substantial direct benefit to the industry) and negative for any taxpayer (because the substantial lobbying cost overwhelms the small individual share of the subsidy that could be saved).

These efforts to influence fiscal decisions take two general forms. Traditional lobbying is personal: "Affable men in suits would hang around swarming, sweaty legislative chambers, buttonholing lawmakers as they swaggered through lustrous bronzed doors, whispering in ears, slapping backs, winking knowingly." The lobbyists know the elected representative and have access to them (usually because they can be counted on for contributions and other campaign assistance), know the unelected administrators carrying out public policies, and use these contacts to deliver the message of their clients on issues. Many former legislators and agency administrators— federal and state—develop lucrative careers as lobbyists, using contacts and friendships to help deliver the message of the interests they represent; their value is in their access to the people who remain in government. In one recent example, the member of Congress primarily responsible for the Medicare Prescription Drug Improvement and Modernization Act of 2003, an act that provided significant new revenue for the pharmaceutical industry and avoided price constraints on prescription medicines, left Congress for a position as chief lobbyist for brand-name drug companies.

Many call this easy mobility between legislative or executive positions and interested private entities "a revolving door," and few believe it to be contributory to fiscal decisions in the public interest. But it is part of the way in which public policies get adopted today. Grassroots lobbying is the mobilization of constituent action, reflected in letters, phone calls, e-mails, faxes, and other direct contacts to the elected representative. Mass campaigns had great successes in getting civil-rights legislation and in shaping other policies, but communications and information technologies make it much easier to generate what appears to be a groundswell of interest and masses of constituent communications of public policy questions, including those of government expenditure and taxation.

A related influence on representative government is the principle of rational ignorance. Citizen effort to acquire information to cast an informed vote is usually irrational. Although the cost of obtaining information may be low, the expected return from an informed vote is even lower. If others vote in an informed manner, a citizen's uninformed vote is irrelevant because the informed majority choice wins. If others vote in an uninformed manner, a citizen's informed vote is irrelevant because the choice of the uninformed majority wins. In either case, the action of the majority produces the election result, so individual effort to become informed yields no return. Thus, electorate choices produce indivisible benefits or costs. Information gathering to cast informed votesproduces no electoral benefits for an individual. That, of course, is a crucial problem in any democratic society. Fortunately, many individuals become informed for other motives, including pure enjoyment.

The power of the vote is an important reason why free, high-quality primary and secondary education is so critical for democratic government. A final important point in the process of representation deals with the intensity of preference. In ordinary voting, there are no methods of representing intensity of preference on particular issues. Each vote has equal weight. In a legislative body, however, the flow of many issues allows legislators to trade a vote on a minor issue (according to that person's preferences) for a vote on a more important one. Trading votes allows adjustments according to intensity of preference. For example, a member of Congress may be particularly interested in the outcome on issue B, but have little concern about issue A. That representative may trade his or her vote on issue A for some other representative's vote on issue B.

This process, called logrolling, can produce wasteful spending (an irrigation project yielding benefit to a small area at great national cost, for instance), but it can also improve the responsiveness of government by ensuring that intense preferences get recognized. Furthermore, the representative process has special devices for protecting the interests of minorities. These do not appear in the general referendum process of choice by direct vote: The required majority of those voting can inflict severe cost on the rest of society with dramatic consequences for the social fabric. Their major disadvantage must emerge from the absence of minority power in the direct legislation system. An initiated referendum has no provision for executive veto, creation of political stalemates in the legislative process, or changed negotiating positions in committees, all vital positions of lawmaking which can serve to protect minorities.

THE LAYERS OF GOVERNMENT

In the United States three layers of governments with sovereignty of their own (not a single government) provide public services, levy taxes, and borrow money. Indeed, there are more than 86,000 governments in the United States, counting federal, state, and local entities. Not all nations are governed in this fashion. Some governments are unitary, meaning that a single national government has legislative authority over the entire country. There may be local councils with certain powers, but they function only on the approval of the national government.

In many unitary states, local revenue and expenditure programmes must be approved by the national government, and a single consolidated financial programme exists for the entire country. Unitary states include Belgium, France, the Netherlands, Norway, Poland, and many countries of the former Soviet Union. The United Kingdom, historically unitary, is devolving some powers to regional parliaments in Scotland and Wales. Other nations are federal: Subnational governments have considerable autonomous authority to make decisions, including difficult decisions about taxing and spending. In no sense are these subnational units a dependent department of the central government, as they may be in a unitary state.

In the United States, states exist as an independent layer of government with full powers (including independent financial authority) and all residual powers. Other important federal states include Argentina, Australia, Austria, Brazil, Canada, Germany, India, Mexico, and the Russian Federation (although recent changes there to reduce sovereign powers of regional and local governments and move them to the national government have moved the nation closer to being a unitary state).

In each instance, to understand government finances—spending, taxing, and borrowing—one must understand the intergovernmental structure in the country. In the U.S. federal system, constitutional terms define the elemental financial powers and limits under which the levels function.

First, there are powers and limits to national authority:

These include the powers:

- To lay and collect taxes, duties, imposts and excises, to pay the debts and provide for the common defence and general welfare of the United States; but all duties, imposts and excises shall be uniform throughout the United States.
- To borrow money on the credit of the United States.
- To regulate commerce with foreign nations, and among the several States, and with the Indian tribes.
- To coin money, regulate the value thereof, and of foreign coin, and fix the standard of weights and measures.
- To establish post-offices and post-roads.
- To raise and support armies, but no appropriation of money to that use shall be for a longer term than two years.
- To provide and maintain a navy.

Article I, Section 9, establishes some fiscal constraints:

- No capitation, or other direct, tax shall be laid, unless in proportion to the census of enumeration herein before directed to be taken.
- No tax or duty shall be laid on articles exported from any State.
- No money shall be drawn from the Treasury, but in consequence of appropriations made by law; and a regular statement and account of the receipts and expenditures of all public money shall be published from time to time.

Of course, legislation and court decisions have, over the years, specifically defined what these powers and constraints mean in practice. The Constitution similarly identifies, in Article I, Section 10, powers specifically denied the states. Of fiscal significance is the prohibition against coining money. The commerce clause prevents state interference with international commerce and commerce among the states, a particularly significant limit on taxing power and regulatory authority in a global economy.

This is referred to as the Commerce Clause, and it plays an important role in many facets of state taxation. A later amendment requires states to follow due process in their actions and to afford equal protection of the law to all within their jurisdictions. These provisions have had substantial impact on service provision in the states, as courts have reminded state and local governments that fiscal processes must meet federal constitutional tests. The federal equal-protection clause has been often copied in state constitutions. The dramatic change in school finance in California generated by the court case Serrano v. Priest resulted from state constitutional provisions copied after those in the federal law.

The major constitutional provision for states appears in the tenth amendment of the Constitution: "The powers not delegated to the United States by the Constitution, nor prohibited by it to the States, are reserved to the States respectively, or to the people." The states thus have residual powers. The Constitution does not need to provide specific authority for a state government to have a particular power: Constitutional silence implies that the state can act in the area in question, thus establishing states as the sovereign "middle layer" in the federal system. Local governments in the United States typically appear as captive creatures of their states, unless state action has specifically altered that relationship.

This principle was defined by Judge J. F. Dillon of Iowa:

- It is a general and undisputed proposition of law that a municipal corporation possesses and can exercise the following powers and no others: First, those granted in express words; second, those necessarily or fairly implied in or incident to the powers expressly granted; third, those essential to the declared objects and purposes of the corporation— not simply convenient, but indispensable. Any fair, reasonable, substantive doubt concerning the existence of power is resolved by the courts against the corporation, and the power denied.

Dillon's rule thus holds that if state law is silent about a particular local power, the presumption is that the local level lacks power. In state-local relationships, state government holds all powers. That is a critical limitation on local government fiscal activity. Several states have altered Dillon's rule by granting home-rule charter powers to particular local governments. Such powers are particularly prevalent in states containing a small group of large metropolitan areas with conditions substantially different from the environment in other areas of the state.

The special conditions of such large cities can be handled by providing them home-rule charter power to govern their own affairs. State law can thus proceed without being cluttered by numerous special enactments for the larger units. When charter powers have been provided, local governments can act in all areas unless state law specifically prohibits those actions. Many times, however, fiscal activities are included in the range of areas that are prohibited under charter powers. Thus, it is better to presume limits than to presume local freedom to choose in fiscal affairs. That presumption is accurate if Dillon's rule applies or if charter powers have been constrained in fiscal activities.

CEASE

An overview of the basis for government action certainly indicates that government choices made in budgeting and revenue raising will not be simple. Government will be unable to sell its services because these services are nonappropriable (neither excludable nor exhaustible). That means that government will not have normal market tests available to help it with choices. Governments surely do not want to waste resources—after all, resources are scarce, and most things used by government do have alternative uses—so the benefits to society from government action ought to exceed the cost to society from that action. Determining whether actions really improve the conditions of the community gets complicated, however, when there is no basis for making comparison of the worth of individuals.

The Pareto criterion for the welfare of a community does not require interpersonal judgments, but it leaves many choices open to political decision. Despite sophistication and rigor, science and analysis will not provide definitive answers to many government choices. Votes, either on issues or for representatives, will settle many decisions. Direct votes, however, will neither guarantee no wasteful public decisions nor choices that satisfy the Pareto criterion for improving society. They may well cause the imposition of substantial costs on minorities.

Some problems of direct choice are reduced when representatives make decisions, but there will remain imbalances of influence and posturing to continue in office rather than to follow clearly defined principles. Lobbying—direct or grassroots—is one way in which some interests obtain extra influence. Finance in a representative democracy is not simple. Governments should be judged on their responsiveness to public preferences and on their refusal to ignore minority positions. Not all governments can meet those simple standards, and not all budget systems used in the United States do much to contribute to those objectives.

The U.S. structure delivers and finances services using three tiers of government— federal, state, and local. Although independent in some respects, there are important mutual constraints. The federal level has powers delimited in the Constitution; the states have residual powers. Local governments—under Dillon's rule—have only powers expressly granted by their states. Some states grant local home rule, giving localities all powers save those expressly prohibited. Few home-rule authorizations are complete, however. Thus, budget and finance functions vary widely across the country.

Bibliography

A. Raja Sekhar: *Advanced Scientific Methods for Environmental Safety and Economic Development*, Serials Publications, Delhi, 2011.

Amlan Datta: *An Introduction To Indias Economic Development Since the Nineteenth Century*, Popular Prakashan, Delhi, 2004

Amod Sharma and Ravishankar Kumar Singh: *Composite Farming Practices and Economic Development*, Abhijeet Publication, Delhi, 2007.

Anjan Chakrabarti: *Economic Development and Employment in Sikkim*, Authors Press, Delhi, 2009.

Ashutosh Kumar: *Economic Development and Income Distribution*, Deep and Deep, Publication, Delhi, 2003.

Bhabesh Sen and Mitali Chinara: *Economic Development and Poverty in India*, New Century Publication, Delhi, 2012.

D.R. Joshi and Sandeep Bajpai: *Economic Development Agricultural and Industrial Growth*, Cyber Tech, 2009.

Debashis Chakraborty and Smita Nath: *Collected Essays on Economic Development : In Honour of Prof. Asok Barman*, Bookwell, Publication, Delhi, 2008.

District Development Profile of Nepal 2010/2011 : A Socio-Economic Development Database of Nepal, Mega Publication, Delhi, 2010.

Hema Khanna and G.S. Bhalla: *Economic Development and Ecological Degradation*, Regal Publications, Delhi, 2010.

Jasmine Y. Damle: *Beyond Economic Development: A Case Study of Marathwada*, Mittal, Publication, Delhi, 2001

L C Mallaiah and L Ratna Kumari: *Economic Development and Dalit Agricultural Workers*, Abhijeet Publication, Delhi, 2007.

M. Lakshmi Narasaiah: *Agriculture and Economic Development*, Sonali, Publication, 2004.

M. Vasu: *Economic Development and Poverty*, Abhijeet Publication, Delhi, 2009.

Man Chand Khandela: *Economic Development: Myth and Reality*, Pointer Publication, Delhi, 2007.

Md. Mukhtar Alam: *Economic Development and Contemporary Geopolitics*, Om Publication, Delhi, 2004.

Misra and Puri: *Economic Development and Policy in India*, Himalaya Publishing House, Delhi, 2010.

N. Kumar and R. Mittal: *Economic Development and Planning*, Anmol, Publication, Delhi, 2002.

Niranjan Roy and M.P. Bezbaruah: *Agricultural Growth and Regional Economic Development*, Mittal, Publication Delhi, 2002.

P.A. Koli: *Economic Development and Environment Issues*, Serials Publication, Delhi, 2005.

P.R. Gopinathan Nair, K.N.S. Nair, Thampi Jose and K.V. Velayudhan: *Dimensions of Economic Development: Spatial and Sectoral Perspectives*, Commonwealth, Delhi, 2004.

Paramjit Singh: *Climate Change and Socio Economic Development: Spatial and Temporal Variation*, Keshav Publications, Delhi, 2012.

Profulla Hazarika: *Economic Development and Ecological Balance in Assam*, D.V.S. Publication, Delhi, 2010.

R.K. Panda and K.C. Patnaik: *Bureaucracy and Economic Development*, Abhijeet, Publication, Delhi, 2010.

R.V. Gangshetty: *Economic Development and Regional Disparities*, Current Publication, Delhi, 2009.

Rajni Saluja: *Banking Performance and Socio Economic Development*, Regal Publications, Delhi, 2014.

Raman Singh: *Economic Development and Planning*, ABD Publication, Delhi, 2011.

Ramprasad Sengupta: *Ecological Limits and Economic Development*, Oxford University Press, Delhi, 2013.

S.D. Chamola: *Economic Development and Ethics: Indian Experience Since Independence*, Global Vision, Delhi, 2011.

S.D. Singh: *Economic Development*, Centrum Press, Delhi, 2010.

S.N. Yogish: *Coconut and Economic Development*, Serials Publications, Delhi, 2004.

Samitha Rani Natarajan: *Economic Development for Women*, Jnanada Prakashan, Delhi, 2013.

Tapas R. Dash and K.K. Sen: *Co-Operatives and Economic Development*, Rawat, Publication, Delhi, 2004.

V. Nath: *Economic Development and Planning in India*, Concept Publication, Delhil, 2010.

Index